Cisco Networking Academy Program: Lab Companion, Volume I
Second Edition

Cisco Systems, Inc.

Cisco Networking Academy Program

Jim Lorenz

Cisco Press

Cisco Press
201 West 103rd Street
Indianapolis, IN 46290 USA

Cisco Networking Academy Program: Lab Companion Volume I, Second Edition

Cisco Systems, Inc.

Cisco Networking Academy Program

Jim Lorenz

Copyright © 2001 Cisco Press

Published by:
Cisco Press
210 West 103rd Street
Indianapolis, IN 46290 USA

Printed in the United States of America   5 6 7 8 9 0

ISBN: 1-58713-027-0

Warning and Disclaimer

This book is designed to provide information on networking fundamentals. Every effort has been made to make this book as complete and as accurate as possible, but no warranty or fitness is implied.

The information is provided on an as-is basis. The author, Cisco Press, and Cisco Systems, Inc., shall have neither liability nor responsibility to any person or entity with respect to any loss or damages arising from the information contained in this book or from the use of the programs that may accompany it.

The opinions expressed in this book belong to the author and are not necessarily those of Cisco Systems, Inc.

Trademark Acknowledgments

All terms mentioned in this book that are known to be trademarks or service marks have been appropriately capitalized. Cisco Press or Cisco Systems, Inc., cannot attest to the accuracy of this information. Use of a term in this book should not be regarded as affecting the validity of any trademark or service mark.

Feedback Information

At Cisco Press, our goal is to create in-depth technical books of the highest quality and value. Each book is crafted with care and precision, undergoing rigorous development that involves the unique expertise of members from the professional technical community.

Readers' feedback is a natural continuation of this process. If you have any comments regarding how we could improve the quality of this book, or otherwise alter it to better suit your needs, you can contact us at networkingacademy@ciscopress.com. Please make sure to include the book title and ISBN in your message.

We greatly appreciate your assistance.

Publisher	John Wait
Executive Editor	Carl Lindholm
Cisco Systems Program Management	Michael Hakkert
	Tom Geitner
	William Warren
Production Manager	Patrick Kanouse
Senior Project Editor	Sheri Replin
Product Manager	Shannon Gross

About the Author

Jim Lorenz is the Lead Instructor and Coordinator for the Cisco Regional Training Academy at Chandler-Gilbert Community College (CGCC) in Chandler, Arizona. He is a full-time faculty member and was also Lead Instructor for the Microsoft Certified Systems Engineering (MCSE) curriculum. He has 20 years of experience in computers and information systems ranging from programming and database administration to network design and implementation. Jim has taught computer and networking courses for both public and private institutions for more than 15 years.

Jim is a Novell Certified NetWare Engineer (CNE), a Microsoft Certified Trainer (MCT), a Cisco Certified Network Associate (CCNA), and a Cisco Certified Academy Instructor (CCAI). He holds a bachelor's degree in Computer Information Systems from Prescott College.

Acknowledgments

Brad Niesluchowski has been a great help in putting these labs together and reviewing them for technical accuracy. Brad is a Network Administrator with Higley Unified School District in Arizona and is a graduate of the Chandler-Gilbert Cisco Academy. Ray Moore, Director of Technology for Fountain Hills School District in Arizona, has also been a big help as an author and technical reviewer. Ray is the president of the Phoenix NT Users Special Interest Group and is also a part-time Cisco instructor at Chandler-Gilbert Community College.

I would like to thank Cisco Press Executive Editor Carl Lindholm, Cisco Networking Academy Editor Vito Amato, and Academy curriculum specialists Kevin Johnston and Dennis Frezzo for their support and guidance.

I would also like to thank the Administration of Chandler-Gilbert Community College for their tremendous support of my efforts and the Cisco Networking Academy Program. Most importantly, I would like to thank my wife, Mary, and my kids, Jessica and Natasha, for their patience and understanding.

Preface

This manual was developed for use with the Cisco CCNA online curriculum and the *Cisco Networking Academy Program: First-Year Companion Guide*, Second Edition, textbook for Semesters 1 and 2. These labs are based on those in the current Cisco Networking Academy Program with some additional information. Most of the labs are hands-on and require access to a Cisco Router Lab or a Simulator. Additional paper-based labs, which are practice exercises for complex topics, are included to supplement the online curriculum.

All labs and exercises are structured in two parts:
1. **Overview Section**: Includes **Objectives**, **Background** information, and a **Tools/Preparation** section to help students, instructors, and lab assistants prepare for the lab.
2. **Worksheet Section**: Includes the steps necessary to complete the lab and progress questions.

Semester 2

Table of Contents

Semester 1 Labs

Cisco Labs–Semester 1–Networking Fundamentals
LAB 1.1.1–PC HARDWARE–OVERVIEW
(Estimated time: 60 minutes)

Objectives:
- Connect peripheral components (monitor, keyboard, and so on) to the main PC system unit
- Name the typical PC components
- Identify major internal PC components and connections
- Document the configuration of a functioning PC
- Boot a system to a Windows operating system (Windows 95, 98, NT, or 2000)
- Use the Control Panel, System icon utility to gather information about the PC configuration

Background:
This lab helps you become familiar with the basic peripheral components of a PC computer system and their connections, including network attachment. You also examine the internal PC configuration and identify major components. You observe the boot process for the Windows operating system and use the Control Panel to find out information about the PC. Knowing the components of a PC is valuable when troubleshooting and is important to your success in the networking field. For some students, this lab is a review.

Tools/Preparation:
Before you begin, the teacher or lab assistant should have a typical desktop Pentium-based PC available with all peripherals, such as keyboard, monitor, mouse, speakers or headphones, a network interface card (NIC), and network cable. The system unit cover should be removed, or tools should be provided to remove it. You can work individually or in teams. Before you begin this lab, you should read the A+ or PC hardware maintenance training materials.

Required Resources:
- PC with monitor, keyboard, mouse, and power cords
- Windows operating system (Windows 95, 98, NT, or 2000)
- Sound card and speakers or headphones
- Network Interface Card and Cat 5 patch cable

Notes:
_____

_____

_____

_____

Cisco Labs–Semester 1–Networking Fundamentals
LAB 1.1.1–PC HARDWARE–WORKSHEET

Step 1. Examine the computer for internal and external components.

Task: Examine the computer and peripheral components, both front and back.

Explanation: The components and configuration of the PC you are working with may vary from the sample answers below.

1. What is the manufacturer and model number of this computer?

Manufacturer	
Model Number	

2. Remove the PC system unit cover. List at least eight major internal components inside the system unit (use the procedure in Step 3 to find the CPU and amount of RAM).

Component Name	Manufacturer/Description/Characteristics

3. What are the major external components of the PC, including the peripherals?

Component Name	Manufacturer/Description/Characteristics

Cisco Labs–Semester 1–Networking Fundamentals
LAB 1.1.1–PC HARDWARE–WORKSHEET

Step 2. Observe the boot process.

Task: Assemble the PC components and attach all peripherals and boot the PC. Observe the boot process.

Explanation: The computer should boot to the Windows operating system. If the computer does not boot, contact the lab assistant.

1. Observe the boot process.
    a. Did the Windows operating system boot OK? _____
    b. Could you see how much memory there was as the system was booting? _____

Step 3. General system information.

Task: Click the Start button and select Settings and Control Panel. Click the System icon and then the General tab.

Explanation: Here, we view information about the computer by using the operating system.

1.
    a. What is the Central Processing Unit? _____
    b. How much RAM is installed? _____

Cisco Labs–Semester 1–Networking Fundamentals
LAB 1.1.4–NIC INSTALLATION–OVERVIEW
(Estimated time: 60 minutes)

Objective:
- Demonstrate proper installation of a NIC card in a workstation

Background:
A network interface card (NIC) allows your computer to connect to a local-area network (LAN) and share resources with other computers on the network, such as printers and Internet connections. The type of NIC installed depends on several factors:

1. **LAN Architecture:** Ethernet and Token Ring are the two primary LAN architectures in use today, with Ethernet being the most widely used. Ethernet switches are the most common choice for connecting LANs today. They are available in various speeds, including Ethernet (10 Mbps), Fast Ethernet (100 Mbps) and Gigabit Ethernet (1000 Mbps). The NIC should be capable of running at the speed of the switch and in full-duplex mode.

2. **Computer Bus Type:** Most NICs you can buy today go into a PCI slot in the computer's bus. Higher-performance NICs are usually available for use in servers. ISA cards are also available.

3. **Computer Operating System:** The NIC and its "driver" must be compatible with the computer operating system. The NIC "driver" is software used to communicate between the NIC and the computer operating system. Operating systems include Windows, Novell, Macintosh, and UNIX.

4. **Media Type:** The NIC connector should match the network media. Some NICs have more than one connector type. The following table shows some types of cable and connectors.

Media (Cable) Type	Ethernet LAN Architecture	Connector Type
Unshielded Twisted-Pair (UTP) Copper (for example, CAT 5)	10Base-T, 100Base-TX	RJ-45 (modular 8-pin)
Coaxial (Thinnet)	10Base-2	BNC
Coaxial (Thicknet)	10Base-5	AUI (DB15-pin)
Fiber Optic (multimode)	10Base-FL, 100Base-FX, 1000Base-SX	ST, SC or MT-RJ

Network cards (also called network adapters) are relatively easy to install, as long as you follow simple guidelines. After installing the network interface card, you have access to your LAN or to the Internet.

Tools/Preparation:
Ensure that a PC is available that can be opened and attached to the network after the NIC is installed. Before beginning this lab, refer to the *Cisco Networking Academy Program: First-Year Companion Guide*, Second Edition. Also review Semester 1 online Lesson 1.

Cisco Labs–Semester 1–Networking Fundamentals
LAB 1.1.4–NIC INSTALLATION–OVERVIEW

Required Resources:
1. A computer system running Windows 95 or 98
2. Empty PCI or ISA expansion slot
3. PCI or ISA network card (Ethernet adapter)
4. Network card driver disk and/or Windows 95 CD
5. Network cable
6. Toolkit set
7. Static mat and wrist strap

Cisco Labs–Semester 1–Networking Fundamentals
LAB 1.1.4–NIC INSTALLATION–WORKSHEET

1. Turn off your computer and unplug the power cable. Use a static mat and wrist strap to ground yourself.

2. Remove the dust plate from computer case for the empty PCI or ISA expansion slot in which you plan to install the NIC card.

3. Remove the network card from the anti-static bag. Handle the top corners of the network card with both hands. Align the tabs of the network card with the slot, and gently rock the card front to rear to insert it into the expansion slot. Finally, secure the card to the case with a screw.

4. Restart the computer. The Windows 95 setup hardware detection automatically determines the adapter driver for your network card. Windows 95 might ask you to supply your computer name and workgroup name. Select a computer name for your PC, and use a specific workgroup name provided by your lab instructor.

5. Double-click the Network Neighborhood icon on the desktop. If you find other computer names displayed in the window, the network card is working properly. If you do not find other computer names, Windows 95 might have installed an incorrect driver for your network card. If so, you need to perform the following steps to add an adapter driver:

   1. Click the Start button, select Settings, and then select Control Panel.
   2. Double-click the Network icon. A network dialog box appears.
   3. Click the Add button. Select adapter and click the Add button once again.
   4. Click the Have Disk button. Insert the network card's driver disk into the floppy drive. Click OK. The Windows 95 setup program installs the driver.
   5. Windows 95 might ask you to reboot your system. After you restart the computer, follow the instructions in the beginning of this exercise to check whether your network card works properly.

Reflection:

Write in your journal the steps that you used to install a network card. Also write what precautions you took and why they were important.

Cisco Labs–Semester 1–Networking Fundamentals
LAB 1.2.1.1–TCP/IP NETWORK SETTINGS–OVERVIEW
(Estimated time: 45 minutes)

Objectives:
- Use the Windows Network icon in Control Panel to determine current network settings
- Use the WINIPCFG.EXE utility (with Windows 95 or 98) to determine network settings
- Identify the type of client software being used and record related settings
- Determine the computer name and domain name
- Determine the NIC manufacturer and driver
- Identify what network (Layer 3) protocols are bound to the NIC (in use)
- Determine the Internet Protocol (IP) Layer 3 address
- Determine the subnet mask and IP address of the default gateway (router)
- Determine whether Domain Name System (DNS), Dynamic Host Configuration Protocol (DHCP), and Windows Internet Name Service (WINS) are being used and the IP addresses of the servers providing these services
- Determine the Media Access Control (MAC) or hardware address of the workstation NIC
- Use the Windows System Device Manager to verify that the NIC is working properly
- Document all findings in this lab

Background:
This lab helps you become familiar with the network settings required to connect your PC to a local-area network and to gain access to the Internet (World Wide Web) and intranet (internal local Web servers). The purpose of this lab is to discover what your workstation's network settings are and how they are used. You review network interface card (NIC) configuration and drivers and TCP/IP protocol settings for a typical Windows client workstation in a server-based Ethernet network. This information is valuable any time you have a problem logging on to a network or when you must set up a new workstation. This lab focuses on the Windows 95 or 98 client.

Tools/Preparation:
Before you begin, the teacher or lab assistant will have a typical desktop Pentium-based (or comparable) PC available. The desktop policies must be set to allow access to the Network icon in Control Panel and either the Run command or the DOS command prompt in order to run the WINIPCFG.EXE utility. The PC should be a classroom/lab computer configured to access the Web-based Cisco curriculum and assessment system. You can work individually or in teams. Before beginning this lab, you should refer to the *Cisco Networking Academy Program: First-Year Companion Guide*, Second Edition. You should also review Semester 1 online Lessons 1 through 4.

Required Resources:
- PC workstation with monitor, keyboard, mouse, and power cords
- Windows operating system (Windows 95, 98, NT, or 2000) installed on PC
- NIC installed and Cat 5 patch cable with connection to the Internet
- Browser software installed (Netscape Navigator 3.0 or higher or Internet Explorer 4.0 or higher)
- Apple QuickTime browser and ShockWave Macromedia browser plug-ins

Cisco Labs–Semester 1–Networking Fundamentals
LAB 1.2.1.1–TCP/IP NETWORK SETTINGS–WORKSHEET

Step 1. Determine the network settings for your workstation.

Task: Boot (start) the PC, log on to the network, and use the following procedures to determine the network settings for your workstation.

Explanation: The primary tools you use for gathering this information are 1) the Network icon in Control Panel, 2) the WINIPCFG.EXE utility (Windows 95 or 98) or IPCONFIG.EXE (Windows NT), and 3) the System icon in Control Panel. You use these tools to verify your network settings and that the NIC is functioning properly. The following procedures focus primarily on a Windows NT server-based network. Answers vary depending on the PC you use and the network you are on.

Step 2. Use Control Panel/Network to determine the workstation computer name, NT domain name, network client, the network Layer 3 protocols in use, and information about the NIC.

Task: Click Start, select Settings, and then Control Panel. Double-click the Network icon. Click the Identification tab to find the computer name and the domain name (Windows NT). Click the Configuration tab and note what networking components are installed.

Explanation: The Network Client has an icon that looks like a computer, the NIC icon looks like a NIC, and the Protocols have an icon that looks like a network cable connection. There might be more than one of each of these.

1. Record your findings in the following table.

Computer (NetBIOS) name	
NT Domain name	
Network client type	
NIC installed (driver name)	
1st Protocol installed	
2nd Protocol installed	
Other network components	
Other network components	

Step 3. Use Control Panel/Network to check the TCP/IP-related settings, such as IP address information, DHCP, and DNS.

Task: Click the TCP/IP protocol while on the Network Configuration tab and then click Properties.

Explanation: Click the tab indicated in the table, and record your findings in this space provided.

Cisco Labs–Semester 1–Networking Fundamentals
LAB 1.2.1.1–TCP/IP NETWORK SETTINGS–WORKSHEET

1. Record your findings in the following table.

Tab	Type of Information	Findings
IP Addr.	How does the workstation get its IP address?	If "obtain IP address automatically" button is selected, go to Step 4.
IP Addr.	Workstation IP Address	
IP Addr.	Workstation Subnet Mask	
Gateway	Default Gateway	
DNS Cfg.	Is DNS enabled?	
DNS Cfg.	DNS Server IP address	
WINS Cfg.	Is WINS enabled?	
WINS Cfg.	WINS Server IP address	

Step 4. Using WINIPCFG.EXE utility.

Task: You can run WINIPCFG.EXE from the Start/Run command or from the DOS command prompt (IPCONFIG.EXE must be run from the DOS prompt). This exercise focuses on the WINIPCFG.EXE utility. To run it from the Start menu, click Start and Run, then type in WINIPCFG in the window. To run it from the DOS prompt, click Start, Programs, MS DOS Prompt, and then type WINIPCFG at the command line. If you enter WINIPCFG/ALL, you get much more information, including the MAC address.

Explanation: The WINIPCFG.EXE utility can be used to check TCP/IP-related settings as well as the MAC address of the NIC installed (also called the hardware address). When the TCP/IP protocol is installed on Windows 95 or 98, the graphical WINIPCFG.EXE utility is included with it. Windows NT uses a different utility, IPCONFIG.EXE, to give similar results. If your workstation obtains its IP address automatically (a DHCP client), you must use one of these utilities to determine its IP address and subnet mask. Be sure to select the proper NIC or Ethernet adapter.

1. Record your findings in the following table (your answers may vary).

Workstation IP Address	
Workstation Subnet Mask	
Workstation MAC Address	
Default Gateway (Router)	
DHCP Server	
DNS Server IP Address	
WINS Server IP Address	

Cisco Labs–Semester 1–Networking Fundamentals
LAB 1.2.1.1–TPC/IP NETWORK SETTINGS–WORKSHEET

Step 5. Use Control Panel/System/Device Manager to verify that the NIC and drivers are functioning properly.

Task: Click Start, select Settings, and then Control Panel. Double-click the System icon, click the Device Manager tab, and click the plus sign on the Network Adapter icon. Select the desired adapter and click Properties. Click the General tab to see the Adapter Manufacturer and check the status. Click the Driver tab to see the version of the driver and files being used.

Explanation: You can also find the operating system version, the CPU type, and the amount of RAM installed.

1. Record your findings in the following table.

Network Adapter (NIC) Manufacturer	
Is the Network Adapter working properly?	
Date of the Driver	
List one of the driver files	

Cisco Labs–Semester 1–Networking Fundamentals
LAB 1.2.1.2–PC SOFTWARE–OVERVIEW
(Estimated time: 30 minutes)

Objectives:
- Determine the PC operating system and version number
- Identify the manufacturer and version number of the BIOS the computer is running
- Learn how to access the CMOS settings for the computer
- Check browser software setup including version and necessary plug-ins

Background:
This lab helps you become familiar with the PC operating system, Basic Input Output System (BIOS), and application software configuration. You verify that the PC is configured properly to run the Cisco Online Curriculum and practice exams that are multimedia-based. This includes the operating system, video settings, browser, and plug-ins required. For some of you, this lab is a review.

Tools/Preparation:
Before you begin, the teacher or lab assistant will have a typical desktop Pentium-based (or comparable) PC available with the following software installed. The PC should be a classroom computer configured to access the Web-based Cisco curriculum and assessment system. You can work individually or in teams. Before you begin this lab, you should read the A+ or PC hardware maintenance training materials.

Required Resources:
- PC workstation with monitor, keyboard, mouse, and power cords
- Windows operating system (Windows 95, 98, NT, or 2000) installed on PC
- NIC installed and Cat 5 patch cable with connection to the Internet
- Browser software installed (Netscape Navigator 3.0 or higher or Internet Explorer 4.0 or higher)
- Apple QuickTime browser plug-in for use with training videos (can be downloaded from www.apple.com)
- ShockWave Macromedia browser plug-in for use with practice quizzes (can be downloaded from www.macromedia.com)

Notes: _____

_____

_____

_____

_____

Cisco Labs–Semester 1–Networking Fundamentals
LAB 1.2.1.2–PC SOFTWARE–WORKSHEET

Step 1. PC software overview.
Task: Before booting the PC, determine the manufacturer and model number.
Explanation: Boot (start) the PC and use the following procedures to determine the BIOS. Answers will vary depending on the PC. You can "cold boot" the PC by turning it off and on again. You can "warm boot" it by holding down the Ctrl and Alt keys and pressing the Delete key. Be sure to shut down Windows properly before rebooting by clicking Start and Shutdown.

1. What is the PC manufacturer and model? _____

Step 2. Determine the operating system.
Task: Determine the operating system and version.
Explanation: You can check the operating system by watching the screen as the computer boots, or by clicking Start, Help after it finishes booting. To verify the exact version number, click Start, Settings, Control Panel, and double-click the System icon. This also shows the manufacturer, model, CPU, and amount of RAM in the PC.

1. What operating system (OS) and version is the computer running? _____

Step 3. CMOS setup.
Task: Determine the keys to press to enter CMOS setup. Then determine the BIOS manufacturer and version number.
Explanation: While booting the system, watch the screen to see what keystroke(s) are required to enter the CMOS Setup mode. CMOS setup can be used to change settings such as the boot sequence (floppy, CD, or hard disk) and power saver options. As the system is booting, you should also see who makes the Basic Input Output System (BIOS) and what version it is.

1. How would you access the CMOS setup to change settings? _____

2. Who is the BIOS manufacturer? _____

Step 4. Verify browser software and plug-ins.
Task: Determine the browser software and version and check for the plug-ins required to view the Cisco online computer-based curriculum.
Explanation: Start the browser (Netscape or Internet Explorer) on the computer and determine the following information. Start one of the lessons from the Cisco online computer-based curriculum and run a movie clip and take a sample quiz. QuickTime (from Apple Computer) is required to run the videos and ShockWave (from Macromedia) is required to run the sample quizzes.

Cisco Labs–Semester 1–Networking Fundamentals
LAB 1.2.1.2–PC SOFTWARE–WORKSHEET

1. What is the browser software and version? _____

2. Is the QuickTime plug-in on this computer? _____

3. Is the ShockWave plug-in on this computer? _____

4. Does the sound work when you play videos? _____

Step 5. Verify your video settings.

Task: Click Start, Settings, Control Panel and then double-click the Display icon. Click the Settings tab.

Explanation: The display settings allow you to confirm that you have at least 800 x 600 resolution with 256 colors.

1. Record the settings on your computer below:

Screen Area (Resolution)	
Colors	

Cisco Labs–Semester 1–Networking Fundamentals
LAB 1.2.2–WEB BROWSER LITERACY–OVERVIEW
(Estimated time: 20 minutes)

Objectives:

- Learn how to use a Web browser to access Internet sites
- Become familiar with the concept of a URL
- Use a search engine to locate information on the Internet
- Access selected Web sites to learn the definitions of networking terms
- Use hyperlinks to jump from the current Web site to other Web sites

Background:

A Web browser is a powerful tool that many people use every day to surf different Web sites on the World Wide Web. With a Web browser, you can find anything from airline flight information to the directions on how to get to a specific address. A browser is a client application program or software that is loaded on the PC to gain access to the Internet and local Web pages.

The name of a Web sight, such as **www.cisco.com**, is also referred to as a Universal Resource Locator (URL). This URL points to the World Wide Web server (WWW) in the Cisco domain (CISCO) under the Commercial domain (COM). The www also refers to an HTTP or Hypertext Transfer Protocol server. You can also type in a slash after the Web site name and then the name of a Web page to get to a specific location on a Web site. When you type in the URL or name of a Web site, your browser makes a request of a Domain Name Server (DNS) in order to convert the URL to an IP address. The IP address is how the server (www.cisco.com) is actually contacted.

Web browsers can provide access to a number of search engines, such as www.yahoo.com, www.excite.com, www.lycos.com, and www.metacrawler.com (among others). You can use these search engines directly by typing in their URL or you can click Search from the Netscape or Internet Explorer menu. A number of Web sites provide definitions of networking and computer-related terms and acronyms. These can help you learn more about networking and do research on the Internet. Two of these are www.whatis.com and www.webopedia.com. Most Web sites contain hyperlinks, which are words that are underlined and highlighted. By clicking a hyperlink you "jump" to another page on the current site or to a page on another Web site.

Tools/Preparation:

Before you begin, the teacher or lab assistant will have a typical desktop Pentium-based (or comparable) PC available with the following software installed. The PC should be a classroom computer configured to access the Web-based Cisco curriculum and assessment system. You should also review Semester 1 online Lesson 1.

Required Resources:

- A computer running Windows 95/98
- Netscape or Internet Explorer software CD-ROM (if not already installed on the computer)
- Access to the Internet via an Internet service provider (ISP) using a local-area network (LAN) or dial-up

Cisco Labs–Semester 1–Networking Fundamentals
LAB 1.2.2–WEB BROWSER LITERACY–WORKSHEET

1. Install Netscape or Internet Explorer on your computer (if it has not already been done).

2. If you are on a LAN, start the Web browser (either Netscape or Internet Explorer). If you are using a modem to make the connection, you must dial your ISP before you can start your Web browser.

3. What version of Netscape or Internet Explorer are you using? _____
   _____

4. After you start your browser, click and highlight the Location field (with Netscape) or Address field (with Internet Explorer). Press the Delete key to delete the current address.

5. When your Location or Address field is empty, type in **www.cisco.com** to get to the Cisco Systems Web site. This is how you can navigate from one site to another on the World Wide Web (WWW).

6. Load a new page (type in a new location, for example, **www.nba.com**). Notice the status on the bottom bar of your browser. What do you see? _____

7. Each of the buttons on top of your browser has a function. Click the Back button. What did it do?
   _____

8. Click the Forward button. Does it take you to the NBA Web site? _____

9. Try clicking the Reload or Refresh button. What do you think they do? _____
   _____

10. Type in a new Web site address and click the Stop button. What happens? _____
    _____

11. Enter the URL for a search engine, such as www.metacrawler.com. Search for the word BROWSER. What was the result? _____
    _____

12. Enter the URL for www.webopedia.com. Enter the keyword BROWSER. What was the result?
    _____ What other hyperlinks were available? _____
    _____
    _____

Reflection Questions:

1. Identify a way in which you can navigate from one site to another. _____
   _____

2. If you see the same graphics or text the next time you go to the NBA site, what should you do to ensure that you could look at updated news? _____

Cisco Labs–Semester 1–Networking Fundamentals
LAB 1.2.3–BASIC TROUBLESHOOTING–OVERVIEW
(Estimated time: 30 minutes)

Objectives:
- Learn the proper sequence for troubleshooting computer- and network-related problems
- Become familiar with some of the more common hardware and software problems
- Given a basic problem situation, be able to troubleshoot and resolve the problem

Background:
The ability to effectively troubleshoot computer-related problems is an important skill. The process of identifying the problem and trying to solve it requires a systematic step-by-step approach. This lab introduces some basic hardware- and software-related problems to solve and helps you become more familiar with PC components and the software required to use the Cisco curriculum. The process of trying to solve a problem is fairly straightforward. Some of the suggestions here are more than what is required to solve basic hardware and software problems, but they help provide a framework and guidelines when more complex problems arise.

Step 1. Gather information:
- Observe the symptoms and try to characterize or identify the problem.
- Try to describe what is happening or not happening using proper terminology.
- Ask a coworker if he or she has encountered a similar problem.
- Get the opinions of others who might have more experience.
- Check Web sites and troubleshooting knowledge databases.

Step 2. Isolate the problem:
- Is it hardware- (check for lights and noises) or software- (errors on screen) related?
- Use substitution to isolate the problem if there is more than one component. (If the monitor does not work, it could be the monitor, video adapter, or cables.)
- Is it local (this workstation only) or remote (possible network-wide problem)?
- Does it affect this software only or more than one application?
- Is this the first time it has happened, or has it happened before?
- Was anything changed recently?

Step 3. Select one or more possible causes and identify potential solutions:
- Rank them in order of most likely to least likely cause.
- Check the simplest possible causes first. (Is the power turned on?)
- Check the easiest-to-check problems first. (Try a system reboot)
- Verify hardware first, then software. (Do any lights come on?)
- Start with the physical, then move to logical (check the NIC before the IP address).
- Troubleshoot from the bottom up. Always check OSI layer 0 first (the power cord layer!). *Note:* There is no OSI layer 0, but it is pretty important to check.

Step 4. Test the most likely solution based on your best guess, and check the results.

Step 5. When you think you have found the problem and corrected it, double-check to make sure everything still works.

Cisco Labs–Semester 1–Networking Fundamentals
LAB 1.2.3–BASIC TROUBLESHOOTING–WORKSHEET

Tools/Preparation:

Before you begin, the teacher or lab assistant will have a typical desktop Pentium-based (or comparable) PC available. The PC should be a classroom computer configured to access the Web-based Cisco curriculum and assessment system. You should also review Semester 1 online Lesson 1.

Required Resources:

- A computer running Windows 95/98
- Netscape or Internet Explorer software CD-ROM (if not already installed on the computer)
- Access to the Internet via an Internet service provider (ISP) using a LAN or dial-up

1. Work in teams of two. Team member A (or the instructor) will select two problems from the list of common hardware- and software-related problems (see answer section) and introduce the problems into the computer. The desired goal will be to run one of the videos from the semester 1 online curriculum. Team member A (or the instructor) should create the hardware- or software-related problems with the computer while the other is out of the room and then turn off the computer and monitor.

2. When team member B identifies the problems and corrects them, switch places and have the other introduce some new problems.

3. Each team member solving the problem should fill in the table based on the symptoms observed, problems identified, and solutions to the problem.

Team Member A

	Symptom Observed	Problem Identified	Solution
1st problem			
2nd problem			

Team Member B

	Symptom Observed	Problem Identified	Solution
1st problem			
2nd problem			

Cisco Labs–Semester 1–Networking Fundamentals
EXERCISE 1.3.6–BINARY NUMBERING–OVERVIEW
(Estimated time: 30 minutes)

Objectives:

- Identify the positions in a binary number and know the value of each
- Identify the positions in a decimal number and know the value of each
- Work with Base 10 exponents (powers of 10) and understand how position defines value
- Work with Base 2 exponents (powers of 2) and understand how position defines value
- Manually convert simple binary numbers and decimal numbers
- Manually convert 32-bit binary IP addresses and dotted decimal IP addresses
- Use the Windows Scientific Calculator to check your answers
- Describe the differences between binary and decimal numbering systems

Background:

This lab helps you learn to work with the binary numbering system. You convert binary numbers (Base 2) to decimal numbers (Base 10) and decimal to binary. Computers and networking equipment, such as routers, work with binary numbers, a series of Bits (short for Binary Digits) that are either on (a binary 1) or off (a binary 0). They are encoded internally in the PC and on networking media (cables) as either electrical voltages on copper cable, such as Unshielded Twisted-Pair (UTP), or as light pulses on fiber cable. The current version of the Internet Protocol (IPv4) uses a 32-bit address (usually divided into 4 "octets" or 8-bit bytes) to identify a particular network and a host on that network. Humans are more comfortable working with decimal numbers, so IP addresses are usually written as four decimal numbers separated by periods (dots), each representing an octet, to make them easier to read. This is referred to as *dotted decimal notation*. Understanding binary numbers and how they relate to decimal numbers is critical to understanding IP addresses, subnets, and network routing.

Tools/Preparation:

This is primarily a written lab exercise, but you do use the Windows Scientific Calculator, so you need access to a PC. You might want to refer to Lab 1.3, "PC Network Settings," for some real IP addresses to convert. Before beginning this lab, you should refer to the *Cisco Networking Academy Program: First-Year Companion Guide*, Second Edition. You should also review Semester 1 online Lesson 9.

Required Resources:

- PC workstation with Windows operating system (Windows 95, 98, NT, or 2000) installed and access to the Windows Calculator.

NOTES:

_____

_____

_____

_____

Cisco Labs–Semester 1–Networking Fundamentals
EXERCISE 1.3.6–BINARY NUMBERING–WORKSHEET

Step 1. **Decimal numbers.**

Explanation: We are most familiar with "decimal" numbers (Base 10). The decimal numbering system is based on the powers of 10. This exercise helps you develop an understanding of the exponentiation or "powers" of numbers using the Base 10 number system, which is what our arithmetic and money systems are based on. With Base 10, the right-most position has a value of 1 (same as Base 2). Each position moving to the left is worth 10 times more. 10 to the zero power (10^0) is 1, 10 to the first power (10^1 or 10 x 1) is 10, 10 to the second power (10^2 or 10 x 10) is 100 and 10 to the third power (10^3 or 10 x 10 x 10) is 1000, and so on. Just multiply the number in each position times the value of each position (for example, $400 = 4 \times 10^2$ or 4 x 100). Remember that any number to the zero power is 1.

Decimal Number Conversion Example

The following chart shows how the decimal number system represents the number 352,481. This helps in understanding the binary numbering system.

Exponent	10^6	10^5	10^4	10^3	10^2	10^1	10^0
Position	7	6	5	4	3	2	1
Value	1000000	100000	10000	1000	100	10	1
Number	0	3	5	2	4	8	1
	0 x 1,000,000	3 x 100,000	5 x 10,000	2 x 1000	4 x 100	8 x 10	1 x 1

The number 352,481 if read from right to left would be (1 x 1) + (8 x 10) + (4 x 100) + (2 x 1000) + (5 x 10,000) + (3 x 100,000) for a total of 352,481 (a 6-digit number).

Here is another way to look at it that makes it easier to add up the decimal number values:

Position of digit (from right)	Value of bit position (10^X or 10 to the power of)	Number value from 0 to 9	Calculation	Decimal Value
1st Decimal Digit	10^0 or 1	1	1 x 1	1
2nd Decimal Digit	10^1 or 2	8	8 x 10	80
3rd Decimal Digit	10^2 or 4	4	4 x 100	400
4th Decimal Digit	10^3 or 8	2	2 x 1000	2000
5th Decimal Digit	10^4 or 16	5	5 x 10,000	50,000
6th Decimal Digit	10^5 or 32	3	3 x 100,000	300,000
Decimal Value (Total of 6 digits)				352,481

Cisco Labs–Semester 1–Networking Fundamentals
EXERCISE 1.3.6–BINARY NUMBERING–WORKSHEET

Step 2. **Binary numbers.**

Explanation: Binary means "two," and each digit in a binary number can only have two values (zero or one). It is also called a Base 2 numbering system. Binary numbers are the key to understanding how routers work and how packets get from one workstation (host) to another server (host) on a TCP/IP network. Internet addresses are made up of 32 bits or four groups of 8 bits known as "octets." Each bit of each octet has a value based on its position. Of the 8 bits in an octet, the left-most bit is worth 128 (2^7) and the right-most bit is worth 1 (2^0). The value of each bit is based on the powers of 2.

The binary numbering system is based on the powers of 2. This exercise helps you develop an understanding of exponentiation or "powers" of numbers using the Base 2 number system, which is what all computers and data communications use. With Base 2, the right-most position has a value of 1, as with base 10. Each position moving to the left is worth 2 times more. 2 to the zero power (2^0) is 1, and 2 to the first power (2^1 or 2 x 1) is 2. 2 to the second power (2^2 or 2 x 2) is 4 and 2 to the third power (2^3 or 2 x 2 x 2) is 8, and so on. Just multiply the number in each position (either a 0 or a 1) times the value of each position (for example, $8 = 1$ x 2^3 or 1 x 8) and add up the total. Remember, any number to the zero power is 1. Convert the following binary numbers to decimal numbers. In the first exercise, you convert a binary number to a decimal number. Starting from the right, the first binary digit is a zero, which is calculated as zero times 2^0 (two to the zero power or 0 x 1–anything to the zero power is 1). The second position from the left is also a zero, so this is zero times 2^1 (or 0 x 2). The third binary number from the right is a 1. This is 1 times 2^2 (two to the 2nd power or 4).

Binary Number Conversion Example

The following table shows the detail calculations (starting from the right side) to convert the binary number 10011100 into a decimal number.

Position of digit (from right)	Value of bit position (2 to the power of)	Is bit a One (on) or a Zero (off)?	Calculation	Decimal Value
1st Binary Digit	2^0 or 1	0	0 x 1	0
2nd Binary Digit	2^1 or 2	0	0 x 2	0
3rd Binary Digit	2^2 or 4	1	1 x 4	4
4th Binary Digit	2^3 or 8	1	1 x 8	8
5th Binary Digit	2^4 or 16	1	1 x 16	16
6th Binary Digit	2^5 or 32	0	0 x 32	0
7th Binary Digit	2^6 or 64	0	0 x 64	0
8th Binary Digit	2^7 or 128	1	1 x 128	128
Decimal Value. (Sum total of 8 bits)				156

Cisco Labs–Semester 1–Networking Fundamentals
EXERCISE 1.3.6–BINARY NUMBERING–WORKSHEET

Step 3. Binary–to–decimal practice exercises.

Task: Practice converting the four binary octets of an IP address to the dotted decimal equivalent.

Explanation: Look at the binary number bit status. If there is a 1 in a position, add the value shown. If there is a 0 in a position, do not add it. Note that 8 bits cannot represent a decimal number greater than 255. (If all eight positions are ones, $128 + 64 + 32 + 16 + 8 + 4 + 2 + 1 = 255$.)

1. Solve for the 1st, 2nd, 3rd, and 4th octet decimal value.

Exponent	2^7	2^6	2^5	2^4	2^3	2^2	2^1	2^0
Bit Position	8	7	6	5	4	3	2	1
Value	128	64	32	16	8	4	2	1
Binary number bit status	1	0	0	1	1	1	0	0

1st Octet Decimal Value: _____

Exponent	2^7	2^6	2^5	2^4	2^3	2^2	2^1	2^0
Bit Position	8	7	6	5	4	3	2	1
Value	128	64	32	16	8	4	2	1
Binary number bit status	1	1	1	0	0	0	1	1

2nd Octet Decimal Value: _____

Exponent	2^7	2^6	2^5	2^4	2^3	2^2	2^1	2^0
Bit Position	8	7	6	5	4	3	2	1
Value	128	64	32	16	8	4	2	1
Binary number bit status	0	1	1	1	0	0	0	0

3rd Octet Decimal Value: _____

Exponent	2^7	2^6	2^5	2^4	2^3	2^2	2^1	2^0
Bit Position	8	7	6	5	4	3	2	1
Value	128	64	32	16	8	4	2	1
Binary number bit status	1	1	0	1	1	0	1	0

4th Octet Decimal Value: _____

2. Enter the dotted decimal octet values for all four octets for the following IP address:

10011100 . 11100011 . 01110000 . 11011010

_____   _____   _____   _____

Cisco Labs–Semester 1–Networking Fundamentals
EXERCISE 2.3.4–OSI MODEL and TCP/IP–OVERVIEW
(Estimated time: 20 minutes)

Objectives:
- Describe the 4 layers of the TCP/IP model
- Relate the 7 layers of the OSI model to the 4 layers of the TCP/IP model
- Name the primary TCP/IP protocols and utilities that operate at each layer

Background:
This lab helps you develop a better understanding of the seven layers of the OSI model as they relate to the most popular functioning networking model in existence, the TCP/IP model. The Internet is based on TCP/IP, which has become the standard language of networking. Although the TCP/IP model is the most widely used, the 7 layers of the OSI model are the ones most commonly used to describe and compare networking software and hardware from various vendors. It is important to know both the OSI and TCP/IP models and to be able to relate (or map) the layers of one to the other. An understanding of the TCP/IP model and the protocols and utilities that operate at each layer is essential to troubleshooting.

Tools/Preparation:
You can work individually or in teams. Before beginning this lab, you should refer to the *Cisco Networking Academy Program: First-Year Companion Guide*, Second Edition. You should also review Semester 1 online Lesson 2.

Required Resources:
- PC workstation with monitor, keyboard, mouse, and power cords
- Windows operating system (Windows 95, 98, NT, or 2000) installed on PC
- NIC installed and Cat 5 patch cable with connection to the Internet
- Browser software installed (Netscape 4.6.1 or Internet Explorer 5.1 Flash Plug-in)
- Apple QuickTime and ShockWave Macromedia browser plug-ins
- Sample Ethernet and Token Ring NICs with different connectors (Coax, AUI, RJ-45)
- Sample hubs, switches, and routers

NOTES: _____

_____

_____

_____

_____

_____

Cisco Labs–Semester 1–Networking Fundamentals
EXERCISE 2.3.4–OSI MODEL and TCP/IP–WORKSHEET

Step 1. The OSI model and associated TCP/IP protocol stack layers.
  Task: Fill out the following chart based on your knowledge of the OSI and TCP/IP models.
  Explanation: Your understanding of the OSI model as it relates to the TCP/IP model greatly
  increases your ability to absorb and categorize networking information as you learn it.

1. List the 7 layers of the OSI model from the top to the bottom with the proper name for each
    layer. List the TCP/IP layer number and its correct name in the next columns. Also list the
    term used for the encapsulation units, the related TCP/IP protocols/utilities, and the devices
    that operate at each layer. *Note:* More than one OSI layer will be related to certain TCP/IP
    layers.

OSI Comparison with TCP/IP Protocol Stack

OSI #	OSI Layer Name	TCP/IP #	TCP/IP Layer Name	Encapsul. Units	TCP/IP Protocols at Each TCP/IP Layer	TCP Utilities
7						
6						
5						
4						
3						
2						
1						

Cisco Labs–Semester 1–Networking Fundamentals
EXERCISE 2.3.5–OSI MODEL LAYERS–OVERVIEW
(Estimated time: 20 minutes)

Objectives:
- Name the seven layers of the OSI model in order using a mnemonic (memory jogger)
- Describe the characteristics, functions, and keywords relating to each layer
- Describe the packaging units used to encapsulate each layer
- Name several protocols and standards that operate at each layer

Background:
This lab helps you develop a better understanding of the seven layers of the OSI model. You identify the characteristics of each layer as well as the terminology at each layer. The OSI model was developed by the ISO to help provide a common framework for the development of both local-area networks (LANs) and wide-area networks (WANs). Most network architectures and companies do not adhere exactly to the OSI model but use it to describe their products and compare them to others. The OSI model helps us troubleshoot networking problems by breaking down the networking process (communication from hosts to servers) into distinct layers where functions must occur and identifying tools that can help isolate the problem. An understanding of the OSI model is essential to success in the world of networking. This lab focuses on the Ethernet network architecture and related physical devices.

Tools/Preparation:
This is primarily a written lab exercise, but you also identify physical devices that relate to the layers of the OSI model. Before you begin this lab, the teacher or lab assistant should have samples of typical networking components such as network interface cards (NICs), hubs, cables, routers, switches, and so on. You can work individually or in teams. Before beginning this lab, you should refer to the *Cisco Networking Academy Program: First-Year Companion Guide*, Second Edition. You should also review Semester 1 online Lesson 2.

Required Resources:
- PC workstation with monitor, keyboard, mouse, and power cords
- Windows operating system (Windows 95, 98, NT, or 2000) installed on PC
- NIC installed and Cat 5 patch cable with connection to the Internet
- Browser software installed (Netscape 4.6.1 or Internet Explorer 5.1 Flash Plug-in)
- Apple QuickTime and ShockWave Macromedia browser plug-ins
- Sample Ethernet and Token Ring NICs with different connectors (Coax, AUI, RJ-45)
- Sample hubs, switches, and routers

NOTES: _____

_____

_____

Cisco Labs–Semester 1–Networking Fundamentals
EXERCISE 2.3.5–OSI MODEL LAYERS–WORKSHEET

Step 1. The OSI Model layers–functions and devices.

Task: Fill out the following charts based on your knowledge of the OSI model.

Explanation: Your understanding of the OSI model will greatly increase your ability to absorb and categorize networking information as you learn it.

1. List the 7 layers of the OSI model from the top to the bottom. Give a mnemonic word for each layer that can help you remember it and then list the keywords and phrases that describe the characteristics and function of each.

Layer #	Name	Mnemonic	Key Words and Description of Function
7			
6			
5			
4			
3			
2			
1			

2. List the 7 layers of the OSI model. List the encapsulation unit used to describe the data grouping at each layer and the corresponding devices or components that operate at this level.

Layer #	Name	Encapsulation Unit or Logical Grouping	Devices or Components That Operate at This Level
7			
6			
5			
4			
3			
2			
1			

Cisco Labs–Semester 1–Networking Fundamentals
LAB 3.4.2–BASIC LAN SETUP–OVERVIEW
(Estimated time: 60 minutes)

Objectives:

- Create a simple LAN with two PCs using a single crossover cable to connect the workstations
- Create a simple LAN with two PCs using an Ethernet hub and two straight-through cables to connect the workstations
- Connect the hub-based mini-LAN to the Internet if a connection is available
- Use the Control Panel/Network utility to verify and configure the network settings
- Use the ICMP Ping command to verify the TCP/IP connection between the two workstations
- Use the WINIPCFG.EXE utility to verify all IP configuration settings

Background:

In this lab, you learn how to connect two PCs to create a simple peer-to-peer LAN or workgroup. The instructions for this lab focus on the Windows 95 or 98 operating system. You share a folder on one workstation and connect to that folder from the other workstation. This lab is divided into three exercises as follows:

Exercise A. The two PCs (or workstations) will be connected directly to each other from one network interface card (NIC) to the other NIC using a crossover cable. This can be useful to allow you to create a mini-lab for testing purposes with the need for a hub. Because the NICs on the workstations are directly connected, you are not able to connect any additional workstations.

Exercise B. The two PCs will be connected with a hub between them. Using a hub allows for more than just two workstations to be connected, depending on the number of ports on the hub. Hubs can have anywhere from 4 to 24 ports.

Note: For both Exercises A and B, you need to verify that the workstations are functioning and that network hardware is installed properly. You also need to verify and configure all TCP/IP protocol network settings for the two workstations to communicate, such as IP address and subnet mask.

Exercise C. (Optional) The two PCs attached to the hub will be connected to the Internet with another straight-through cable connected to a live hub or switch. You will use your browser to access a Web site.

Tools/Preparation:

It is best to start with a fresh install of Windows 98. The workstations should have network interface cards (NICs) installed with the proper drivers (floppy disk or CD) available. Before beginning this lab, you should refer to *Cisco Networking Academy Program: First-Year Companion Guide*, Second Edition. You should also review Semester 1 online Lesson number 1.

Required Resources:

- Two Pentium-based workstations with a NIC in each (NIC drivers should be available)
- Exercise A: One CAT5 Crossover cable to connect the workstations without a hub
- Exercise B: An Ethernet hub (4 or 8 port) and two CAT5 straight-wired cables
- Exercise C: A connection to the Internet if available with a third straight-through cable on the hub
- Windows 98 CD-ROM to do fresh install or to use when network setting changes are made

Cisco Labs–Semester 1–Networking Fundamentals
LAB 3.4.2–BASIC LAN SETUP–WORKSHEET

In this lab, you set up a small peer-to-peer Ethernet LAN workgroup using two workstations. Answer the following questions with each step as you check and/or configure the necessary components.

Note: Steps 1 and 2 (physical LAN connections) are different between Exercises A and B. The steps from 3 on should be the same because they relate only to the workstations and should be performed on both workstations.

Step 1. Check local-area network (LAN) connections.
  Task: Verify the cables.
  Explanation:
  Exercise A. A single CAT 5 crossover cable is used to connect the workstations together. Verify that the pins are wired as a crossover by holding both RJ45 connectors side by side with the clip down and inspect them. Pairs 2 and 3 should be reversed. Refer to Lab 5.3.4.1 for correct wire color and pin locations.

  Exercise B. Check each of the two CAT 5 cables from each workstation to the hub. Verify that the pins are wired straight through by holding the two RJ-45 connectors for each cable side by side with the clip down and inspect them. All pins should have the same color wire on the same pin at both ends of the cable. (Pin 1 should match pin 1 and pin 8 should match pin 8, and so on.) Refer to Lab 5.3.4.1 for correct pin locations.

  1. Are the cable(s) wired correctly? _____

Step 2. Plug in and connect the equipment.
  Task: Check the workstations (and hub for Exercise B).
  Explanation:
  Exercises A. Check to make sure that the NICs are installed correctly in each workstation. Plug in the workstations and turn them on.

  Exercise B. Plug the hub or its AC adapter into a power outlet. Plug the straight-through cable from workstation 1 into port 1 of the hub and the cable from workstation 2 into port 2 of the hub. After the workstations have booted, check the green link light on the back of each NIC and the green lights on ports 1 and 2 of the hub to verify that they are communicating. This also verifies a good physical connection between the hub and the NICs in the workstations (OSI Layers 1 and 2). If the link light is not on, it usually indicates a bad cable connection or an incorrectly wired cable, or the NIC or hub might not be functioning correctly.

  1. Are the NIC and hub link lights on? _____

Cisco Labs–Semester 1–Networking Fundamentals
LAB 3.4.2–BASIC LAN SETUP–WORKSHEET

Step 3. Network adapters and protocols.

   Task: Check the Network Adapter (NIC): Use the Control Panel, System, Device Manager utility to verify that the Network Adapter (NIC) is functioning properly for both workstations. Double-click Network Adapters and then right-click the NIC adapter in use. Click Properties to see if the device is working properly.

   Explanation: If there is a problem with the NIC or driver, the icon shows a yellow circle with an exclamation mark in it with (possible resource conflict) or a red X indicating a serious problem (device could cause Windows to lock up).

   1. What does the NIC properties screen say about the Network Adapter?

   _____

Step 4. Check the TCP/IP protocol settings.

   Task: Use the Control Panel, Network utility and select the TCP/IP protocol from the Configuration Tab and click Properties. Check the IP address and subnet mask for both workstations on the IP Address tab.

   Explanation: The IP addresses can be set to anything as long as they are compatible and on the same network. Record the existing settings before making any changes in case they need to be set back (for instance, they might be DHCP clients now). For this lab, use the Class C network address of 200.150.100.0 and set workstation 1 to the static IP address 200.150.100.1 and set workstation 2 to 200.150.100.2. Set the default subnet mask on each workstation to 255.255.255.0.

   1. Have the IP addresses and subnet mask been set? _____

Step 5. Check the TCP/IP settings with the WINIPCFG utility.

   Task: Use the winipcfg.exe command to see your TCP/IP settings on one screen. Click Start, Programs, and select the MS-DOS Prompt.

   Explanation: Enter the winipcfg /all command (you do not need the .exe because this is an executable command) to see all TCP/IP-related settings for your workstation.

   1. Using the results of the winipcfg command, fill in the blanks for each workstation:

Workstation 1 Name:	Workstation 2 Name:
IP Address:	IP Address:
Subnet Mask:	Subnet Mask:
MAC (Hardware) Address:	MAC (Hardware) Address:

Step 6. Check the network connection with the Ping utility.

   Task: Use the Ping command to check for basic TCP/IP connectivity. Click Start, Programs and the MS-DOS Prompt. Enter the Ping command followed by the IP address of the other workstation.

   Explanation: This verifies that you have a good OSI Layers 1 through 3 connection.

   1. What was the result of the Ping command?_____

   _____

Cisco Labs–Semester 1–Networking Fundamentals
LAB 3.4.2–BASIC LAN SETUP–WORKSHEET

Step 7. Windows Networking options.

Task: Check Network Configuration: Use the Control Panel, Network utility, Configuration tab and check to be sure that you have the following networking components installed:
1. Microsoft Family or Microsoft Windows Logon Client (small computer icon)
2. The NIC adapter (small NIC icon)
3. The TCP/IP Protocol (small network cable connection icon)

There might be other adapters and protocols listed, but these are the ones required for this lab. Click the Access Control tab and verify that the Share Level Access Control button is selected. Select the Microsoft Family or Windows client and click Properties. Click the Identification tab and enter a name for the first computer of PC1. Name the other computer PC2. The Workgroup should be WORKGROUP and the Computer Description is optional.

Explanation: You need to reboot the computer and insert the Windows 98 CD when prompted.

1. List the networking components installed:

Client (computer icon)	
Adapter (NIC icon)	
Protocol (net connection icon)	
Other Client/Adapter/Protocol	

Step 8. Check File and Print Sharing.

Task: Use the Control Panel, Network utility, Configuration tab and click the File and Print Sharing button. On the workstation that will have the folder to be shared, check the box that says, "I want to be able to give others access to my files" to allow each workstation to share its folders. You can also check the box that says, "I want to be able to allow others to print to my printers" to allow the other workstation to print if you have a shared printer attached to one of the workstations.

Step 9. File folders and sharing options.

Task: Set up a file folder to share: On workstation one, use Windows Explorer to create a folder to be shared Called "Testfolder." Using Windows Explorer, My Computer, or Network Neighborhood, select the folder and right-click to share it. Enter the name of the share and click OK. From the other workstation, click Network Neighborhood and select the first workstation and the shared folder.

Explanation: You can map a drive to the shared folder if you wish. While working in the shared folder on the other workstation, create a new document and save it. If you have a printer shared, you might want to print the document.

1. Document the results of the folder sharing and file creating process:

_____
_____
_____

Cisco Labs–Semester 1–Networking Fundamentals
LAB 4.2.1–SAFE HANDLING and USE OF A MULTIMETER–OVERVIEW
(Estimated time: 15 minutes)

Objective:
- Learn how to use or handle a multimeter correctly

Background:
A multimeter is a powerful electrical testing tool that can detect voltage levels, resistance levels, and open/closed circuits. It can check both Alternating Current (AC) and Direct Current (DC) voltage. Open and closed circuits are indicated by resistance measurements in Ohms. Each computer and networking device consists of millions of circuits and small electrical components. A multimeter can be used to debug electrical problems within a computer/networking device or between networking devices.

Tools/Preparation:
Prior to starting the lab, the teacher or lab assistant should have several multimeters available (one for each team of two students) and various batteries for testing. Work in teams of two. You should review Semester 1 online Lesson 4.

Required Resources:
- A digital multimeter (Fluke 12B or similar) for each team
- A manual for the multimeter
- A battery (for example, a 9v, 1.5V or lantern; it doesn't matter) for each team to test

Cisco Labs–Semester 1–Networking Fundamentals
LAB 4.2.1–SAFE HANDLING and USE OF A MULTIMETER–
WORKSHEET

Note: The multimeter is a sensitive piece of electronic test equipment. Be sure that you do not drop it or throw it around. Be careful not to accidentally nick or cut the red or black wire leads (probes). Because it is possible to check high voltages, extra care should be taken when doing so to avoid electrical shock.

Perform the following steps to become familiar with the handling of the multimeter:

Step 1. Insert the red and black leads (probes) into the proper jacks on the meter. The black probe should go in the COM jack and the red probe should go in the + (plus or positive) jack.

Step 2. Turn on the multimeter (click/turn to the on button). What model of multimeter are you working with? _____
What action must you take to turn the meter on?
_____

Step 3. Switch or turn to different measurements (for example, voltage, ohms, and so on). How many different switch positions does the multimeter have? _____
What are they? _____
_____

Step 4. Switch or turn the multimeter to the voltage measurement. What is the symbol for this? ____

Step 5. Put the tip of the red (positive) lead on one end of a battery (+ side), and put the tip of the black (negative) lead on the other end of a battery. Is any number showing up on the multimeter? _____ If not, make sure you switch to the correct type of measurement (Vol, voltage, or V). If the voltage is negative, reverse your leads.

Reflection:

1. Name one thing that you should not do to a multimeter.

2. Name one important function of a multimeter.

3. If you get a negative voltage when measuring a battery, why is that?

Cisco Labs–Semester 1–Networking Fundamentals
LAB 4.2.2–RESISTANCE MEASUREMENTS–OVERVIEW
(Estimated time: 30 minutes)

Objective:
- Demonstrate your ability to measure resistance and continuity with the multimeter

Background:
The digital multimeter is a versatile testing and troubleshooting device. In this lab, you learn how to perform resistance measurements, and related measurements called continuity. Resistance is measured in Ohms (indicated by the Greek letter Omega or Ω). Copper wires (conductors) such as those commonly used in network cabling (UTP and coax) normally have very low resistance or "good" continuity (the wire is continuous) if you check them from end to end. If there is a break in the wire, it is called "open," which creates very high resistance (air has nearly infinite resistance, indicated by the infinity symbol or ∞, a sideways 8). The multimeter has a battery in it, which it uses to test the resistance of a conductor (wire) or insulator (wire sheathing). When the probes are applied to the ends of a conductor, the battery current flows and the meter measures the resistance it encounters. If the battery in the multimeter is low or dead, you must replace it or you will not be able to take resistance measurements.

With this lab, you test common networking materials so that you can become familiar with them and their resistance characteristics. You first learn to use the resistance setting on the multimeter. As you measure small resistances, you should also note the continuity feature. The instructions provided are for the Fluke 12B. Other meters will function in a similar way.

Tools/Preparation:
Prior to starting the lab, the teacher or lab assistant should have several multimeters available (one for each team of two students) and various networking-related items for testing resistance. Work in teams of two. You should review Semester 1 online Lesson 4.

Required Resources:
- Fluke 12B multimeter or equivalent
- 1000 Ohm resistor
- 10,000 Ohm resistor
- Pencil for creating graphite paths on paper
- Cat 5 jack
- Small (0.2m or approximately 6 to 8 inches) section of Cat 5 UTP solid cable
- BNC terminated coaxial cable
- Unconnected DB9 to RJ-45 adapter
- Terminated Cat 5 UTP patch cable

Cisco Labs–Semester 1–Networking Fundamentals
LAB 4.2.2–RESISTANCE MEASUREMENTS–WORKSHEET

Step 1. Move the rotary selector to the Omega symbol for Ohms (red Ω) in order to measure resistance. Press the button that has the Ohms symbol (red Ω) on it to select between resistance measurements and continuity.

Resistance Measurements: The screen will show Ω (ohms), KΩ (kilohms = thousands of Ohms) or MΩ (megohms = millions of Ohms). Use the Range button to change the range of resistance to be measured based on what resistance you expect to get. If you expect low resistance (less than 10 ohms), select a low scale (like Ω). If you expect a high reading (over 10,000 ohms), select a high scale (like KΩ). If the resistance reading is over the range selected, the OL or Over Limit indicator will be displayed on the screen. The resistance setting is for measuring exact amounts of resistance.

Continuity Measurements: The screen will show a diode symbol, which is a small black triangle pointing to a vertical bar. A diode is an electronic device that either passes or blocks electrical current. You might see a small sound symbol next to it, which means that when there is good continuity (no resistance), the beep will sound. The continuity setting is used when you just want to know if there is a good path for electricity and don't care about the exact amount of resistance.

Step 2. Check the following resistances. Turn the meter off when finished or battery will drain.

Item to Measure the Resistance of	Set Selector and Range Scale to	Resistance Reading
1000 Ω Resistor		
10 kΩ Resistor		
Graphite marking from a pencil on a piece of paper		
Cat 5 jack		
0.2 m section of Cat 5 UTP solid cable		
Touch red and black probe contacts together		
Your own body (touch the tips of the probes with your fingers)		
BNC terminated coaxial cable		
Unconnected DB9 to RJ-45 adapter		
Terminated Cat 5 UTP patch cable		

Reflection Question: What purpose might the multimeter serve in maintaining and troubleshooting a computer network? _____

Cisco Labs–Semester 1–Networking Fundamentals
LAB 4.2.3–VOLTAGE MEASUREMENTS–OVERVIEW
(Estimated time: 30 minutes)

Objective:
- Demonstrate your ability to measure voltage safely with the multimeter

Background:
The digital multimeter is a versatile testing and troubleshooting device. In this lab, you learn how to perform both Direct Current (DC) and Alternating Current (AC) voltage measurements. Voltage is measured in either AC or DC volts (indicated by a V). Voltage is the pressure that moves electrons through a circuit from one place to another. Voltage differential is essential to the flow of electricity. The voltage differential between a cloud in the sky and the earth is what causes lightning to strike. *Note:* It is very important to be careful when taking voltage measurements because it is possible to receive an electrical shock.

Direct Current (DC): DC voltage rises to a set level and then stays at that level and flows in one direction (positive or negative). Batteries produce DC voltage and are commonly rated at 1.5v or 9v (flashlight batteries) and 6v (lantern and vehicle batteries). Typically, the battery in your car or truck is a 12v battery. When an electrical "load" such as a light bulb or motor is placed between the positive (+) and negative (-) terminals of a battery, electricity flows.

Alternating Current (AC): AC voltage rises above zero (positive) and then falls below zero (negative) and actually changes direction very rapidly. The most common example of AC voltage is the wall outlet in your house or business. These outlets provide approximately 120 volts of AC directly to any electrical appliance that is plugged in, such as a computer, toaster, or television. Some devices, such as small printers and laptop computers, have a transformer (small black box) that plugs into a 120V AC wall outlet and then converts the AC voltage to DC voltage for use by the device. Some AC outlets can provide a higher voltage of 220V for use by devices and equipment with heavier requirements, such as clothes dryers and arc welders.

Tools/Preparation:
Prior to starting the lab, the teacher or lab assistant should have several multimeters available (one for each team of students) and various items for testing voltage. Work in teams of two. You should review Semester 1 online Lesson 4.

Required Resources:
Required voltage measurement items:
- Fluke 12B multimeter (or equivalent)
- An assortment of batteries: A cell, C cell, D cell, 9 Volts, 6 V lantern
- Duplex wall outlet (typically 120v)
- Power supply (for laptop or other networking electrical device)
Optional voltage measurement items:
- A lemon with a galvanized nail stuck in one side and a piece of uninsulated copper wire stuck in the opposite side
- Solar cell with leads attached
- Homemade generator (wire wound around a pencil 50 times and a magnet)

Cisco Labs–Semester 1–Networking Fundamentals
LAB 4.2.3–VOLTAGE MEASUREMENTS–WORKSHEET

Step 1. Move the rotary selector to the V symbol for voltage (black V) in order to be able to measure voltage. Press the button that has the VDC and VAC symbol to select between Direct Current (DC) and Alternating Current (AC) measurements.

Direct Current Measurements: The screen will show a V (voltage) with a series of dots and a line over the top. There are several scales available depending on the voltage to be measured. They start from millivolts (abbreviated mV = 1000th of a volt) to voltages up to hundreds of volts. Use the Range button to change the range of DC voltage to be measured based on what voltage you expect to measure. Batteries (less than 15 volts) can typically be measured accurately with the VDC scale and 0.0 range. DC voltage measurements can be used to determine if batteries are good or if there is voltage coming out of an AC adapter (transformer or converter). These are common and are used with hubs, modems, laptops, printers, and other peripherals. These adapters can take wall outlet AC voltage and step it down to lower AC voltages for the device attached or can convert the AC voltage to DC and step it down. Check the back of the adapter to see what the input (AC) and output voltages (AC or DC) should be.

Alternating Current Measurements: The screen will show a V (voltage) with a tilde (~) after it. This represents alternating current. There are several scales available depending on the voltage to be measured. They start from millivolts (abbreviated mV = 1000th of a volt) to voltage up to hundreds of volts. Use the Range button to change the range of AC voltage to be measured based on what voltage you expect to measure. Voltage from power outlets (120v or greater) can typically be measured accurately with the VAC scale and 0.0 range. AC voltage measurements are useful in determining if there is adequate voltage coming from an AC outlet to power the equipment plugged in.

Use a Fluke 12B multimeter (or equivalent) to measure the voltage of each of the following:

Step 2. Check the following voltages. Be sure to turn the meter off when finished.

Item to Measure the Voltage Of	Set Selector and Range Scale to	Voltage Reading
Batteries: A cell (AA, AAA), C cell, D cell, 9 Volts, 6 V lantern		
Duplex wall outlet (typically 120v)		
Power supply (converts AC to lower AC or DC) for laptop, mobile phone, or other networking electrical device		
(Optional) A lemon with a galvanized nail stuck in one side and a piece of uninsulated copper wire stuck in the opposite side		

Reflection Question: Why might you want to measure voltage when troubleshooting a network?

Cisco Labs–Semester 1–Networking Fundamentals
LAB 4.2.4–SERIES CIRCUITS–OVERVIEW
(Estimated time: 30 minutes)

Objective:
- Build series circuits and explore their basic properties

Background:
One of the most basic concepts in electronics is that of a continuous loop through which electrons flow, and which is called a circuit. Throughout networking there are references to ground loop circuit, circuit versus packet switching, and virtual circuits, in addition to all the real circuits formed by networking media and networking devices. One of the fundamental electrical circuits is the series circuit. While most networking devices and networks are built from very complex circuits that are beyond the scope of the lessons included in this course, the process of building some series circuits will help you with some of the terminology and concepts of networking. This lab also helps increase your overall understanding of some of the most basic electrical circuit building blocks.

Tools/Preparation:
Prior to starting the lab, the teacher or lab assistant should have several multimeters available (one for each team of students) and various items for testing voltage. Work in teams of two. You should review Semester 1 online Lesson 4.

Required Resources:
- Fluke 12B multimeter (or equivalent)
- Light switch
- Wire cutters/stripper
- Copper wire
- 2 light bulbs (6v) with bulb bases
- 6-Volt lantern battery

Cisco Labs–Semester 1–Networking Fundamentals
LAB 4.2.4–SERIES CIRCUITS–WORKSHEET

Step 1. Measure the resistances of all devices and components except the battery. Measure the voltage of the battery. All resistances should be less than 1 Ω (Ohm), except the light bulbs. All the devices except the battery should register continuity (with the tone), indicating a short circuit or a conducting path.

Check the following resistances. Turn the meter off when finished or it drains the battery.

Item to Measure the Resistance of	Set Selector and Range Scale to	Resistance Reading
Pieces of wire to connect components		
Light switch		
Light bulbs		

Step 2. Measure the voltage of the battery, unloaded (with nothing attached to it).

Item to Measure the Voltage of	Set Selector and Range Scale to	Voltage Reading
Lantern battery: (6 V) with no load		

Step 3. Build a series circuit, one device at a time (use 1 battery, 1 switch, 1 bulb, and connecting wires). Connect the battery positive lead to the end of one wire and connect the negative lead to the other wire. If the switch is turned on, the bulb should light. Disconnect one thing and see that the circuit is broken. Did the bulb go out? _____

Step 4. Measure the battery voltage while the circuit is running. The switch should be turned on and the light bulb should be lit. What was the voltage of the battery with the light bulb on? _____

Step 5. Add the second bulb in series and measure the battery voltage again. What was the voltage of the battery with the light bulb on? _____

Reflection:

How do series circuits apply to networking?

_____

_____

Cisco Labs–Semester 1–Networking Fundamentals
LAB 4.2.5–COMMUNICATIONS CIRCUIT–OVERVIEW
(Estimated time: 50 minutes)

Objective:

- Design, build, and test a simple, complete, fast, and reliable communication system, using common materials

Background:

For reliable communications to take place on a network, many things must be defined ahead of time, including the physical method of signaling and the meaning of each signal or series of signals. With this lab, you create a simple physical network and agree on some basic rules for communication in order to send and receive data. This will be a digital network based on the American Standard Code for Information Interchange (ASCII). It will be somewhat similar to the old telegraph Morse code-based systems where the only means of communicating over long distances was by sending a series of dots and dashes as electrical signals over wires between locations. Although the technology used will be simpler than real systems, many of the key concepts of data communications between computers will arise. This lab also helps to clarify the functions of the layers of the OSI model.

Tools/Preparation:

Prior to starting the lab, the teacher or lab assistant should have several multimeters available (one for each team of students) and various items for construction of a simple communication network. Work in teams of 2 to 4. Review Semester 1 online Lesson 4 prior to starting this lab.

Required Resources:

Review the purpose of each of the following required items because it will help in designing your network.

Network Construction Item Required	Purpose
Fluke 12B multimeter (or equivalent)	For testing communication connections
20' Cat 5 UTP cable	For the physical communications lines (the cabling medium)
ASCII chart	To help with coding and interpretation of signals (If you do not have a hardcopy of the 7-bit ASCII code chart, search the Internet for the words "ACSII chart" and you will find several listed.)
Light switch	To activate the signaling device in order to create the digital on/off (binary) signals
Light bulbs (6v) with bulb bases	To act as the signaling device
6-Volt lantern battery	To power the signaling device
Wire cutters/stripper	To adjust the length and prepare the ends of the communication lines

Cisco Labs–Semester 1–Networking Fundamentals
LAB 4.2.5–COMMUNICATIONS CIRCUIT–WORKSHEET

Lab Goals:

Your group must design, build, and test a communications circuit with another team. You must communicate as much data as possible, quickly and with as few errors as possible. Spoken, written, or miscellaneous nonverbal communication of any kind is not allowed–only communication over the wire. You will agree as a team on the physical connections and on the coding you will use. One of the main goals is to send a message to the other team and have it interpret what you intended without it knowing ahead of time what your message was. Keep the OSI model in mind as you design your system.

1. **Layer 1 issues**–You must connect 2 pairs of wire in order to have communication in both directions (half or full duplex).

2. **Layer 2 issues**–You must communicate some sort of frame start and stop sequence. This is a sequence of bits that is different than the character and number bits you will be transmitting.

3. **Layer 3 issues**–You must invent an addressing scheme (for hosts and networks) if it is more than point-to-point communication.

4. **Layer 4 issues**–You must include some form of control to regulate quality of service (for example, error correction, acknowledgment, windowing, flow controls, and so on).

5. **Layer 5 issues**–You must implement some way of synchronizing or pausing long conversations.

6. **Layer 6 issues**–You must use some means of data representation (for example, ASCII encoded as optical bits).

7. **Layer 7 issues**–You must be able to communicate an idea supplied by your instructor or come up with a message on your own.

Reflection Questions:

1. What issues arose as you tried to build your communications system that you think apply to data communications between computers?

_____
_____
_____
_____

2. Analyze your communications system in terms of the OSI layers.

_____
_____
_____
_____

Cisco Labs–Semester 1–Networking Fundamentals
LAB 5.3.1–BASIC CABLE TESTER–OVERVIEW
(Estimated time: 30 minutes)

Objective:
- Use a cable tester to verify that a straight-through or crossover path cable is good or bad

Background:
UTP Ethernet Cabling: Cabling is one of the most critical areas of network design and implementation. Cabling is expected to last from 10 to 15 years. The quality of cable and connections is a major factor in reducing network problems and time spent troubleshooting. Unshielded Twisted-Pair (UTP) copper cable is the most common in use in today's Ethernet networks. There are various categories (CAT 3, CAT 5, CAT 5e, and so on) but all of them contain 8 wires or conductors and use RJ45 connectors. A UTP patch cable in a network is usually wired as a straight-through or crossover. In order to follow proper specifications, all 8 conductors must be used even though with most earlier versions of Ethernet, not all 8 conductors were used. You create these cables in the future labs. In this lab, you work with several cables that have already been made and will test them for basic continuity (breaks in wires) and shorts (2 or more wires touching) using a basic cable tester (refer to the lab on resistance measurements).

Basic Cable Testers: There are a number of very simple and inexpensive basic cable testers available (less than $100). They usually consist of one or two small boxes with RJ-45 jacks in them to plug the cables to be tested into. Many of these are designed specifically to test only the Ethernet UTP type of cable. The testers will have more than one jack to allow for testing of straight-through or crossover cable. Both ends of the cable are plugged in to the proper jacks, and the tester will test all 8 wires and indicate whether the cable is good or bad. If any of the eight wires has a break or is shorted to any of the other wires, the cable is bad. The simple testers might just have a single light to indicate this; others might have eight lights to tell you which wire is bad. These testers have internal batteries and are doing continuity checks on the wires.

Advanced Cable Testers: Advanced cable testers, such as the Fluke 620 LAN CableMeter, are sophisticated cable testers that have basic cable testing functions and much more. You will use an advanced cable tester in future labs to do wire maps, and so on. If an inexpensive basic cable tester is unavailable, the Fluke (or equivalent) is more than adequate. Advanced cable testers can cost from hundreds to thousands of dollars.

Tools/Preparation:
Prior to starting the lab, the teacher or lab assistant should have several basic cable testers available (one for each team of students) or several Fluke cable meters and various lengths of wire with induced problems. Work in teams of two. Before beginning this lab, you might want to refer to the *Cisco Networking Academy Program: First-Year Companion Guide*, Second Edition. You should also review Semester 1 online Lesson 5.

Required Resources:
- Basic cable tester
- Advanced cable tester (Fluke 620 or equivalent)
- 2 lengths of *good* CAT 5 cable (one crossover and one straight-through; use different colors or labels)

Cisco Labs–Semester 1–Networking Fundamentals
LAB 5.3.1–BASIC CABLE TESTER–WORKSHEET

If you are using a basic cable tester, refer to the instructions from the manufacturer and insert the ends of the cable to be tested into the jacks accordingly. If you are using the Fluke 620, use the following instructions to test the four cables. Insert the RJ-45 from one end of the cable into the UTP/FTP jack on the tester and turn the dial to test. All conductors will be tested to verify they are not broken or shorted. (*Note:* This test does not verify that the pins are connected correctly from one end to the other.)

Step 1. **1st Cable test**–Insert the cable into the RJ-45 jack(s) of the cable tester.
    a. What is the color or cable number of this cable? _____
    b. What category type of cable is it (CAT 3, CAT 5, and so on)? _____
    c. How is the cable wired (straight-through or crossover)? _____
    d. How long is the cable? _____
    e. Did the cable test OK? _____

Step 2. **2nd Cable test**–Insert the cable into the RJ-45 jack(s) of the cable tester.
    a. What is the color or cable number of this cable? _____
    b. What category type of cable is it (CAT 3, CAT 5, and so on)? _____
    c. How is the cable wired (straight-through or crossover)? _____
    d. How long is the cable? _____
    e. Did the cable test OK? _____

Step 3. **3rd Cable test**–Insert the cable into the RJ-45 jack(s) of the cable tester.
    a. What is the color or cable number of this cable? _____
    b. What category type of cable is it (CAT 3, CAT 5, and so on)? _____
    c. How is the cable wired (straight-through or crossover)? _____
    d. How long is the cable? _____
    e. Did the cable test OK? _____

Step 4. **4th Cable test**–Insert the cable into the RJ-45 jack(s) of the cable tester.
    a. What is the color or cable number of this cable? _____
    b. What category type of cable is it (CAT 3, CAT 5, and so on)? _____
    c. How is the cable wired (straight-through or crossover)? _____
    d. How long is the cable? _____
    e. Did the cable test OK? _____

Cisco Labs–Semester 1–Networking Fundamentals
LAB 5.3.2–STRAIGHT-THROUGH CABLE–OVERVIEW
(Estimated time: 30 minutes)

Objective:

- Build a straight-through Ethernet patch cable to T568-B (or T568-A) standards for connection from workstation to hub/switch or patch panel to hub/switch.

Background:

In this lab, you learn how to build a Category 5 (CAT 5) Unshielded Twisted-Pair (UTP) Ethernet network patch cable (or patch cord) and test it for good connections (continuity) and correct pinouts (correct color of wire on the right pin). This will be a 4-pair (8 wires) "straight-through" cable, which means that the color of wire on pin 1 on one end of the cable will be the same as pin 1 on the other end. Pin 2 will be the same as pin 2, and so on. It will be wired to EIA/TIA 568-B or A standards for 10Base-T Ethernet, which determines what color wire is on each pin. T568-B (also called AT&T specification) is more common, but many installations are also wired to T568-A (also called ISDN).

This patch cable will conform to the structured cabling standards and is considered to be part of the "horizontal" cabling, which is limited to 99 meters total between workstation and hub or switch. It can be used in a workstation area to connect the workstation NIC to the wall plate data jack, or it can be used in the wiring closet to connect the patch panel (horizontal cross connect) to an Ethernet hub or switch. Patch cables are wired straight thru because the cable from the workstation to the hub or switch is normally crossed over automatically at the switch or the hub. Note that the ports on most hubs have an X next to them. This means the send and receive pairs will be crossed when the cabling reaches the switch. The pinouts will be T568-B, and all 8 conductors (wires) should be terminated with RJ-45 modular connectors (only 4 of the 8 wires are used for 10/100Base-T Ethernet; all 8 are used for 1000Base-T Ethernet).

Tools/Preparation:

Prior to starting the lab, the teacher or lab assistant should have a spool of Cat 5 Unshielded Twisted-Pair (UTP) cable, RJ-45 (8-pin) connectors, an RJ-45 crimping tool, and an Ethernet/RJ-45 continuity tester available. Work individually or in teams. Before beginning this lab, you might want to refer to the *Cisco Networking Academy Program: First-Year Companion Guide*, Second Edition. You should also review Semester 1 online Lesson 5.

Required Resources:

- Two- to three-foot length of Cat 5 cabling (one per person or one per team)
- Four RJ-45 connectors (two extra for spares)
- RJ-45 Crimping Tools to attach the RJ-45 connectors to the cable ends
- Ethernet cabling continuity tester that can test straight-through or crossover type cables (T568-A or T568-B)
- Wire cutters

Cisco Labs–Semester 1–Networking Fundamentals
LAB 5.3.2–STRAIGHT-THROUGH CABLE–WORKSHEET

Step 1. Cabling information.

Explanation: Instructions are provided here for building a T568-A or T568-B cable. Either can be used as long as all connections (pinouts) from the workstation to the wiring closet and terminating electronics (hubs or switches) are consistent. If cables are to be built for an existing network, it is important to keep the same standard that already exists (either T568-A or B). A patch cable that is wired "straight through" will have the same color of wire on the same pin (1–8) at both ends. A straight-through patch cable (T568-A or B) can be used to connect a PC workstation to a wall plate in a work area, or it can be used to connect from a patch panel in a wiring closet to a hub or a switch. A PC can also be connected directly to a port on a hub or switch with this cable. If a cable will be used to connect from an "Uplink" port on one hub to a "crossover" front port on another hub, a straight-through cable should be used.

Step 2. Create a T568-B straight-through patch panel cable.

Task: Use the following tables, diagrams, and steps to create a T568-B patch panel cable.

Explanation: Both cable ends should be wired the same when looking at the conductors. Only four wires are used with 10Base-T or 100Base-TX Ethernet.

T568-B Cabling

Pin #	Pair #	Function	Wire Color	Used with 10/100 Base-T Ethernet?	Used with 100Base-T4 and 1000Base-T Ethernet?
1	2	Transmit	White/Orange	Yes	Yes
2	2	Transmit	Orange/White	Yes	Yes
3	3	Receive	White/Green	Yes	Yes
4	1	Not used	Blue/White	No	Yes
5	1	Not used	White/Blue	No	Yes
6	3	Receive	Green/White	Yes	Yes
7	4	Not used	White/Brown	No	Yes
8	4	Not used	Brown/White	No	Yes

Diagram showing both T568-A and T568-B cabling wire colors.

Created by Anixter Inc., based on TIA source materials.

Cisco Labs–Semester 1–Networking Fundamentals
LAB 5.3.2–STRAIGHT-THROUGH CABLE–WORKSHEET

1. Determine the distance between devices, or device and plug, and add at least 12" to it. The maximum length for this cord is 3 m; standard lengths are 6' and 10'.

2. Cut a piece of stranded Cat 5 unshielded twisted-pair cable to a determined length. You need to use stranded cable for patch cables because it is more durable when bent repeatedly. Solid wire is fine for cable runs that are punched down into jacks.

3. Strip 2" of jacket off one end of the cable.

4. Hold the 4 pairs of twisted cables tightly where the jacket was cut away, and then reorganize the cable pairs into the order of the 568-B wiring standard. Take care to maintain the twists because this provides noise cancellation (orange pair, green pair, blue pair, brown pair).

5. Hold the jacket and cable in one hand, untwist a short length of the green and blue pairs, and reorder them to reflect the 568-B wiring color scheme. Untwist and order the rest of the wire pairs according to the color scheme.

6. Flatten, straighten, and line up the wires, then trim them in a straight line to within 1/2"–3/4" from the edge of the jacket. Be sure not to let go of the jacket and the wires, which are now in order! You should minimize the length of untwisted wires because overly long sections that are near connectors are a primary source of electrical noise.

7. Place an RJ-45 plug on the end of the cable, with the prong on the underside and the orange pair at the top of the connector.

8. Gently push the plug onto the wires until you can see the copper ends of the wires through the end of the plug. Make sure the end of the jacket is inside the plug and all wires are in the correct order. If the jacket is not inside the plug, it will not be properly strain-relieved and will eventually cause problems. If everything is correct, crimp the plug hard enough to force the contacts through the insulation on the wires, thus completing the conducting path.

9. Repeat Steps 3–8 to terminate the other end of the cable, using the same scheme to finish the straight-through cable.

10. Test the finished cable and have the instructor check it. How can you tell if your cable is functioning properly? _____

Cisco Labs–Semester 1–Networking Fundamentals
LAB 5.3.3–ROLLOVER CABLE–OVERVIEW
(Estimated time: 30 minutes)

Objective:

- Build a rollover cable for connection from a workstation to the console port on a router or switch

Background:

In this lab, you learn how to build a Category 5 (CAT 5) Unshielded Twisted-Pair (UTP) console rollover cable and test it for good connections (continuity) and correct pinouts (correct wire on the right pin). This will be a 4-pair (8 wires) "rollover" cable.

This cable should be approximately 10 feet in length but can be as long as 25 feet. It can be used to connect a workstation or dumb terminal to the console port on the back of a router or Ethernet switch in order to be able to configure the router or switch. This cable uses an asynchronous serial interface to the router or switch (8 data bits, no parity, and 2 stop bits). Both ends of the cable you build will have RJ-45 connectors on them. One end plugs directly into the RJ-45 console management port on the back of the router or switch, and the other end plugs into an RJ-45-to-DB9 terminal adapter. This adapter converts the RJ-45 to a 9-pin female D connector that plugs into the DB9 serial port male adapter on the back of a PC running terminal emulation software such as HyperTerminal. A DB25 terminal adapter is also available to connect with a dumb terminal that has a 25-pin connector.

A rollover cable uses 8 pins but is different from the straight-through cable or crossover cable that you will build in other labs. With a rollover cable, pin 1 on one end connects to pin 8 on the other end. Pin 2 connects to pin 7, pin 3 connects to pin 6, and so on. This is why it is referred to as a rollover, because the pins on one end are all reversed on the other end as though one end of the cable was just rotated or rolled over.

A flat black rollover cable comes with each new router or switch, along with the terminal adapters for both DB9 and DB25 connections to terminals or PC serial ports. It is approximately 8 feet long. This lab enables you to build another cable if the one that comes with the router or switch is damaged or lost. It also allows you to connect to routers or switches from workstations that are more than 8 feet away by building your own longer cables.

Tools/Preparation:

Prior to starting the lab, the teacher or lab assistant should have a spool of Cat 5 Unshielded Twisted-Pair (UTP) cable, RJ-45 (8-pin) connectors, an RJ-45 crimping tool, and a continuity tester available. Work individually or in teams. Before beginning this lab, you might want to refer to the *Cisco Networking Academy Program: First-Year Companion Guide*, Second Edition. You should also review Semester 1 online Lesson 5.

Required Resources:

- 10- to 20-foot length of Cat 5 cabling (one per person or one per team)
- Four RJ-45 connectors (two extra for spares)
- RJ-45 crimping tools to attach the RJ-45 connectors to the cable end
- An RJ-45 to DB9 female terminal adapter (available from Cisco)
- Cabling continuity tester
- Wire cutters

Cisco Labs–Semester 1–Networking Fundamentals
LAB 5.3.3–ROLLOVER CABLE–WORKSHEET

Step 1. Review cable connections and pin locations.

Use the following table as a reference to answer the following questions and to help you create a rollover console cable.

Questions:

1. Which signal on the Router port (column 1 of the table) will be used to transmit data to the PC when the PC is first connected and HyperTerminal is started (this is what displays the router prompt on the workstation)? _____

2. Which pin is this connected to on the router end of the RJ-45 cable? _____

3. Which pin is this connected to on the other end of the RJ-45 cable? _____

4. Which pin is this connected to in the DB9 connector? _____

5. Which console device signal does this connect to? _____

6. What would happen if pin 3 on the left cable end were attached to pin 3 as with a straight-through cable? _____
_____

Rollover Console Cable Table

For connecting from a router or switch console port to a PC workstation running HyperTerminal terminal emulation software. Console port signaling and cabling using an RJ-45 rollover and DB9 adapter.

Router or Switch Console Port (DTE)	RJ-45 to RJ-45 Rollover Cable (Left End)	RJ-45 to RJ-45 Rollover Cable (Right End)	RJ-45 to DB9 Adapter	Console Device (PC Work-station Serial Port)
Signal	From RJ-45 Pin No.	To RJ-45 Pin No.	DB9 Pin No.	Signal
RTS	1	8	8	CTS
DTR	2	7	6	DSR
TxD	3	6	2	RxD
GND	4	5	5	GND
GND	5	4	5	GND
RxD	6	3	3	TxD
DSR	7	2	4	DTR
CTS	8	1	7	RTS

Signal Legend: RTS = Request To Send, DTR = Data Terminal Ready, TxD = Transmit Data, GND = Ground (one for TxD and one for RxD), RxD = Receive Data, DSR = Data Set Ready, CTS = Clear To Send

Cisco Labs–Semester 1–Networking Fundamentals
LAB 5.3.3–ROLLOVER CABLE–WORKSHEET

Step 2. Use the following steps to build the rollover console cable.

1. Determine the distance between devices, and then add at least 12" to it. Make your cable about 10 feet unless you are connecting to a router or switch from a greater distance. The maximum length for this cable is about 8m (approximately 25 feet).

2. Strip 2" of jacket off one end of the cable.

3. Hold the 4 pairs of twisted cables tightly where the jacket was cut away, and then reorganize the cable pairs and wires into the order of the 568-B wiring standard. You can order them in any sequence but use the 568-B sequence to become more familiar with it.

4. Flatten, straighten, and line up the wires, and then trim them in a straight line to within 1/2"–3/4" from the edge of the jacket. Be sure not to let go of the jacket and the wires, which are now in order!

5. Place an RJ-45 plug on the end of the cable, with the prong on the underside and the orange pair at the top of the connector.

6. Gently push the plug onto the wires until you can see the copper ends of the wires through the end of the plug. Make sure the end of the jacket is inside the plug and all wires are in the correct order. If the jacket is not inside the plug, it will not be properly strain-relieved and will eventually cause problems. If everything is correct, crimp the plug hard enough to force the contacts through the insulation on the wires, thus completing the conducting path.

7. Repeat Steps 2–6 to terminate the other end of the cable, but reversing every pair of wires as indicated in the table above (pin 1 to pin 8, pin 2 to pin 7, pin 3 to pin 6, and so on).

8. Test the finished cable and have the instructor check it. How can you tell if your cable is functioning properly?

_____

_____

_____

_____

_____

Cisco Labs–Semester 1–Networking Fundamentals
LAB 5.3.4–CROSSOVER CABLE–OVERVIEW
(Estimated time: 30 minutes)

Objective:
- Build a crossover Ethernet patch cable to T568-B (or T568-A) standards for connection from workstation to workstation or from switch to switch

Background:
In this lab, you learn how to build a Category 5 (CAT 5) Unshielded Twisted-Pair (UTP) Ethernet crossover network cable and test it for good connections (continuity) and correct pinouts (correct color of wire on the right pin). This will be a 4-pair (8 wires) "crossover" cable, which means that pairs 2 and 3 on one end of the cable will be reversed on the other end. It will be wired to EIA/TIA 568-B and A standards for 10Base-T Ethernet, which determines what color wire is on each pin. The pinouts will be T568-A on one end and T568-B on the other end. All eight conductors (wires) should be terminated with RJ-45 modular connectors.

This patch cable conforms to the structured cabling standards and, if it is used between hubs or switches, is considered to be part of the "vertical" cabling, also known as backbone cable. A crossover cable can be used as a backbone cable to connect two or more hubs or switches in a LAN or to connect two isolated workstations to create a mini-LAN. This allows you to connect two workstations together or a server and a workstation without the need for a hub between them. This can be helpful for training and testing. If you want to connect more than two workstations, you need a hub or a switch.

Tools/Preparation:
Prior to starting the lab, the teacher or lab assistant should have a spool of Cat 5 Unshielded Twisted-Pair (UTP) cable, RJ-45 (8-pin) connectors, an RJ-45 crimping tool, and an Ethernet/RJ-45 continuity tester available. Work individually or in teams. Before beginning this lab, you might want to refer to the *Cisco Networking Academy Program: First-Year Companion Guide*, Second Edition. You should also review Semester 1 online Lesson 5.

Required Resources:
- Two- to three-foot length of Cat 5 cabling (one per person or one per team)
- Four RJ-45 connectors (two extra for spares)
- RJ-45 crimping tools to attach the RJ-45 connectors to the cable ends
- Ethernet cabling continuity tester that can test crossover type cables (T568-A to T568-B)
- Wire cutters

Cisco Labs–Semester 1–Networking Fundamentals
LAB 5.3.4–CROSSOVER CABLE–WORKSHEET

Step 1. Create a crossover patch panel cable.

Use the following tables, diagrams, and steps to create a crossover cable. One end of the cable should be wired to the T568-A standard and the other end to the T568-B standard. This crosses the transmit and receive pairs (2 and 3) to allow communication to take place. Only four wires are used with 10Base-T or 100Base-TX Ethernet.

T568-A Cabling

Pin #	Pair #	Function	Wire Color	Used with 10Base-T and 100 Base-TX Ethernet?	Used with 100Base-T4 and 1000Base-T Ethernet?
1	3	Transmit	White/Green	Yes	Yes
2	3	Transmit	Green/White	Yes	Yes
3	2	Receive	White/Orange	Yes	Yes
4	1	Not used	Blue/White	No	Yes
5	1	Not used	White/Blue	No	Yes
6	2	Receive	Orange/White	Yes	Yes
7	4	Not used	White/Brown	No	Yes
8	4	Not used	Brown/White	No	Yes

T568-B Cabling

Pin #	Pair #	Function	Wire Color	Used with 10/100 Base-T Ethernet?	Used with 100Base-T4 and 1000Base-T Ethernet?
1	2	Transmit	White/Orange	Yes	Yes
2	2	Transmit	Orange/White	Yes	Yes
3	3	Receive	White/Green	Yes	Yes
4	1	Not used	Blue/White	No	Yes
5	1	Not used	White/Blue	No	Yes
6	3	Receive	Green/White	Yes	Yes
7	4	Not used	White/Brown	No	Yes
8	4	Not used	Brown/White	No	Yes

Created by Anixter Inc., based on TIA source materials.

Cisco Labs–Semester 1–Networking Fundamentals
LAB 5.3.4–CROSSOVER CABLE–WORKSHEET

1. Determine the distance between devices, or device and plug, and then add at least 12" to it. The maximum length for this cord is 3 m; standard lengths are 6' and 10'.

2. Cut a piece of stranded Cat 5 unshielded twisted-pair cable to the determined length. You need to use stranded cable for patch cables because it is more durable when bent repeatedly. Solid wire is fine for cable runs that are punched down into jacks.

3. Strip 2" of jacket off one end of the cable.

4. Hold the 4 pairs of twisted cables tightly where the jacket was cut away, and reorganize the cable pairs into the order of the 568-B wiring standard. Take care to maintain the twists because this provides noise cancellation (orange pair, green pair, blue pair, brown pair).

5. Hold the jacket and cable in one hand, untwist a short length of the green and blue pairs, and reorder them to reflect the 568-B wiring color scheme. Untwist and order the rest of the wire pairs according to the color scheme.

6. Flatten, straighten, and line up the wires, then trim them in a straight line to within 1/2"–3/4" from the edge of the jacket. Be sure not to let go of the jacket and the wires, which are now in order! You should minimize the length of untwisted wires because overly long sections that are near connectors are a primary source of electrical noise.

7. Place an RJ-45 plug on the end of the cable, with the prong on the underside and the orange pair at the top of the connector.

8. Gently push the plug onto the wires until you can see the copper ends of the wires through the end of the plug. Make sure the end of the jacket is inside the plug and all wires are in the correct order. If the jacket is not inside the plug, it will not be properly strain-relieved and will eventually cause problems. If everything is correct, crimp the plug hard enough to force the contacts through the insulation on the wires, thus completing the conducting path.

9. Repeat Steps 3–8 to terminate the other end of the cable, using the 568-A scheme to finish the crossover cable.

10. Test the finished cable and have the instructor check it. How can you tell if your cable is functioning properly? _____

Cisco Labs–Semester 1–Networking Fundamentals
LAB 5.3.5–CABLE TESTER–WIRE MAP–OVERVIEW
(Estimated time: 45 minutes)

Objectives:
- Demonstrate skill with a cable tester more advanced than a simple continuity/pin-out tester
- Use the wire mapping features of the tester to check for opens and shorts with UTP cable
- Perform wire mapping on cables, detecting faults that are not detectable with simple continuity measuring devices such as crossed and split pairs

Background:
In this lab, you learn the wire mapping features of the Fluke 620 LAN CableMeter (or its equivalent). Wire maps can be helpful in troubleshooting cabling problems with UTP cable. Wire maps are not used with coaxial cable because there is only one wire and no map is needed. A wire map allows the network technician to verify which pins on one end of the cable are connected to which pins on the other end. With an understanding of the proper wiring connections, you can determine when a cable is wired improperly, depending on its intended use. You learn how to use a cable tester to check for the proper installation of Unshielded Twisted-Pair (UTP) Category 5 (CAT 5) according to EIA/TIA 568 cabling standards in an Ethernet network. You test different cables using all four pairs to determine some problems that can occur from incorrect cabling installation and termination.

The cabling infrastructure (or cable plant) in a building is expected to last at least 10 years. Cabling-related problems are one of the most common causes of network failure. The quality of cabling components used, the routing and installation of the cable and quality of the connector terminations will be the main factors in determining how trouble-free the cabling will be.

Tools/Preparation:
Prior to starting the lab, the teacher or lab assistant should have several correctly wired CAT 5 cables (both straight-through and crossover) to test. There should also be several CAT 5 cables created with problems such as poor connections and split pairs to test. Cables should be numbered to simplify the testing process and to maintain consistency. A cable tester should be available that can test at least continuity, cable length, and wire map. Work individually or in teams. Before beginning this lab, you should refer to the *Cisco Networking Academy Program: First-Year Companion Guide*, Second Edition. You should also review Semester 1 online Lesson 5.

Required Resources:
- CAT 5 straight-wired cables of different colors
- CAT 5 crossover-wired cable (T568A on one end and T568B on the other)
- CAT 5 straight-wired cables with open wire connections in the middle or one or more conductors shorted at one end of different colors and different lengths
- CAT 5 straight-wired cable with a split-pair miswire
- Cable tester (Fluke 620 LAN CableMeter or similar) to test cable length, continuity, wire map

Web Site Resources:
www.bicsi.org/techsem
www.fluke.com/

Cisco Labs–Semester 1–Networking Fundamentals
LAB 5.3.5–CABLE TESTER–WIRE MAP–WORKSHEET

Step 1. Set the advanced cable tester for the desired cable.

These instructions pertain to the Fluke 620 LAN CableMeter. Turn the rotary switch selector on the tester to the WIRE MAP position. Press the SETUP button to enter the setup mode and observe the LCD screen on the tester. The first option should be CABLE. Press the UP or DOWN buttons until the desired cable type of UTP is selected. Press ENTER to accept that setting and go to the next one. Continue pressing the UP/DOWN arrows and pressing ENTER until the tester is set to the following cabling characteristics:

Tester Option	Desired Setting
CABLE:	UTP
WIRING:	10BASE-T or EIA/TIA 4PR
CATEGORY:	CAT 5
WIRE SIZE	AWG 24
CAL to CABLE?	NO
BEEPING:	ON or OFF
LCD CONTRAST	From 1 thru 10 (brightest)

Step 2. Set up the Cable to be tested.

For each cable to be tested with the following tests, place the near end of the cable into the RJ-45 jack labeled UTP/FTP on the tester. Place the RJ-45-RJ-45 female coupler on the far end of the cable and then insert the Cable Identifier into the other side of the coupler. The coupler and the cable identifier are accessories that come with the Fluke 620 LAN CableMeter.

Step 3. Perform Wire Map testing.

Using the tester's Wire Map function and a Cable ID unit, you can determine the wiring of both the near and far ends of the cable. The top set of numbers displayed on the LCD screen is the near end and the bottom set is the far end. Perform a Wire Map test on each of the cables provided and fill in the following table based on the result for each CAT 5 cable tested. For each cable, write down the number and color, whether the cable is straight-through or crossover, the tester screen test results, and what you think the problem is.

Cable Number	Cable Color	How Cable Is Wired (Straight-Through or Crossover)	Tester Displayed Test Results (_Note:_ Refer to the Fluke manual for detailed description of test results for wire map.)	Problem Description
1			Top: Bot:	
2			Top: Bot:	
3			Top: Bot:	
4			Top: Bot:	
5			Top: Bot:	

Cisco Labs–Semester 1–Networking Fundamentals
LAB 5.3.6–STRAIGHT-THROUGH CABLE TESTER–OVERVIEW
(Estimated time: 45 minutes)

Objectives:
- Demonstrate skill with a cable tester more advanced than a simple continuity/pin-out tester
- Use the Test feature of the tester to check for opens and shorts with coax and UTP cable
- Understand the use of the Cable ID feature

Background:
In this lab, you learn the Cable Test–Pass/Fail features of the Fluke 620 LAN CableMeter (or its equivalent). Basic cable tests can be helpful in troubleshooting cabling problems with UTP and coaxial cable. You learn how to use a cable tester to check for the proper installation of Unshielded Twisted-Pair (UTP) and Coaxial (Thinnet) for an Ethernet network. You test different cables to determine some problems that can occur from incorrect cabling installation and termination.

The cabling infrastructure (or cable plant) in a building is expected to last at least 10 years. Cabling-related problems are one of the most common causes of network failure. The quality of cabling components used, the routing and installation of the cable, and the quality of the connector terminations will be the main factors in determining how trouble-free the cabling will be.

Tools/Preparation:
Prior to starting the lab, the teacher or lab assistant should have several correctly wired CAT 5 cables (both straight-through and crossover) to test. There should also be several CAT 5 cables created with problems and a coaxial cable to test. Cables should be numbered to simplify the testing process and to maintain consistency. A cable tester should be available that can do a basic cable test for UTP and coax. Work individually or in teams. Before beginning this lab, you should refer to the *Cisco Networking Academy Program: First-Year Companion Guide*, Second Edition. You should also review Semester 1 online Lesson 5.

Required Resources:
- CAT 5 straight-through and crossover wired cables of different colors (some good and some bad)
- CAT 5 straight-through and crossover wired cables with open wire connections in the middle or one or more conductors shorted at one end of different colors and different lengths
- Coax cable with a short in it
- Cable tester (Fluke 620 LAN CableMeter or similar) to test cable length, continuity, wire map

Web Site Resources:
www.bicsi.org/techsem
www.fluke.com/

Cisco Labs–Semester 1–Networking Fundamentals
LAB 5.3.6–STRAIGHT-THROUGH CABLE TESTER–WORKSHEET

Step 1. Set the advanced cable tester for the desired cable (UTP or COAX).

These instructions pertain to the Fluke 620 LAN CableMeter. Turn the rotary switch selector on the tester to the TEST position. Press the SETUP button to enter the setup mode and observe the LCD screen on the tester. The first option should be CABLE. Press the UP or DOWN buttons until the desired cable type of UTP or COAX (thinnet) is selected. Press ENTER to accept that setting and go to the next one. Continue pressing the UP/DOWN arrows and pressing ENTER until the tester is set to the following cabling characteristics, depending on the type of cable you will be testing:

Tester Option	Desired Setting—UTP	Desired Setting—COAX
CABLE	UTP	COAX
WIRING	10BASE-T or EIA/TIA 4PR	10BASE-2 or RG58 (thinnet)
CATEGORY	CAT 5	N/A
WIRE SIZE	AWG 24	N/A
CAL to CABLE?	NO	NO
BEEPING	ON or OFF	ON or OFF
LCD CONTRAST	From 1 through 10 (brightest)	From 1 through 10 (brightest)

Step 2. Set up the cable to be tested (UTP or COAX).

For each UTP cable to be tested with the following tests, place the near end of the cable into the RJ-45 jack labeled UTP/FTP on the tester. Place the RJ-45-RJ-45 female coupler on the far end of the cable and then insert the Cable Identifier into the other side of the coupler. The coupler and the cable identifier are accessories that come with the Fluke 620 LAN CableMeter. Multiple Cable IDs with different numbers can be purchased to help in identifying which cable you are working with. For coax cables, insert one end of the BNC connector into the jack labeled COAX on the tester. Coax cables should not have a terminating resistor.

Step 3. Perform basic cable test–Pass/Fail function.

Using the tester's Test function and a Cable ID unit (for UTP), you can determine the functionality of the cable. Perform a basic cable test on each of the cables provided and fill in the following table based on the result for each cable tested. For each cable, write down the number and color, whether the cable is straight-through, crossover, or coaxial, the tester screen test results, and what you think the problem is. The Cable ID can be used to identify a particular cable by moving it to another cable.

Cable No.	Cable Color	How Cable Is Wired (UTP or COAX)	Tester Displayed Test Results (*Note:* Refer to the Fluke manual for detailed description of test results.)	Problem Description
1				
2				
3				
4				

Cisco Labs–Semester 1–Networking Fundamentals
LAB 5.3.7–CABLE TESTER–LENGTH–OVERVIEW
(Estimated time: 45 minutes)

Objectives:
- Demonstrate skill with a cable tester more advanced than a simple continuity/pin-out tester
- Use the Length features of the tester to check for opens and shorts with coax and UTP cable

Background:
In this lab, you learn the Cable Length feature of the Fluke 620 LAN CableMeter (or its equivalent). Cable length tests can be very helpful in troubleshooting cabling problems with UTP and coaxial cable. You learn how to use a cable tester to check the length of Ethernet cabling to verify that it is within the standards specified and that the wires inside are the same length (for UTP). You test different cables including UTP and Coax to determine their length.

The cabling infrastructure (or cable plant) in a building is expected to last at least 10 years. Cabling-related problems are one of the most common causes of network failure. The quality of cabling components used, the routing and installation of the cable, and quality of the connector terminations will be the main factors in determining how trouble-free the cabling will be.

Tools/Preparation:
Prior to starting the lab, the teacher or lab assistant should have several correctly wired CAT 5 cables (both straight-through and crossover) and several Coaxial (thinnet) cables to test. Cables should be numbered to simplify the testing process and to maintain consistency. A cable tester should be available that can do cable length tests for UTP and coax. Work individually or in teams. Before beginning this lab, you should refer to the *Cisco Networking Academy Program: First-Year Companion Guide*, Second Edition. You should also review Semester 1 online Lesson 5.

Required Resources:
- CAT 5 straight-through or crossover cables of different colors (some good and some bad)
- Coax (thinnet) cables of different lengths
- Cable Tester (Fluke 620 LAN CableMeter or similar) to test cable length

Web Site Resources:
www.bicsi.org/techsem
www.fluke.com/

Cisco Labs–Semester 1–Networking Fundamentals
LAB 5.3.7–CABLE TESTER–LENGTH–WORKSHEET

Step 1. Set the advanced cable tester for the desired cable (UTP or COAX).

These instructions pertain to the Fluke 620 LAN CableMeter. Turn the rotary switch selector on the tester to the LENGTH position. Press the SETUP button to enter the setup mode and observe the LCD screen on the tester. The first option should be CABLE. Press the UP or DOWN buttons until the desired cable type of UTP or COAX (thinnet) is selected. Press ENTER to accept that setting and go to the next one. Continue pressing the UP/DOWN arrows and pressing ENTER until the tester is set to the following cabling characteristics, depending on the type of cable you are testing:

Tester Option	Desired Setting—UTP	Desired Setting—COAX
CABLE	UTP	COAX
WIRING	10BASE-T or EIA/TIA 4PR	10BASE-2 or RG58 (thinnet)
CATEGORY	CAT 5	N/A
WIRE SIZE	AWG 24	N/A
CAL to CABLE?	NO	NO
BEEPING	ON or OFF	ON or OFF
LCD CONTRAST	From 1 through 10 (brightest)	From 1 through 10 (brightest)

Step 2. Set up the cable to be tested (UTP or COAX).

For each UTP cable to be tested with the following tests, place the near end of the cable into the RJ-45 jack labeled UTP/FTP on the tester. Place the RJ-45-RJ-45 female coupler on the far end of the cable and then insert the Cable Identifier into the other side of the coupler. The coupler and the cable identifier are accessories that come with the Fluke 620 LAN CableMeter. For coax cables, insert one end of the BNC connector into the jack labeled COAX on the tester. Coax cables should not be terminated. If tested with a terminating resistor (50Ω), the display will be the resistance of the cable plus the terminating resistor.

Step 3. Perform cable length Test function.

Using the tester's Test function and a Cable ID Unit (for UTP), you can determine the functionality of the cable. Perform a basic cable test on each of the cables provided and fill in the following table based on the result for each CAT 5 cable tested. For each cable, write down the number and color, whether the cable is straight-through, crossover, or coaxial, the tester screen test results, and what you think the problem is. For UTP cables, press the down arrow or up arrow to see all pairs.

Cable No.	Cable Color	How Cable Is Wired (UTP or COAX)	Tester Displayed Test Results (*Note:* Refer to the Fluke manual for detailed description of test results.)	Problem
1				
2				
3				

Cisco Labs–Semester 1–Networking Fundamentals
LAB 7.6.2–NETWORK DISCOVERY–OVERVIEW
(Estimated time: 20 minutes)

Objective:

- Use Network Inspector (or equivalent) software to perform network discovery

Background:

One of the most powerful tools for troubleshooting computer networks is Network Management software. There are many fine programs for performing various network discovery, monitoring, and analysis tasks. In this lab, you explore a basic network management application: Fluke Network Inspector 3.0 (or equivalent). You use the Network Inspector to perform a process called network discovery. As the number of computers, servers, printers, switches, and routers on a network grows, it can be difficult to keep track of all the relevant characteristics of the devices. Such information as MAC addresses, IP addresses, and topologies is crucial for troubleshooting a network. You use Network Inspector to perform a network discovery on an Ethernet 10Base-T (or 100Base-TX) network.

Tools/Preparation:

Each PC must be running Windows 95, 98, or NT, Microsoft TCP/IP stack, and Winsock 2.0. Fluke Network Inspector 3.0 (or equivalent) must be installed on each PC. During the installation of the software, you must specify which network adapter (NIC, dial-up, and so on) you wish to monitor. Specify the NIC that attaches the PC to an Ethernet. The PCs should be on either a 10Base-T or 100Base-TX Ethernet network that preferably includes servers, switches, routers, and printers (this makes the network discovery more interesting). Before beginning this lab, you should refer to the *Cisco Networking Academy Program: First-Year Companion Guide*, Second Edition, Chapter 29. You should also review Semester 1 online Lesson 7.

Required Resources:

- PC with Windows 95, 98, or NT, Microsoft TCP/IP stack, and Winsock 2.0
- Fluke Network Inspector 3.0 software

Cisco Labs–Semester 1–Networking Fundamentals
LAB 7.6.2–NETWORK DISCOVERY–WORKSHEET

1. If you have not done so already, install Network Inspector software (the "Agent" and the "Console") on your PC. How will you know this step was done correctly?

    _____

2. Make sure you are connected to a working Ethernet network. What are some signs that you are on the network? _____

    _____

3. Open Fluke Network Inspector Agent. You will be prompted to do something. What are you prompted to do and why do you suppose you must do this? Click OK when finished.

    _____

4. Now the Agent prompts you with a status screen. Click the tabs and write down what are the major categories of things you can control about the Agent. Under the Database/Address tab, click "overwrite" so that the new data you are collecting will be stored in the database. Click Apply. _____

5. Start the Agent. What is the status shown? What does the status change to after a few minutes? What do you suppose is happening? Minimize the Agent.

    _____

    _____

6. Open Fluke Network Inspector Console. What do you see? _____

    _____

7. Allow the Agent to run for a few minutes. What do you see? _____

8. Stop the Agent and minimize the Agent screen. What significant information about the network have you obtained? Write down a few complete lines of the database.

    _____

    _____

    _____

9. In the left of the Control Panel, click each of the "Devices" and explain briefly what they are: "Fluke Tools," "Key Devices," "Utilization Sources," "SNMP Agents," "Servers," "Routers," "Switches," "Printers," and "Hosts."

    _____

    _____

    _____

10. Close the Agent and the Console. You have begun using a very powerful piece of software.

Reflection:

Imagine you have earned your CCNA and are working in a medium-sized company. Write in your journal what value you see in using Network Management software.

Cisco Labs–Semester 1–Networking Fundamentals
LAB 7.6.3–NETWORK INSPECTOR PROBLEM LOG–OVERVIEW
(Estimated time: 20 minutes)

Objective:
- Use Network Inspector (or equivalent) software problem logging function to monitor network management information such as errors, warnings, and changes

Background:
Network Management is an important part of a networking professional's responsibilities. One of the most common network management tasks is keeping track of IP addresses. You have been reading about IP addresses and subnets. The Network Analysis software allows you to get the "big picture" of how IP addresses are assigned on your networks and subnetworks. It alsos allow you to access detailed information from the problem log for errors (such as incorrect subnet mask), warnings (such as incorrect IP address), and changes (such as IP address change).

Tools/Preparation:
Each PC must be running Windows 95, 98, or NT, Microsoft TCP/IP stack, and Winsock 2.0. Fluke Network Inspector 3.0 (or equivalent) must be installed on each PC. During the installation of the software, you must specify which network adapter (NIC, dial-up, and so on) you wish to monitor. Specify the NIC that attaches the PC to an Ethernet. The PCs should be on either a 10Base-T or 100Base-TX Ethernet network that preferably includes servers, switches, routers, and printers (this makes the network discovery more interesting). Before beginning this lab, you should read the *Cisco Networking Academy Program: First-Year Companion Guide*, Second Edition, Chapter 29. You should also review Semester 1 online Lesson 7.

Required Resources:
- PC with Windows 95, 98, or NT, Microsoft TCP/IP stack, and Winsock 2.0
- Fluke Network Inspector 3.0 software

Cisco Labs–Semester 1–Networking Fundamentals
LAB 7.6.3–NETWORK INSPECTOR PROBLEM LOG–WORKSHEET

1. Make sure you are connected to the network. How can you verify this? _____
   _____

2. Log on to Network Inspector Agent, set the Database tab to overwrite, and start the agent running.
   _____

3. Open Network Inspector Console, and watch until network discovery appears to have stopped.
   Stop the agent. _____

4. Go to Help/About the problem log and troubleshooting problems/errors, warnings, and changes
   that can be discovered–does a list appear? _____
   _____

5. Review the list. Choose 3 errors, 3 warnings, and 3 changes that you believe are important, and
   describe them in your own words. _____
   _____
   _____
   _____

6. Return to database view. Are there any errors, warnings, and changes that have appeared? If your
   instructor tells you, try starting and stopping the agent again, rediscovering the network, and
   seeing if the instructor has caused any errors, warnings, or changes. Note these changes in your
   journal. _____
   _____

7. Can you draw a topology of the network based on the IP addresses and subnetwork information
   obtained? Go ahead and try. _____
   _____

Reflection:
Imagine you are a network administrator. Describe how this software would be useful to you.
_____
_____
_____
_____
_____

Cisco Labs–Semester 1–Networking Fundamentals
LAB 7.6.4–PROTOCOL INSPECTOR FRAME STATS–OVERVIEW
(Estimated time: 35 minutes)

Objective:
- Use Protocol Inspector (or equivalent) software to examine some simple network utilization and frame statistics, in order to make more real the concept of frame flow as the heartbeat of the LAN

Background:
Protocol analysis software, often called protocol "sniffers," allows an in-depth view of the amazing diversity of network processes. Protocol analysis software often lets you study protocols at various layers of the OSI model, especially Layers 2, 3, 4, 5, and 7. In this lab, you focus on Layer 2 information. You have been studying frames, the Layer 2 protocol data unit (PDU). Frames might seem like an abstract thing, hard to imagine, but they are constantly being sent and received by your PC on a network. One feature of protocol analysis software is the ability to gather statistics about frames on the "wire" in real time so you can see some of the frame processes occurring. This is one indication of the health of a network, and helps in troubleshooting network problems. Most protocol analyzers can capture frames to and from a host based on MAC address, IP address, and the type of traffic to be monitored. Be warned that this is an amazingly powerful piece of software with many features, so you will learn them in small labs.

Tools/Preparation:
Each PC must be running Windows 95, 98, or NT, Microsoft TCP/IP stack, and Winsock 2.0. Fluke Protocol Inspector 3.0 (or equivalent) must be installed on each PC. During the installation of the software, you must specify which network adapter (NIC, dial-up, and so on) you wish to monitor. Specify the NIC that attaches the PCs to an Ethernet. The PCs should be on either a 10Base-T or 100Base-TX Ethernet network that preferably includes servers, switches, routers, and printers and a connection to a web server, or preferably the Internet (this will make the protocol analysis more interesting). Before beginning this lab, you should refer to the *Cisco Networking Academy Program: First-Year Companion Guide*, Second Edition, Chapter 29. You should also review Semester 1 online Lesson 7.

Required Resources:
- PC with Windows 95, 98, or NT, Microsoft TCP/IP stack, and Winsock 2.0
- Fluke Protocol Inspector 3.0 software

Cisco Labs–Semester 1–Networking Fundamentals
LAB 7.6.4–PROTOCOL INSPECTOR FRAME STATS–WORKSHEET

1. Make sure the PC is connected to your local-area network (LAN), which preferably is connected to the Internet. What are some ways to determine if your PC is connected to the LAN?

   _____

   _____

2. Install the protocol analysis software onto your computer (unless you have already done so). For Protocol Inspector, you must be sure that you have installed the correct NDIS 802.3 module as a Resource in Protocol Inspector. You probably need to see several NDIS 802.3 modules as resources, corresponding to different installed adapters on your PC. The Protocol Inspector can only look at one of these adapters at a time, which you must choose. Open the Protocol Inspector program. Do you see multiple adapters in the resource window? (Your instructor might need to specify which one. Note that if you are doing captures and you see no traffic whatsoever, you are probably looking at the wrong resource.)

   _____

3. Choose the correct module with a double-click. Describe the 2 graphs and the 6 tabs that appear. Write down and explain everything that appears in the Description tab.

   _____

   _____

4. Click the start button (1st line of icons, 3rd icon from the left) and see if the utilization graph increases above zero (displayed as blue sections on the graph). This indicates network traffic (perhaps switch or router or DNS updates). If after about 20 seconds you don't see anything, that's OK; click the stop button. You are about to start your own traffic.

   _____

   _____

5. In another window, open your e-mail program and prepare to send a simple e-mail to yourself. But don't send it yet! _____

6. Click the start button. Watch the utilization graph as your e-mail is transmitted and then received. Check your e-mail until you get the second blue "bump" indicating receipt of the e-mail, then click the stop icon. If your network is such that the delay for receipt of e-mails is too long for class time, just watching the transmitted e-mail is fine._____

7. Check the RX tab. Look at the MAC counters column. What types of frames were received? What does each type mean? Look at the errors column (7 are listed). Imagine what the different types of frame errors are, and put, in your own words, what you think they mean. Frame types include broadcast (to all MAC addresses), multicast (to a group of MAC addresses), or unicast (to one MAC address). _____

   _____

8. At the top left of the window, there should be two lines of icons. On the second line of icons, 6th from the left, is the Detail View icon. Click it and describe what happens.

   _____

   _____

Cisco Labs–Semester 1–Networking Fundamentals
LAB 7.6.4–PROTOCOL INSPECTOR FRAME STATS–WORKSHEET

9. From detail view, stop the capture. On the first line of icons, select the yellow "file cabinet," 8th from the left of "Capture View." What happens? _____

_____

10. Take a view, scrolling down looking at all the frames and all of the protocols involved in a simple e-mail. _____

11. Now try out the other views: MAC statistics, Frame Size Distribution Monitor, Protocol statistics, Network Layer Host Table, Application Layer Host Table, Host Matrix, Network Layer Matrix. Comment on each. _____

_____

_____

Reflection:

1. Has this program given you a new perspective on frames? Explain. _____

_____

2. Does the number of protocol frames for even a simple e-mail request surprise you? Why or why not? _____

_____

3. Did this lab change the way you view the functioning of computer networks? Explain.

_____

_____

_____

Cisco Labs–Semester 1–Networking Fundamentals
LAB 9.2.12–RJ-45 JACK INSTALL–OVERVIEW
(Estimated time: 45 minutes)

Objectives:
- Learn the correct process for terminating (punching down) an RJ-45 jack
- Learn the correct procedure for installing the jack in a wall plate

Background:
In this lab, you learn to wire an RJ-45 data jack for installation in a wall plate using a punch-down tool. These skills are useful when you must install a small amount of cabling in an office or residence. A punch tool is a device that uses spring-loaded action to push wires between metal pins, while at the same time skinning the sheath away from the wire. This ensures that the wire makes a good electrical connection with the pins inside the jack. The punch tool also cuts off any extra wire.

You will work with CAT 5 cabling and CAT 5 rated T568-B jacks. A CAT 5 straight-wired patch cable with an RJ-45 connector will normally plug into this data jack (or outlet) to connect a PC in a work area to the network. It is important that you use CAT 5 rated jacks and patch panels with CAT 5 cabling in order to support higher-speed versions of Ethernet such as Fast Ethernet, which is 100Mbps. The process of punching down wires into a data jack in an office area is the same as punching them down in a patch panel in a wiring closet such as a Main Distribution Facility (MDF) or Intermediate Distribution Facility (IDF).

Tools/Preparation:
Prior to starting the lab, the teacher or lab assistant should have a spool of Cat 5 Unshielded Twisted-Pair (UTP) cable, several RJ-45 data jacks, a 110 Punch down tool and an Ethernet/RJ45 continuity tester available. Work individually or in teams. *Cisco Networking Academy Program: First-Year Companion Guide,* Second Edition, and Semester 1 online Lesson 9 should be reviewed prior to starting this lab.

Required Resources:
- Two- to three-foot length of CAT 5 cabling (one per person or one per team).
- Two CAT 5 RJ-45 data jacks (one extra for spare). If RJ-45 data jacks are installed on both ends of the cable, the installation can be tested by inserting cable with RJ-45 connectors and a simple cable continuity tester.
- CAT 5 wall plate.
- 110 type punch-down tool.
- Wire cutters.

Cisco Labs–Semester 1–Networking Fundamentals
LAB 9.2.12–RJ-45 JACK INSTALL–WORKSHEET

Use the following procedure and diagram to punch down the wires into the RJ-45 jack and install the jack into the wall plate:

Step 1. Remove the jacket 1" from the end of the cable.

Step 2. Position wires in the proper channels on the jack, according to the following color chart.

Step 3. Use the 110 punch-down tool to push conductors into the channels. Make sure that you position the cut side of the punch-down tool so that it faces the outside of the jack, or you will cut the wire you are trying to punch down. (*Note:* If you tilt the handle of the punch tool a little to the outside, it will cut better.) If any wire remains attached after you have used the punch tool, simply twist the ends gently to remove them, then place the clips on the jack, and tighten them. *Note:* Make sure that no more than .5" of untwisted wire is between the end of the cable jacket and the channels on the jack.

Step 4. Snap the jack into its faceplate by pushing it in from the back side. Make sure, when you do this, that the jack is right-side up (clip faces down when wall plate is mounted).

Step 5. Use the screws to attach the faceplate to either the box, or to the bracket. If you have surface-mounted the box, keep in mind that it might hold 1'–2' of excess cable. Then you need to either slide the cable through its tie-wraps, or pull back the raceway that covers it, in order to push the rest of the excess cable back into the wall. If you have flush-mounted the jack, all you need to do is push the excess cable back into the wall.

Category 5 568-B Jack Wiring Color Scheme
Hold the jack with the 8-pin jack receptacle (the part that the RJ-45 connector goes into) facing up or away from you while looking at the wire channels or slots. There should be four wire channels on each side.

8-pin receptacle	
White Green	White Blue
Green	Blue
White Brown	White Orange
Brown	Orange

Cisco Labs–Semester 1–Networking Fundamentals
LAB 9.5.1–DEMO CABLE INSTALLATION–OVERVIEW
(Estimated time: 50 minutes)

Objective:
- To learn three crucial cable installation skills: stringing, running, and mounting Cat 5 cable

Background:
How you do this lab depends on your instructor's choice of project. You can simply string, run, and mount some cable temporarily for practice. Or, you might actually be wiring some or part of your lab. Or, you might be doing your structured cabling project, installing networks in some other part of the school or some small business. Regardless of where you are doing your project, you should follow the same professional standards. Assume that one end of your cable run will terminate, via punchdown, in an RJ-45 jack. Assume the other end of your cable run will terminate, via punchdown, in an RJ-45 Patch panel. Assume you will put the cable in raceway, in ceilings, around obstructions–various conditions you will likely encounter.

Tools/Preparation:
Basic materials include spools of Cat 5 cable, wire cutter/strippers, punchdown tools, raceway, various mounting consumables like cable ties, cable label, surface mounts, RJ-45 jacks and outlets, rack-mounted patch panels, a mock wall, fish tape and telepole, safety goggles, a ladder. The actual complete list and quantity of materials depends heavily on your actual project. Use the Cost Calculator, available on the Community Server, for a complete lab list and estimated quantities and costs. In other words, actual tools and preparation depend heavily on local conditions and resources. Before beginning this lab, you should refer to the *Cisco Networking Academy Program: First-Year Companion Guide*, Second Edition. You should also review Semester 1 online Lesson 9.

Required Resources:
Equipment/Tools
- Wire cutter/strippers
- Fish tape
- Telepole
- Safety goggles
- Ladder
- Punchdown tools

Consumables
- Cat 5 cable
- Raceway
- Cable ties
- Cable label
- Surface mounts
- RJ-45 jacks and outlets
- Rack-mounted patch panels
- Mock wall (2 x 4 with drywall)

Cisco Labs–Semester 1–Networking Fundamentals
LAB 9.5.1–DEMO CABLE INSTALLATION–WORKSHEET

Before starting the lab, you and your group should plan your cable run. Walk from where the RJ-45 jack and outlet will be to where the patch panel will be. Look for hazards, obstructions, light fixtures, difficult-to-reach places, and places where cable and raceway will be difficult to mount. Prepare a plan, which includes a diagram of your entire run, the total lengths of cable and raceway you will need, and how you plan to actually install the cable. (For example, will you need a ladder to reach a high point in the room?) After your plan is approved by your instructor, follow the procedures your instructor has described for you and your team to demonstrate the following procedures/techniques:

1. Fish cable from above.

2. Fish cable from below.

3. String cable through a dropped ceiling space.

4. Wall mount cable by using tie-wraps.

5. Wall mount cable by using decorative raceway.

6. Wall mount cable by using gutter.

7. Mount cable by using a ladder rack.

8. String cable by using a telepole.

9. String cable by using fish tape.

10. String cable using pull string.

Cisco Labs–Semester 1–Networking Fundamentals
LAB 9.7.13–DEMO CABLE TESTING–OVERVIEW
(Estimated time: 50 minutes)

Objective:

- Use the Fluke 620 (or equivalent) to perform cable verification experiments on newly installed cable runs

Background:

In Lab 9.5.1.1, you did a cable installation. As part of that lab, or as part of a project, you should complete the cable run installation by punching down into an RJ-45 jack on one end and a patch panel on the other. In this lab, you are called upon to test this cable run. There are a wide variety of tests and a wide variety of equipment that you could use. In this lab, you learn two techniques, one using a simple cable continuity meter and the other using a more sophisticated cable test meter.

Students should demonstrate the ability to use simple continuity-level cable testers. Instructors should at least demonstrate cable testing to the level of a Fluke 620 Cablemeter or equivalent. If more Fluke meters (or equivalent) are available, training all students on these meters will give them enhanced professional skills. If available (perhaps on loan from your regional academy or a local cable installation company), demonstrate the use of the higher-end cable testers—they are truly remarkable devices that measure many of the cable parameters discussed throughout the curriculum.

Tools/Preparation:

You should be familiar with the use of the Fluke 620 and basic cable testers from the Lesson 5 labs on media. Before beginning this lab, refer to the *Cisco Networking Academy Program: First-Year Companion Guide*, Second Edition. You should do the Lesson 5 labs and also review Semester 1 online Lessons 5 and 9.

Required Resources:

- One completely installed but untested cable run (RJ-45 wall jack to cable to patch panel) per student group
- Fluke 620 Cablemeter or equivalent
- Common RJ-45 cable continuity meter
- Journals
- Tools and materials for Lab 9.5.1.1 if the cable run fails the test and must be redone
- High-end cable testers (attenuation, NEXT, FEXT) if one can be borrowed from a local company or regional academy

Cisco Labs–Semester 1–Networking Fundamentals
LAB 9.7.13–DEMO CABLE TESTING–WORKSHEET

You should be able to take the cable run created in Lab 9.5.1.1 and test it. Your instructor will demonstrate some of the tests that can be performed with a cable tester. In some instances, the tests will indicate that problems exist. You are asked to outline how you would determine what the problem is, and describe how you would fix it.

1. Complete a cable run: _____
_____

2. Use the Fluke 620 Meter on Wire Map to test the installation: _____
_____

3. Identify any faults as near-end, along the cable, or far-end: _____
_____

4. Correct the faults: _____
_____

5. Retest until the cable run passes on the Fluke Meter: _____
_____

6. Label the cable run (alphanumeric identification) as passed and record in your journal: _____
_____

7. (Optional) Using the continuity meter, test two straight-through patch cords–one can be short, but the other must make up the entire rest of the distance from jack to patch panel. Test both patch cables on the continuity tester: _____

8. (Optional) Connect both cables to the continuity tester. If all of the light pairs (1 to 1, 2 to 2, 3 to 3, and so on; up to 8 to 8) light up, you have demonstrated at least the continuity.

9. (Optional) Perform high-end tests on the cable run with more expensive test equipment.

Cisco Labs–Semester 1–Networking Fundamentals
LAB 10.4.1–IP ADDRESSING–OVERVIEW
(Estimated time: 30 minutes)

Objectives:

- Name the five different classes of IP addresses
- Describe the characteristics and use of the different IP address classes
- Identify the class of an IP address based on the network number
- Determine which part (octet) of an IP address is the network ID and which part is the host ID
- Identify valid and invalid IP host addresses based on the rules of IP addressing
- Define the range of addresses and default subnet mask for each class

Background:

This lab helps you develop an understanding of IP addresses and how TCP/IP networks operate. IP addresses are used to uniquely identify individual TCP/IP networks and hosts (computers and printers) on those networks in order for devices to communicate. Workstations and servers on a TCP/IP network are called "hosts," and each has a unique IP address, which is referred to as its "host" address. TCP/IP is the most widely used protocol in the world. The Internet or World Wide Web uses only IP addressing. In order for a host to access the Internet, it must have an IP address.

In its basic form, the IP address has two parts: a network address and a host address. The network portion of the IP address is assigned to a company or organization by the Internet Network Information Center (InterNIC). Routers use the IP address to move data packets between networks. IP addresses are 32 bits long (with current version IPv4) and are divided into 4 octets of 8 bits each. They operate at the network Layer 3 of the OSI model (the Internetwork layer of the TCP/IP model) and are assigned statically (manually) by a network administrator or dynamically (automatically) by a Dynamic Host Configuration Protocol (DHCP) Server. The IP address of a workstation (host) is a "logical address," meaning it can be changed. The MAC address of the workstation is a 48-bit "physical address," which is burned into the NIC and cannot change unless the NIC is replaced. The combination of the logical IP address and the physical MAC address helps route packets to their proper destination.

There are five different classes of IP addresses, and depending on the class, the network and host part of the address will use a different number of bits. In this lab, you work with the different classes of IP addresses and become familiar with the characteristics of each. The understanding of IP addresses is critical to your understanding of TCP/IP and internetworks in general.

Tools/Preparation:

This is primarily a written lab exercise, but you might want to use Control Panel/Network to review some real network IP addresses. Before beginning this lab, you should refer to the *Cisco Networking Academy Program: First-Year Companion Guide*, Second Edition. You should also review Semester 1 online Lesson 10.

Required Resources:

- PC workstation with Windows operating system (Windows 95, 98, NT, or 2000) installed on PC and access to the Windows Calculator

Cisco Labs–Semester 1–Networking Fundamentals
LAB 10.4.1–IP ADDRESSING–WORKSHEET

Step 1. Review IP address classes and their characteristics.

Explanation: There are five classes of IP addresses (A through E). Only the first three classes are used commercially. We discuss a Class A network address in the table to get started. The first column is the class of IP address. The second column is the first octet, which must fall within the range shown for a given class of address. The Class A address must start with a number between 1 and 126. The first bit of a Class A address is always a zero, meaning the High Order Bit (HOB) or the 128 bit cannot be used. 127 is reserved for loopback testing. The first octet alone defines the network ID for a Class A network address. The default subnet mask uses all binary ones (decimal 255) to mask the first 8 bits of the Class A address. The default subnet mask helps routers and hosts determine if the destination host is on this network or another one. Because there are only 126 Class A networks, the remaining 24 bits (3 octets) can be used for hosts. Each Class A network can have 2^{24} (2 to the 24th power) or over 16 million hosts. It is common to subdivide the network into smaller groupings called subnets by using a custom subnet mask, which is discussed in the next lab.

The network or host portion of the address cannot be all ones or all zeros. As an example, the Class A address of 118.0.0.5 is a valid IP address because the network portion (first 8 bits, equal to 118) is not all zeros and the host portion (the last 24 bits) is not all zeros or all ones. If the host portion were all zeros, it would be the network address itself. If the host portion were all ones, it would be a broadcast for the network address. The value of any octet can never be greater than decimal 255 or binary 11111111.

Class	1st Octet Decimal Range	1st Octet High Order Bits	Network/Host ID (N=Network, H=Host)	Default Subnet Mask	Number of Networks	Hosts per Network (Usable Addresses)
A	1–126*	0	N.H.H.H	255.0.0.0	126 (2^7–2)	16,777,214 (2^{24}–2)
B	128–191	1 0	N.N.H.H	255.255.0.0	16,382 (2^{14}–2)	65,534 (2^{16}–2)
C	192–223	1 1 0	N.N.N.H	255.255.255.0	2,097,150 (2^{21}–2)	254 (2^8–2)
D	224–239	1 1 1 0	Reserved for Multicasting			
E	240–254	1 1 1 1 0	Experimental; used for research			

* Class A address 127 cannot be used and is reserved for loopback and diagnostic functions.

Cisco Labs–Semester 1–Networking Fundamentals
LAB 10.4.1–IP ADDRESSING–WORKSHEET

Step 2. Basic IP addressing.

Task: Use the IP address chart and your knowledge of IP address classes to answer the following questions.

1. What is the decimal and binary range of the first octet of all possible Class B IP addresses?
   Decimal: From: _____   To: _____
   Binary: From: _____   To: _____

2. Which octet(s) represent the network portion of a Class C IP address? _____

3. Which octet(s) represent the host portion of a Class A IP address? _____

Step 3. Determine the host and network portions of the IP address.

Task: With the following IP host addresses, indicate the class of each address, the network address or ID, the host portion, the broadcast address for this network, and the default subnct mask.

Explanation: The host portion will be all zeros for the network ID. Enter just the octets that make up the host. The host portion will be all ones for a broadcast. The network portion of the address will be all ones for the subnet mask.

1. Fill in the following table:

Host IP Address	Address Class	Network Address	Host Address	Network Broadcast Address	Default Subnet Mask
216.14.55.137					
123.1.1.15					
150.127.221.244					
194.125.35.199					
175.12.239.244					

2. Given an IP address of **142.226.0.15**,

   a. What is the binary equivalent of the second octet? _____
   b. What is the class of the address? _____
   c. What is the network address of this IP address? _____
   d. Is this a valid IP host address (Y/N)? _____
   e. Why or why not? _____

   _____
   _____
   _____

Cisco Labs–Semester 1–Networking Fundamentals
LAB 10.4.1–IP ADDRESSING–WORKSHEET

3. What is the maximum number of hosts you can have with a Class C network address? _____

4. How many Class B networks are there? _____

5. How many hosts can each Class B network have? _____

6. How many octets are there in an IP address? _____ How many bits per octet? _____

Step 4. Determine which IP host addresses are valid for commercial networks.

  Task: For the following IP host addresses, determine which are valid for commercial networks. Why or why not?

  Explanation: Valid means it could be assigned to a workstation, server, printer, router interface, and so on.

1. Fill in the following table.

IP Host Address	Valid Address? (Yes/No)	Why or Why Not
150.100.255.255		
175.100.255.18		
195.234.253.0		
100.0.0.23		
188.258.221.176		
127.34.25.189		
224.156.217.73		

Cisco Labs–Semester 1–Networking Fundamentals
LAB 10.6.6–SUBNET MASK 1–CLASS C WITH 2 SUBNETS–OVERVIEW
(Estimated time: 45 minutes)

Objectives:
- Cite some reasons why a subnet mask would be needed
- Distinguish between a default subnet mask and a custom subnet mask
- Determine the subnets available with a particular IP network address and subnet mask
- Given a network address and requirements for how many subnets and hosts, be able to determine what subnet mask should be used
- Given a network address and a subnet mask, be able to determine the number of subnets and hosts per subnet that can be created as well as useable subnets and useable number of hosts
- Use the "ANDing" process to determine if a destination IP address is local or remote
- Identify valid and invalid IP host addresses based on a given a network number and subnet mask

Background:
This lab helps you understand the basics of IP subnet masks and their use with TCP/IP networks. The subnet mask can be used to split up an existing network into "subnetworks" or "subnets." This can be done to 1) reduce the size of the broadcast domains (create smaller networks with less traffic), 2) to allow LANs in different geographical locations to communicate, or 3) for security reasons to separate one LAN from another. Routers separate subnets, and the router determines when a packet can go from one subnet to another. Each router a packet goes through is considered a "hop." Subnet masks help workstations, servers, and routers in an IP network determine if the destination host for the packet they want to send is on their own network or another network. Default subnet masks were discussed in a prior lab. This lab reviews the default subnet mask and then focus on custom subnet masks, which uses more bits than the default subnet mask by "borrowing" these bits from the host portion of the IP address. This creates a three-part address: 1) The original network address assigned by InterNIC, 2) The subnet address made up of the bits borrowed, and 3) The host address made up of the bits left after borrowing some for subnets.

Tools/Preparation:
This is primarily a written lab exercise, but you might want to use Control Panel/Network to review some real network IP addresses. Before beginning this lab, you should refer to the *Cisco Networking Academy Program: First-Year Companion Guide*, Second Edition. You should also review Semester 1 online Lesson 10.

Required Resources:
- PC workstation with Windows operating system (Windows 95, 98, NT, or 2000) installed on the PC and access to the Windows Calculator.

Notes:
_____
_____
_____

Cisco Labs–Semester 1–Networking Fundamentals
LAB 10.6.6–SUBNET MASK 1–CLASS C WITH 2 SUBNETS– WORKSHEET

Step 1. IP address basics.

Explanation: IP network addresses are assigned by the Internet Network Information Center (InterNIC). If your organization has a class A IP network address, the first octet (8 bits) is assigned by InterNIC and your organization can use the remaining 24 bits to define up to 16,777,214 hosts on your network. This is a lot of hosts! It is not possible to put all of these hosts on one physical network without separating them with routers and subnets. A workstation might be on one network or subnet and a server might be on another network or subnet. When the workstation needs to retrieve a file from the server it will need to use its subnet mask to determine the network or subnet that the server is on. The purpose of a subnet mask is to help hosts and routers determine the network location where a destination host can be found. Refer to the following table to review IP address classes, default subnet masks, and the number of networks and hosts that can be created with each class of network address.

Adress Class	1st Octet Decimal Range	1st Octet High Order Bits	Network/Host ID (N=Network, H=Host)	Default Subnet Mask	Number of Networks	Hosts per Network (Usable Addresses)
A	1–126*	0	N.H.H.H	255.0.0.0	126 $(2^7 - 2)$	16,777,214 $(2^{24} - 2)$
B	128–191	1 0	N.N.H.H	255.255.0.0	16,382 $(2^{14} - 2)$	65,534 $(2^{16} - 2)$
C	192–223	1 1 0	N.N.N.H	255.255.255.0	2,097,150 $(2^{21} - 2)$	254 $(2^8 - 2)$
D	224–239	1 1 1 0	Reserved for Multicasting			
E	240–254	1 1 1 1 0	Experimental; used for research			

* Class A address 127 cannot be used and is reserved for loopback and diagnostic functions.

Step 2. The "ANDing" process.

Explanation: Hosts and routers use the "ANDing" process to determine if a destination host is on the same network or not. The ANDing process is done each time a host wants to send a packet to another host on an IP network. If you want to connect to a server, you might know the IP address of the server you want to connect to or you can just enter the host name (for example, www.cisco.com), and a Domain Name Server (DNS) will convert the host name to an IP address. First, the source host will compare (AND) its own IP address to its own subnet mask. The result of the ANDing is to identify the network where the source host resides. It will then compare the destination IP address to its own subnet mask. The result of the 2nd ANDing will be the network that the destination host is on. If the source network address and the destination network address are the same, they can communicate directly. If the results are different, they are on different networks or subnets and will need to communicate through routers or might not be able to communicate.

Cisco Labs–Semester 1–Networking Fundamentals
LAB 10.6.6–SUBNET MASK 1–CLASS C WITH 2 SUBNETS– WORKSHEET

ANDing depends on the subnet mask. Subnet masks are always all ones. A default subnet mask for a Class C network is 255.255.255.0 or 11111111.11111111.11111111.00000000. This is compared to the source IP address bit for bit. The first bit of the IP address is compared to the first bit of the subnet mask and the second bit to the second, and so on. If the two bits are both ones, the **ANDing result is a ONE.** If the two bits are a zero and a one or two zeros, the **ANDing result is a ZERO.** Basically, this means that a combination of 2 ones results in a ONE, anything else is a zero. The result of the ANDing process is the network or subnet number that the source or destination address is on.

Step 3. Two Class C networks using the default subnet mask.

Explanation: This example shows how a Class C default subnet mask can be used to determine which network a host is on. A default subnet mask does not break an address into subnets. If the default subnet mask is used, the network is not being "subnetted." Host X (source) on network 200.1.1.0 has an IP address of 200.1.1.5 and wants to send a packet to Host Z (destination) on network 200.1.2.0 and has an IP address of 200.1.2.8. All hosts on each network are connected to hubs or switches and then to a router. Remember that with a Class C network address, InterNIC assigns the first 3 octets (24 bits) as the network address, so these are two different Class C networks. This leaves one octet (8 bits) for hosts, so each Class C network could have up to 254 hosts ($2^8 = 256 - 2 = 254$).

Source net: 200.1.1.0
Subnet mask: 255.255.255.0

Destination net: 200.1.2.0
Subnet mask: 255.255.255.0

Host IP 200.1.1.5

Router interface
IP 200.1.1.1

Router interface
IP 200.1.2.1

Host 200.1.2.8

The ANDing process helps the packet get from Host 200.1.1.5 on network 200.1.1.0 to Host 200.1.2.8 on network 200.1.2.0 by using the following steps:

a.   Host X compares its own IP address to its own subnet mask using the ANDing process.

Host X IP address 200.1.1.5	11001000.00000001.00000001.00000101
Subnet Mask 255.255.255.0	11111111.11111111.11111111.00000000
ANDing Result (200.1.1.0)	11001000.00000001.00000001.00000000

Note: The result of step 3a of the ANDing process is the network address of Host X, which is 200.1.1.0.

Cisco Labs–Semester 1–Networking Fundamentals
LAB 10.6.6–SUBNET MASK 1–CLASS C WITH 2 SUBNETS–WORKSHEET

b. Next, Host X compares the IP address of the Host Z destination to its own subnet mask using the ANDing process.

Host Z IP address 200.1.2.8	11001000.00000001.00000010.00001000
Subnet Mask 255.255.255.0	11111111.11111111.11111111.00000000
ANDing Result (200.1.2.0)	11001000.00000001.00000010.00000000

Note: The result of Step3b ANDing process is the network address of Host Z, which is 200.1.2.0.

Host X compares the ANDing results from Step A and the ANDing results from Step B, and they are different. Host X now knows that Host Z is not in its local-area network (LAN), and it must send the packet to its "Default Gateway," which is the IP address of the router interface of 200.1.1.1 on network 200.1.1.0. The router then repeats the ANDing process to determine which router interface to send the packet out.

Step 4. One Class C network using a custom subnet mask.

Explanation: This example uses a single Class C network address (200.1.1.0) and shows how a Class C custom subnet mask can be used to determine which subnetwork (or subnet) a host is on and to route packets from one subnetwork to another. Remember that, with a Class C network address, InterNIC assigns the first 3 octets (24 bits) as the network address. This leaves 8 bits (one octet) for hosts, so each Class C network could have up to 254 hosts ($2^8 = 256 - 2 = 254$).

Perhaps you want less than 254 hosts (workstations and servers) all on one network and you want to create two subnetworks and separate them with a router for security reasons or to reduce traffic. This will create smaller independent broadcast domains and can improve network performance and increase security because these subnetworks will be separated by a router. Assume you will need at least 2 subnetworks and at least 50 hosts per subnetwork. Because you only have one Class C network address, you have only 8 bits in the fourth octet available for a total of 254 possible hosts, so you must create a custom subnet mask. You will use the custom subnet mask to "borrow" bits from the host portion of the address. The following steps help accomplish this:

a. The first step to "subnetting" is to determine how many subnets are needed. In this case, you need 2 subnetworks. To see how many bits you should borrow from the host portion of the network address, add the bit values from right to left until the total is equal to or greater than the number of subnets you need. Because we need two subnets, add the one bit and the two bit, which equals three. This is over the number of subnets we need, so we need to borrow at least two bits from the host address starting from the left side of the octet that contains the host address.

Cisco Labs–Semester 1–Networking Fundamentals
LAB 10.6.6–SUBNET MASK 1–CLASS C WITH 2 SUBNETS–WORKSHEET

Network address: 200.1.1.0

4th octet Host address bits:	1	1	1	1	1	1	1	1
Host address bit values (from right)	128	64	32	16	8	4	**2**	**1**

(Add bits starting from the right side (the 1 and the 2) until you get more than the number of subnets needed.)

b. After we know how many bits to borrow, we take them from the left side of the first octet of the host address. Every bit we borrow from the host leaves fewer bits for the hosts. Even though we increase the number of subnets, we decrease the number of hosts per subnet. Because we need to borrow two bits from the left side, we must show that new value in our subnet mask. Our existing default subnet mask was 255.255.255.0 and our new "custom" subnet mask is 255.255.255.192. The 192 comes from the value of the first two bits from the left (128 + 64 = 192). These bits now become 1s and are part of the overall subnet mask. This leaves 6 bits for host IP addresses or $2^6 = 64$ hosts per subnet.

4th Octet borrowed bits for subnet:	1	1	0	0	0	0	0	0
Subnet bit values: (from left side)	**128**	**64**	32	16	8	4	2	1

With this information, you can build the following table. The first two bits are the subnet binary value. The last 6 bits are the host bits. By borrowing 2 bits from the 8 bits of the host address you can create 4 subnets with 64 hosts each. The 4 networks created are the "0" net, the "64" net, the "128" net, and the "192" net. The "0" net and the "192" net are considered unusable. This is because the "0" net has all zeros in the subnet portion of the address and the 192 net has all ones in the subnet portion of the address.

Subnet No.	Subnet Bits Borrowed Binary Value	Subnet Bits Decimal Value	Host Bits Possible Binary Values (Range) (6 Bits)	Subnet/Host Decimal Range	Useable?
0 Subnet	00	0	000000–111111	0–63	No
1st Subnet	01	64	000000–111111	64–127	Yes
2nd Subnet	10	128	000000–111111	128–191	Yes
3rd Subnet	11	192	000000–111111	192–254	No

Notice that the first subnet always starts at 0 and, in this case, increases by 64, which is the number of hosts on each subnet. One way to determine the number of hosts on each subnet or the start of each subnet is to take the remaining host bits to the power of 2. Because we borrowed two of the 8 bits for subnets and have six bits left, the number of hosts per subnet is 2^6 or 64. Another way to figure the number of hosts per subnet or the "increment" from one subnet to the next is to subtract the subnet mask value in decimal (192 in the fourth octet) from 256 (which is the maximum number of possible combinations of 8 bits), which equals 64. This means you start at 0 for the first network and add 64 for each additional subnetwork. If we take the second subnet (the 64 net) as an example, the IP address of 200.1.1.64 cannot be used for a host ID because it is the "network ID" of the "64" subnet (host portion is all zeros). The IP address of 200.1.1.127 cannot be used because it is the broadcast address for the 64 net (host portion is all ones).

Cisco Labs–Semester 1–Networking Fundamentals
LAB 10.6.6–SUBNET MASK 1–CLASS C WITH 2 SUBNETS–
WORKSHEET

Step 5. One Class C network using a custom subnet mask.

Task: Use the following information and the previous examples to answer the following subnet-related questions.

Explanation: Your company has applied for and received a Class C network address of 197.15.22.0. You want to subdivide your physical network into 4 subnets, which will be interconnected by routers. You need at least 25 hosts per subnet. You need to use a Class C custom subnet mask and have a router between the subnets to route packets from one subnet to another. Determine the number of bits you need to borrow from the host portion of the network address and then the number of bits left for host addresses. (*Hint:* There will be 8 subnets.)

1. Fill in the following table and answer the following questions:

Subnet No.	Subnet Bits Borrowed Binary Value	Subnet Bits Decimal and Subnet No.	Host Bits Possible Binary Values (Range) (6 Bits)	Subnet/Host Decimal Range	Use?
0 Subnet					
1st Subnet					
2nd Subnet					
3rd Subnet					
4th Subnet					
5th Subnet					
6th Subnet					
7th Subnet					

NOTES:

_____
_____
_____
_____
_____
_____
_____

Cisco Labs–Semester 1–Networking Fundamentals
LAB 10.6.6–SUBNET MASK 1–CLASS C WITH 2 SUBNETS– WORKSHEET

Use the table you just developed to help answer the following questions:

1. Which octet(s) represent the network portion of a Class C IP address? _____

2. Which octet(s) represent the host portion of a Class C IP address? _____

3. What is the binary equivalent of the Class C network address in the scenario (**197.15.22.0**)?

Decimal network address: _____ . _____ . _____ . _____
Binary network address: _____ . _____ . _____ . _____

4. How many high-order bits were borrowed from the host bits in the fourth octet? _____

5. What subnet mask must you use (show the subnet mask in decimal and binary)?

Decimal subnet mask: _____ . _____ . _____ . _____
Binary subnet mask: _____ . _____ . _____ . _____

6. What is the maximum number of subnets that can be created with this subnet mask? _____

7. What is the maximum number of useable subnets that can be created with this mask? _____

8. How many bits were left in the 4th octet for host IDs? _____

9. How many hosts per subnet can be defined with this subnet mask? _____

10. What is the maximum number of hosts that can be defined for all subnets with this scenario (assuming you cannot use the lowest and highest subnet numbers and cannot use the lowest and highest host ID on each subnet)? _____

11. Is **197.15.22.63** a valid host IP address with this scenario? _____

12. Why or why not? _____

13. Is **197.15.22.160** a valid host IP address with this scenario? _____

14. Why or why not? _____

15. Host A has an IP address of **197.15.22.126**. Host B has an IP address of **197.15.22.129**. Are these hosts on the same subnet? _____ Why? _____

    _____

Cisco Labs Workbook–Semester 1–Networking Fundamentals
LAB 10.7.5–SUBNET MASK 2–CLASS B WITH 3 SUBNETS– OVERVIEW
(Estimated time: 45 minutes)

Objectives:
- Work with Class B network addresses and subnets
- Determine the subnets available with a particular IP network address and subnet mask
- Given a network address and requirements for how many subnets and hosts, be able to determine what subnet mask should be used
- Given a network address and a subnet mask, be able to determine the number of subnets and hosts per subnet that can be created, as well as useable subnets and useable number of hosts
- Assign IP addresses and subnet masks to hosts and router interfaces
- Use the "ANDing" process to track an IP packet from a local host to a remote host through a router

Background:
This lab builds on the prior labs and helps you develop a better understanding of IP subnet masks using a larger, more complex scale real-world example. Additional worksheet exercises are based on foundations established in Labs 1.10 and 1.11. This lab focuses on a Class B network with three subnets and using a subnet mask.

Tools/Preparation:
This is primarily a written lab exercise, but you will want to use Control Panel/Network to review some real network IP addresses and the basics covered in Labs 1.10 and 1.11. Before you begin this lab, you should refer to *Cisco Networking Academy Program: First-Year Companion Guide*, Second Edition. You should also review Semester 1 online Lessons 12 through 14.

Required Resources:
- PC workstation with Windows operating system (Windows 95, 98, NT, or 2000) installed on a PC to the Windows Calculator.

Notes:
_____

_____

_____

_____

_____

_____

_____

_____

Cisco Labs Workbook–Semester 1–Networking Fundamentals
LAB 10.7.5–SUBNET MASK 2–CLASS B WITH 3 SUBNETS–WORKSHEET

Step 1. IP Address: Basics.
Explanation: For reference, the IP addressing table from Lab 1.10 is included here. IP network addresses are assigned by the Internet Network Information Center (InterNIC). You will work with a Class B address.

Address Class	First Octet Decimal Range	First Octet High Order Bits	Network/ Host ID (N=Network, H=Host)	Default Subnet Mask	Number of Networks	Hosts per Network (Usable Addresses)
A	1–126*	0	N.H.H.H	255.0.0.0	126 (2^7-2)	16,777,214 $(2^{24}-2)$
B	128–191	1 0	N.N.H.H	255.255.0.0	16,382 $(2^{14}-2)$	65,534 $(2^{16}-2)$
C	192–223	1 1 0	N.N.N.H	255.255.255.0	2,097,150 $(2^{21}-2)$	254 (2^8-2)
D	224–239	1 1 1 0	Reserved for multicasting			
E	240–254	1 1 1 1 0	Experimental, used for research			

* Class A address 127 cannot be used and is reserved for loopback and diagnostic functions.

Step 2. Class B network address with three subnets.
Task: Use the information here and from previous labs to help determine your valid subnets and host IP addresses. Answer the following question.

Explanation: Your institution has a Class B network address of 150.193.0.0. This Class B network address will be subdivided to accommodate your physical network, and you will need at least 50 subnets interconnected with routers. Each subnet needs to be capable of handling at least 750 hosts per subnet (workstations, servers, and router interfaces). As the network manager for your local campus at the institution, you were given the first ten of these subnets for use with your local campus. You will be using six of these subnets now and will keep the others for future growth. Do NOT use the first or last subnet.

1. What is the binary equivalent of the Class B network address 150.193.0.0 in the exercise?

   _____ . _____ . _____ . _____

2. Which octet(s) and how many bits are used to represent the network portion of this network address? _____

3. Which octet(s) and how many bits represent the host portion of this Class B network address?

   _____

4. How many original Class B networks are there? _____

Cisco Labs Workbook–Semester 1–Networking Fundamentals
LAB 10.7.5–SUBNET MASK 2–CLASS B WITH 3 SUBNETS–
WORKSHEET

5. What is the total number of hosts that can be created with a Class B network address if it has not been subdivided? _____

6. How many bits must you borrow from the host portion of the network address to provide at least 50 subnets and at least 750 hosts per subnet? _____

7. What will the subnet mask be (using dotted decimal notation) based on the number of bits borrowed in item 6? _____

8. What is the binary equivalent of previous the subnet mask?

    _____ . _____ . _____ . _____

Step 3. Class B network address with three subnets.
> **Task:** Use the diagram at the end of the worksheet to answer the following questions.
> **Explanation:** Be sure to specify all four octets for subnet address and subnet mask. The same subnet mask should be used for all hosts, router interfaces, and subnets. Having a common subnet mask allows hosts and routers to determine the subnet for which the IP packet is intended. Router interfaces will usually be numbered first when assigning IP addresses, and hosts will receive higher numbers.

9. Fill in the following table for each of the possible subnets that can be created by borrowing 6 bits for subnets from the third octet (first host octet). Identify the network address, the subnet mask, the subnetwork address, the range of possible host IP addresses for each subnet, and the broadcast address of each subnet. Also indicate whether the subnet is useable. You will use only three of these subnets for the exercise.

Subnet	Network Address	Subnet Mask	Subnetwork Address	Range of Possible Host IP Addresses	Broadcast Address	Use?
1st						
2nd						
3rd						
4th						
5th						
6th						
7th						
8th						
9th						
10th						

Cisco Labs Workbook–Semester 1–Networking Fundamentals
LAB 10.7.5–SUBNET MASK 2–CLASS B WITH 3 SUBNETS–
WORKSHEET

10. Assign an IP address and subnet mask to router interface A; write it here.

_____ / _____

11. Assign an IP address and subnet mask to router interface B; write it here.

_____ / _____

12. Assign an IP address and subnet mask to router interface C; write it here.

_____ / _____

13. Assign a host IP address to Host X on Subnet A, and assign an IP address to Host Z on Subnet C (answers may vary). Describe the steps (using ANDing) for the process of sending an IP packet from Host X to Host Z through the router. Remember, when ANDing two 1s together, the result is a 1; ANDing any other combination (1 and 0, 0 and 1, or 0 and 0) results in a zero (0). Also, when ANDing two network IP addresses together, the result of the ANDing process will be the network (or subnetwork) address of the destination IP address in the packet. Use the information from the previous diagram and Lab 1.10 to help assign IP addresses and subnet masks.

_____
_____
_____
_____
_____
_____
_____
_____
_____
_____
_____

14. What is the result of the ANDing process for Host X?
    Decimal Host X IP address: _____ . _____ . _____ . _____
    Binary Host X IP address: _____ . _____ . _____ . _____
    Binary subnet mask: _____ . _____ . _____ . _____
    Binary ANDing result: _____ . _____ . _____ . _____
    Decimal ANDing result: _____ . _____ . _____ . _____

15. What is the result of the ANDing process for Host Z?
    Decimal Host Z IP address: _____ . _____ . _____ . _____
    Binary Host Z IP address: _____ . _____ . _____ . _____
    Binary subnet mask: _____ . _____ . _____ . _____
    Binary ANDing result: _____ . _____ . _____ . _____
    Decimal ANDing result: _____ . _____ . _____ . _____

16. The decimal ANDing result from Question 14 is the network/subnet that Host X is on. The result from Question 15 is the network/subnet that Host Z is on. Are Host X and Host Z on the same network/subnet? _____

Cisco Labs Workbook–Semester 1–Networking Fundamentals
LAB 10.7.5–SUBNET MASK 2–CLASS B WITH 3 SUBNETS–WORKSHEET

17. What will Host X now do with the packet ? _____
_____

18. Fill in the blanks in the following diagram with the correct network and IP addresses.

Cisco Labs–Semester 1–Networking Fundamentals
LAB 10.7.7–SUBNET MASK 3–CLASS C WITH 3 SUBNETS–OVERVIEW
(Estimated time: 45 minutes)

Objectives:
- Work with a more complex Class C subnet scenario
- Determine the subnets available with a particular IP network address and subnet mask
- Given a network address and requirements for how many subnets and hosts, be able to determine what subnet mask should be used
- Given a network address and a subnet mask, be able to determine the number of subnets and hosts per subnet that can be created as well as useable subnets and useable number of hosts
- Assign IP addresses and subnet masks to hosts and router interfaces
- Use the "ANDing" process to move an IP packet from a local host to a remote host through a router

Background:
This lab builds on Lab Subnet Mask 1 and helps you develop a better understanding of IP subnet masks using a real-world example with additional worksheet exercises based on foundations established in the prior lab. This lab focuses on a Class C network with three subnets and uses a custom subnet mask.

Tools/Preparation:
This is primarily a written lab exercise, but you need to use Control Panel/Network some real network IP addresses and the basics covered in the prior lab. Before beginning this lab, you should refer to the *Cisco Networking Academy Program: First-Year Companion Guide*, Second Edition. You should also review Semester 1 online Lesson 10.

Required Resources:
- PC workstation with Windows operating system (Windows 95, 98, NT, or 2000) installed on the PC and access to the Windows Calculator

Notes:

_____

_____

_____

_____

_____

_____

_____

_____

Cisco Labs–Semester 1–Networking Fundamentals
LAB 10.7.7– SUBNET MASK 3–CLASS C WITH 3 SUBNETS– WORKSHEET

Step 1. IP Address: Basics.

    Explanation: For reference, the IP addressing table from the prior lab is included here. IP network addresses are assigned by the Internet Network Information Center (InterNIC). You will work with Class C.

Address Class	1st Octet Decimal Range	1st Octet High Order Bits	Network/Host ID (N=Network, H=Host)	Default Subnet Mask	Number of Networks	Hosts per Network (Usable Addresses)
A	1–126*	0	N.H.H.H	255.0.0.0	126 $(2^7 - 2)$	16,777,214 $(2^{24} - 2)$
B	128–191	1 0	N.N.H.H	255.255.0.0	16,382 $(2^{14} - 2)$	65,534 $(2^{16} - 2)$
C	192–223	1 1 0	N.N.N.H	255.255.255.0	2,097,150 $(2^{21} - 2)$	254 $(2^8 - 2)$
D	224–239	1 1 1 0	Reserved for Multicasting			
E	240–254	1 1 1 1 0	Experimental; used for research			

* Class A address 127 cannot be used and is reserved for loopback and diagnostic functions.

Step 2. Class C network address with three subnets.

    Task: Use the following information and use the information from the worksheet in the prior lab to help determine your valid subnets and host IP addresses. Do NOT use subnet zero or the last subnet.

    Explanation: Your company has a Class C network address of 200.10.57.0. You want to subdivide your physical network into 3 subnets (A, B, and C) using a router, as shown in the diagram at the end of the worksheet. You will need at least 20 hosts per subnet. Answer the following questions:

1. What is the binary equivalent of the Class C network address **200.10.57.0** in the exercise?

    _____ . _____ . _____ . _____

2. Which octet(s) represent the network portion and which octet(s) represent the host portion of this Class C network address?

    _____

3. How many bits must you borrow from the host portion of the network address in order to provide at least 3 subnets and at least 20 hosts per subnet? _____

4. What will the subnet mask be (using dotted decimal notation) based on the number of bits borrowed in Step 3?

    _____ . _____ . _____ . _____

5. What is the binary equivalent of the subnet mask previously?

    _____ . _____ . _____ . _____

Cisco Labs–Semester 1–Networking Fundamentals
LAB 10.7.7– SUBNET MASK 3–CLASS C WITH 3 SUBNETS– WORKSHEET

Step 3. Class C network address with 3 subnets.

Task: Use the following diagram to fill in the blanks and answer the following questions.

Explanation: Be sure to specify all four octets for subnet address and subnet mask. The same subnet mask should be used for all hosts, router interfaces, and subnets. Having a common subnet mask allows hosts and routers to determine which subnet the IP packet is intended for. Router interfaces are usually numbered first when assigning IP addresses and hosts will receive higher numbers.

1. Fill in the following table for each of the possible subnets that can be created by borrowing 3 bits for subnets from the fourth octet (host octet). Identify the network address, the subnet mask, the subnetwork address, the range of possible host IP addresses for each subnet, the broadcast address of each subnet, and also indicate whether the subnet is useable or not. You will only use 3 of these subnets for the exercise.

SN #	Network Address	Subnet Mask	Subnetwork Address	Range of Possible Host IP Addresses	Broadcast Address	Use ?
0						
1st						
2nd						
3rd						
4th						
5th						
6th						
7th						

2. Assign an IP address and subnet mask to router interface A and write it here.

   _____ / _____

3. Assign an IP address and subnet mask to router interface B and write it here.

   _____ / _____

4. Assign an IP address and subnet mask to router interface C and write it here.

   _____ / _____

5. Assign a host IP address to Host X on Subnet A and assign an IP address to Host Z on Subnet C (answers will vary). Describe the steps (using ANDing) for the process of sending an IP packet from Host X to Host Z through the router. Remember, when ANDing two 1s together, the result is a 1. ANDing any other combination (1 and 0, 0 and 1, or 0 and 0) results in a zero. Also, when ANDing two network IP addresses together the result of the ANDing process will be the network (or subnetwork) address of the destination IP address in the packet. Use the information from the diagram above and the prior lab to help assign IP addresses and subnet masks.

   _____
   _____
   _____
   _____

Cisco Labs–Semester 1–Networking Fundamentals
LAB 10.7.7– SUBNET MASK 3–CLASS C WITH 3 SUBNETS– WORKSHEET

6. What is the result of the ANDing process for Host X?
    Decimal Host X IP addr: _____ . _____ . _____ . _____
    Binary Host X IP addr: _____ . _____ . _____ . _____
    Binary Subnet Mask: _____ . _____ . _____ . _____
    Binary ANDing Result: _____ . _____ . _____ . _____
    Decimal ANDing Result: _____ . _____ . _____ . _____

7. What is the result of the ANDing process for Host Z?
    Decimal Host Z IP addr: _____ . _____ . _____ . _____
    Binary Host Z IP addr: _____ . _____ . _____ . _____
    Binary Subnet Mask: _____ . _____ . _____ . _____
    Binary ANDing Result: _____ . _____ . _____ . _____
    Decimal ANDing Result: _____ . _____ . _____ . _____

8. The decimal ANDing result from question 6 is the network/subnet that Host X is on. The result from question 7 is the network/subnet that Host Z is on. Are Host X and Host Z on the same network/subnet? _____

9. What will Host X now do with the packet? _____

10. Fill in the blanks in the following diagram with the correct network and IP addresses.

Cisco Labs–Semester 1–Networking Fundamentals
LAB 11.9.1–PROTOCOL INSPECTOR and ARP–OVERVIEW
(Estimated time: 20 minutes)

Objective:

• Use Protocol Inspector (or equivalent) software to study ARP requests and replies.

Background:

Protocol analysis software has a feature called capture. This feature allows all frames through an interface to be captured for analysis. With this feature, we can peek in on the Address Resolution Protocol process. You might have found ARP a bit abstract. With the protocol analyzer, we can see how important ARP is to the normal functioning of a network.

Tools/Preparation:

• Each PC must be running Windows 95, 98, or NT, Microsoft TCP/IP stack, and Winsock 2.0. Fluke Protocol Inspector 3.0 (or equivalent) must be installed on each PC. During the installation of the software you must specify which network adapter (NIC, dial-up, and so on) you wish to monitor. Specify the NIC that attaches the PCs to an Ethernet. The PCs should be on either a 10Base-T or 100Base-TX Ethernet network that preferably includes servers, switches, routers, printers, and a connection to a Web server, or preferably the Internet (this makes the protocol analysis more interesting). Before beginning this lab, you should refer to the Cisco Networking Academy Program: First Year Companion Guide, Second Edition. You should also review Semester 1 online Lessons 7 and 11.

Cisco Labs–Semester 1–Networking Fundamentals
LAB 11.9.1–PROTOCOL INSPECTOR and ARP–WORKSHEET

1. Open Protocol Inspector (or equivalent) software. _____

2. Go to detail view. What do you see? _____
   _____

3. Start a capture. What happens? _____
   _____

4. Open an MS-DOS window. _____

5. Using arp -a examine the contents of the ARP table. What do you see? _____
   _____

6. Using arp -d a.b.c.d delete all entries in the ARP table. Use arp -a to re-examine the ARP table.
   What has happened? _____

7. Use ping a.b.c.d to trigger an ARP frame. What happens? Ping your own machine or another
   machine on the network. _____
   _____

8. Stop the capture. What happens? _____
   _____

9. Study the ARP frames, ping frames, and statistics using various views, especially the detail view.
   Describe the various views and what you learned about ARP. _____
   _____
   _____

10. Start another capture to examine the network you are on.

11. Use the network for a minute or so (sending e-mails, requesting Web pages, and so on) over
    some period of time (say two minutes) and see in detail how many ARP frames occur. Are any
    occurring? If so, why? _____
    _____

Reflection:

Why is ARP necessary for LANs to function? _____
_____
_____
_____

Cisco Labs–Semester 1–Networking Fundamentals
LAB 12.4.1–PROTOCOL INSPECTOR and TCP–OVERVIEW
(Estimated time: 30 minutes)

Objective:

- Use Protocol Inspector (or equivalent) software to view dynamic TCP operations

Background:

Protocol analysis software has a feature called capture. This feature allows all frames, through an interface, to be captured for analysis. With this feature, we can peek in on Transmission Control Protocol (TCP) as it moves segments filled with user data across the network. You might have found TCP to be a bit abstract, but with the protocol analyzer, we can see just how important TCP is to network processes (such as e-mail and Web-browsing).

Tools/Preparation:

Each PC must be running Windows 95, 98, or NT, Microsoft TCP/IP stack, and Winsock 2.0. Fluke Protocol Inspector 3.0 (or equivalent) must be installed on each PC. During the installation of the software, you must specify which network adapter (NIC, dial-up, and so on) you wish to monitor. Specify the NIC that attaches the PCs to an Ethernet. The PCs should be on either a 10Base-T or 100Base-TX Ethernet network. Preferably, this should include servers, switches, routers, printers, and a connection to a Web server, or ideally, the Internet. Before beginning this lab, you should refer to the *Cisco Networking Academy Program: First-Year Companion Guide*, Second Edition. You should also review Semester 1 online Lessons 7 and 11.

Required Resources:

- PC with Windows 95, 98, or NT, Microsoft TCP/IP stack, and Winsock 2.0
- Fluke Protocol Inspector 3.0 software
- Browser and e-mail applications installed and running

Cisco Labs–Semester 1–Networking Fundamentals
LAB 12.4.1–PROTOCOL INSPECTOR and TCP–WORKSHEET

1. Open protocol inspector and your browser. _____

2. Go to detail view. _____
   _____

3. Start a capture. _____

4. Request a Web page: _____

5. Watch the monitor view while the Web page is requested and delivered. _____
   _____

6. Stop the capture. _____

7. Study the TCP frames, HTTP frames, and statistics using various views, especially the detail view.
   _____
   _____
   _____

8. Using the detail view, explain what evidence it provides about a) TCP handshakes, b) TCP acknowledgements, c) TCP segmentation and segment size, d) TCP sequence numbers, and e) TCP sliding windows.
   _____
   _____
   _____
   _____
   _____

Reflection:

Did this lab help you to visualize the TCP protocol in action? Why or why not?
_____
_____
_____

Semester 2 Labs

Cisco Labs–Semester 2–Router Configuration
LAB 2.2.2–ROUTER CHARACTERISTICS–OVERVIEW
(Estimated time: 30 minutes)

Router Name - LAB A
Router Type - 2514
E 0 = 192.5.5.1
E 1 = 205.7.5.1
S 0 = 201.100.11.1
SM = 255.255.255.0

Router Name - LAB B
Router Type - 2503
E 0 = 219.17.100.1
S 0 = 199.6.13.1
S 1 = 201.100.11.2
SM = 255.255.255.0

Router Name - LAB C
Router Type - 2503
E 0 = 223.8.151.1
S 0 = 204.204.7.1
S 1 = 199.6.13.2
SM = 255.255.255.0

Router Name - LAB D
Router Type - 2501
E 0 = 210.93.105.1
S 1 = 204.204.7.2
SM = 255.255.255.0

Router Name - LAB E
Router Type - 2501
E 0 = 210.93.105.2
SM = 255.255.255.0

LEGEND

= ROUTER   User Exec Password = cisco

= HUB   Enable Secret Exec Password = class

= LAN SWITCH   Terminal vty Password = cisco

= CONSOLE CABLE

Objectives:

- Determine the model number of a Cisco router and what physical interfaces (ports) it has
- Identify the cables attached to the router and what they connect to
- Check and/or modify HyperTerminal configuration parameters
- Connect to the router as its console using the PC and HyperTerminal program
- Determine the IOS version and filename
- Determine the CPU type, amount of RAM, NVRAM, and Flash memory

Background:

In this lab, you examine a Cisco router to gather information about its physical characteristics and begin to relate Cisco router products to their function. You determine the model number and features of a specific Cisco router, including which interfaces are present and to which cabling and devices they are connected.

A router is basically a dedicated microcomputer. It has a Central Processing Unit (CPU), an operating system (Cisco IOS), RAM, and ROM inside. Routers do not have disk drives, keyboards, or monitors. One of the ways to configure or program the router is to connect directly to it with a PC or a dumb terminal. The PC provides a monitor and keyboard for the router, which is referred to as its "console." The PC becomes the console, which allows you to enter commands and communicate directly with the router. In this lab, you work with a PC workstation using the Windows HyperTerminal (terminal emulation) program to act as a console to the router, and you configure the proper PC serial port settings in order to connect to and communicate with it.

Cisco Labs–Semester 2–Router Configuration
LAB 2.2.2–ROUTER CHARACTERISTICS–OVERVIEW

Tools/Preparation:

Prior to starting the lab, the teacher or lab assistant needs to check that a router is available and that a PC workstation is connected as a console with HyperTerminal installed and properly configured to access the router. The router should be exposed with all sides clearly visible so that all physical connections and cables can be inspected. Work in teams of two or more. Before beginning this lab, you should refer to the *Cisco Networking Academy Program: First-Year Companion Guide*, Second Edition, and Semester 2 online Chapter 2.

Required Resources:

- Windows PC with HyperTerminal installed and configured to access the router
- Cisco router (16xx or 25xx model)
- Console cable (roll-over) connecting the PC serial port to the router console port
- CAT 5 Ethernet cable attached to an Ethernet port
- Ethernet hub or switch
- WAN cable attached to a serial port

Web Site Resources:

- **Routing basics**—www.cisco.com/univercd/cc/td/doc/cisintwk/ito_doc/routing.htm
- **General information on routers**—www.cisco.com/univercd/cc/td/doc/pcat/#2
- **2500 series routers**—www.cisco.com/warp/public/cc/cisco/mkt/access/2500/index.shtml
- **1600 series routers**—www.cisco.com/warp/public/cc/cisco/mkt/access/1600/index.shtml
- **Terms and acronyms**—www.cisco.com/univercd/cc/td/doc/cisintwk/ita/index.htm
- **IP routing protocol IOS command summary**—www.cisco.com/univercd/cc/td/doc/product/software/ios120/12cgcr/rbkixol.htm

Notes:

_____
_____
_____
_____
_____
_____
_____
_____
_____
_____
_____
_____

Cisco Labs–Semester 2–Router Configuration
LAB 2.2.2–ROUTER CHARACTERISTICS–WORKSHEET

Step 1. Examine the router.

1. What is the model number? _____

2. Do you see a console port? (Y/N) _____   What port is it connected to on the console terminal (PC workstation)? _____

3. What type of cable is the console cable, and is it a roll-over, cross-connect, or straight-through cable? _____

Step 2. Record all router interfaces, connectors, and cables.

Explanation: If the port has a cable attached, identify the cable type, connector, and the device attached to the other end. (If a port does not have a cable, you should be able to identify the connector type that would be used.)

4. Fill in the following table.

Router Interface/Port Identifier	Cable Type/Connector	Device and Port to Which the Cable Is Connected

Step 3. Review the workstation's HyperTerminal configuration.

Explanation: Click Start/Programs/Accessories/Communications/HyperTerminal. Right-click the icon that is defined for console access to the Cisco router, and then click Properties. The icon might be named **Cisco.ht** or something similar. If one does not exist, you can create it using the settings shown in the answers to the worksheet. On the Properties screen, click the Phone Number tab, and then click the Configure button.

Cisco Labs–Semester 2–Router Configuration
LAB 2.2.2–ROUTER CHARACTERISTICS–WORKSHEET

5. Fill in the following table with the information indicated.

Configuration Option	Current Setting(s)
COM port	
Bits per second	
Data bits	
Parity	
Stop bits	
Flow control	

Step 4. Display IOS version and other important information related to RAM, NVRAM, and Flash memory with the show version command.

Task: Connect to the console port on the router, and enter the **show version** command.
Explanation: The router will return information about the IOS and memory.

6. What is the IOS version? _____

7. What is the name of the system image (IOS) file? _____

8. From where was the router IOS image booted? _____

9. What type of processor (CPU) and how much RAM does this router have? _____
   _____

10. How many Ethernet interfaces does this router have? _____

11. How many serial interfaces? _____

12. The router backup configuration file is stored in Non-Volatile Random Access Memory (NVRAM). How much NVRAM does this router have? _____

13. The router operating system (IOS) is stored in Flash memory. How much flash memory does this router have? _____

Cisco Labs–Semester 2–Router Configuration
LAB 2.2.3.1–ROUTER LAB SETUP–OVERVIEW
(Estimated time: 30 minutes)

Router Name - LAB A
Router Type - 2514
E 0 = 192.5.5.1
E 1 = 205.7.5.1
S 0 = 201.100.11.1
SM = 255.255.255.0

Router Name - LAB B
Router Type - 2503
E 0 = 219.17.100.1
S 0 = 199.6.13.1
S 1 = 201.100.11.2
SM = 255.255.255.0

Router Name - LAB C
Router Type - 2503
E 0 = 223.8.151.1
S 0 = 204.204.7.1
S 1 = 199.6.13.2
SM = 255.255.255.0

Router Name - LAB D
Router Type - 2501
E 0 = 210.93.105.1
S 1 = 204.204.7.2
SM = 255.255.255.0

Router Name - LAB E
Router Type - 2501
E 0 = 210.93.105.2
SM = 255.255.255.0

LEGEND

= ROUTER	User Exec Password = cisco
= HUB	Enable Secret Exec Password = class
= LAN SWITCH	Terminal vty Password = cisco
= CONSOLE CABLE	

Objectives:

- Set up the Cisco lab equipment according to the semester 2 topology diagram shown or analyze the physical connections of an existing lab setup
- Document the cabling and connections between devices
- Draw a diagram of your lab equipment setup

Background:

This lab helps you develop an understanding of how the Cisco lab routers are set up and connected for the Semester 2 topology (see the previous diagram). You examine and document the physical connections between these routers and the other lab hardware components such as hubs, switches, and workstations. This lab utilizes the standard setup consisting of five routers, four hubs, one switch, and at least five workstations, plus all associated cabling and adapters. Lab 2.2.10.2 will give you an opportunity to document the IP addressing and internal IOS configuration of the routers if they are already configured. If they are not configured, instructions will be provided to configure and test them.

Cisco Labs–Semester 2–Router Configuration
LAB 2.2.3.1–ROUTER LAB SETUP–OVERVIEW

Tools/Preparation:

Prior to starting this lab, you need to have the equipment from the standard five-router lab available (routers, hubs, switch, and so on). The routers and hubs should be disconnected and stacked. Each cabling type (WAN, LAN, console, power) should be grouped together. If it is not possible to start with equipment disconnected, you should review the steps of the lab with the equipment already connected. This familiarizes you with the physical connections and device interfaces.

The routers might be preconfigured by the instructor or lab assistant with the correct IP interface settings, and so on. The workstations might also be preconfigured to have the correct IP address settings prior to starting the lab. Lab 2.2.10.2 will provide instructions for analyzing and configuring the routers and workstations using IOS commands if they are not already configured. The routers and workstations should be labeled as indicated in this lab.

Start with the routers, switches, hubs, and cabling disconnected if possible. Your team needs to connect them according to the topology diagram in the overview at the beginning of this lab and then document your findings. This lab requires that you assemble the routers into the standard lab topology or as close as possible, depending on the equipment you have. You should work in teams of three or more. Before beginning this lab, refer to the *Cisco Networking Academy Program: First-Year Companion Guide,* Second Edition, and Semester 2 online Chapter 2.

Required Resources:

- Five PC workstations (minimum) with Windows operating system and HyperTerminal installed
- Five Cisco routers (model 1600 series or 2500 series with IOS 11.2 or later)
- Four Ethernet hubs (10Base-T with 4 to 8 ports)
- One Ethernet switch (Cisco Catalyst 1900 or comparable)
- Five serial console cables to connect the workstation to the router console port (with RJ-45 to DB9 converters)
- Three sets of V.35 WAN serial cables (DTE male/DCE female) to connect from router to router
- CAT5 Ethernet cables wired straight through to connect routers and workstations to hubs and switches
- AUI (DB15) to RJ-45 Ethernet transceivers (the quantity depends on the number of routers with AUI ports) to convert router AUI interfaces to 10Base-T RJ-45

Cisco Labs–Semester 2–Router Configuration
LAB 2.2.3.1–ROUTER LAB SETUP–WORKSHEET

Web Site Resources:

- **Routing basics**—www.cisco.com/univercd/cc/td/doc/cisintwk/ito_doc/routing.htm
- **General information on routers**—www.cisco.com/univercd/cc/td/doc/pcat/#2
- **2500 series routers**—www.cisco.com/warp/public/cc/cisco/mkt/access/2500/index.shtml
- **1600 series routers**—www.cisco.com/warp/public/cc/cisco/mkt/access/1600/index.shtml
- **Terms and acronyms**—www.cisco.com/univercd/cc/td/doc/cisintwk/ita/index.htm
- **IP routing protocol IOS command summary**—www.cisco.com/univercd/cc/td/doc/ product/software/ios120/12cgcr/rbkixol.htm

Notes:

_____

_____

_____

_____

_____

_____

Cisco Labs–Semester 2–Router Configuration
LAB 2.2.3.1–ROUTER LAB SETUP–WORKSHEET

Step 1. Plan router lab LAN/WAN arrangement.
A. When setting up the lab equipment from scratch, you need to give some thought to the following questions. Even if you are starting with an existing assembled lab setup, you should review all steps and answer all questions to become more familiar with how the routers are connected. Even though you might not actually be connecting the equipment, you should locate, examine, and document the cabling and physical connections between routers, hubs, and workstations.

- Where should the PCs be placed?
- Where should the routers be placed?
- Where should the switch and hubs be placed?
- How should the Ethernet, serial, and power cables be run?
- How many outlets and power strips will be needed?
- Which PC connects to which router?
- Which PC connects to which hub or switch?
- Which router connects to which hub or switch?
- How should devices and cabling be labeled?

Step 2. Arrange lab equipment.
Your arrangement of the routers and equipment can vary depending on space and physical setup of your lab area. The goal is to group each combination of router/hub/workstation closely because they can represent separate LANs and geographical locations in the real world. It is easier to see the relationships between equipment with this arrangement. Equipment should be positioned so that all interfaces are facing the same direction and so that cabling and connections can be accessed easily.

A. **Table or work surface setup**—If you are setting the routers out over tables or desks, place the labeled routers side by side in order from left to right (Lab-A, Lab-B...). Place the switch on top of router Lab-A. Place hub 1 on top of the switch and hubs 2, 3, and 4 on top of routers B, C, and D. Place router Lab-D with its hub on top of Lab-E because they are connected to the same LAN. Workstations should be located close to or on the tables for the routers and hubs to which they connect.

B. **Single rack setup**—If you have a single 19-inch network equipment rack, mount the first router, Lab-A, up high in the rack, and mount the switch just above it. Mount the other routers in the rack in sequence from top to bottom with about 4 to 6 inches between each router. Place a hub on top of the switch above router Lab-A and on top of routers B, C, and D. Workstations should be spread out around the rack to allow workspace and will be numbered from left to right.

C. **Multiple rack setup**—If you have multiple racks, put a router and hub in each rack from top to bottom and left to right, depending on how many racks you have. Place workstations as close to the routers as possible while still allowing workspace.

Cisco Labs–Semester 2–Router Configuration
LAB 2.2.3.1–ROUTER LAB SETUP–WORKSHEET

Step 3. Connect serial WAN cabling.

Next, you connect serial cables (DCE-DTE) between routers. With this lab setup, the router interface serial 0 (S0) is connected to the DCE cable. DCE refers to Data Circuit-Terminating Equipment (or Data Communications Equipment) connections and represents the clocking end of the synchronous WAN link. The DCE cable has a large female V.35 (34-pin) connector on one end and a DB60 connector on the other end that attaches to the router serial interface. Interface serial 1 (S1) is connected to the DTE (Data Terminal Equipment) cable. The DTE cable has a large male V.35 connector on one end and a DB60 on the other end that attaches to the router serial interface. Cables are also labeled as DCE or DTE.

1. Examine the cables and connections on the routers, and document the connections in this table:

From Router Name	Interface	To Router Name	Interface

Step 4. Connect the router Ethernet cabling.

For routers that have an AUI (Attachment Unit Interface) Ethernet 0 (E0) or E1 port, you will need an external transceiver that converts the DB15 AUI to an RJ-45 10Base-T connector. The 2500 series routers usually have an AUI port. The 1600 series has both AUI and RJ-45 ports, and you can use the RJ-45 port without the need for the external transceiver. All Ethernet cabling from routers to hubs or switches must be Category 5 (Cat 5) and wired straight-through (pin 1 to pin 1, pin 2 to pin 2, and so on). Connect the Ethernet cabling as indicated in the diagram, and then label the cabling at each end. Hubs should be numbered Hub 1, Hub 2, and so on.

2. Record the router Ethernet interfaces in use and which hub (or switch) they attach to in this table:

From Router Name	Router Interface	To Which Ethernet Device
Lab-A		
Lab-A		
Lab-B		
Lab-C		
Lab-D		
Lab-E		

Step 5. Connect the workstation Ethernet cabling.

Place the PCs at their planned locations and label them (WS-1, WS-2...) from left to right according to the diagram. Run straight-through CAT 5 cables from each PC to where the switch and hubs are located. Connect the Ethernet cabling as indicated, and then label the cables at each end depending on what device and interface they connect to. The following table shows the connections for all 10 workstations. Connect at least one workstation to each hub or switch.

Cisco Labs–Semester 2–Router Configuration
LAB 2.2.3.1–ROUTER LAB SETUP–WORKSHEET

3. Indicate which Ethernet device each workstation connects to in this table:

From Workstation	To Which Ethernet Device
WS-1	
WS-2	
WS-3	
WS-4	
WS-5	
WS-6	
WS-7	
WS-8	
WS-9	
WS-10	

Step 6. Connect the console workstations to routers.
Connect one end of the roll-over cables from workstations 4, 6, 8, 9, and 10 to the console interface of routers Lab-A, B, C, D, and E. Connect the other end of each of the roll-over cables to an RJ-45-to-DB9 serial connector. Connect the serial connector to the serial ports of the five workstations. Label the cables at each end.

4. What type of cable is the console cable? _____

Step 7. Connect power cords to all devices.
Plug in and turn on all devices. Verify all of them are activated by checking their indicator lights.

5. Are the link lights for the switch, the hubs, and the Network Interface Cards (NICs) in the workstations on? _____ Are the OK lights on the back of the routers on? _____

Step 8. Draw your lab diagram.

6. In the space provided, or in your engineering journal, redraw the router lab diagram to match your physical setup. Label all LAN (Ethernet) and WAN (serial) interfaces and cabling.

Cisco Labs–Semester 2–Router Configuration
LAB 2.2.3.2–ROUTER LAB CONFIGURATION–OVERVIEW
(Estimated time: 30 minutes)

Router Name - LAB A
Router Type - 2514
E 0 = 192.5.5.1
E 1 = 205.7.5.1
S 0 = 201.100.11.1
SM = 255.255.255.0

Router Name - LAB C
Router Type - 2503
E 0 = 223.8.151.1
S 0 = 204.204.7.1
S 1 = 199.6.13.2
SM = 255.255.255.0

Router Name - LAB E
Router Type - 2501
E 0 = 210.93.105.2
SM = 255.255.255.0

Router Name - LAB B
Router Type - 2503
E 0 = 219.17.100.1
S 0 = 199.6.13.1
S 1 = 201.100.11.2
SM = 255.255.255.0

Router Name - LAB D
Router Type - 2501
E 0 = 210.93.105.1
S 1 = 204.204.7.2
SM = 255.255.255.0

LEGEND
= ROUTER   User Exec Password = cisco
= HUB   Enable Secret Exec Password = class
= LAN SWITCH   Terminal vty Password = cisco
= CONSOLE CABLE

Objectives:

- Analyze the routers in an existing lab setup and document the IOS configuration
- Use the **show running-config** command at each router to determine attached IP network numbers, interfaces, IP addresses, and subnet mask information for the local-area networks (LANs) and wide-area networks in use
- Use Control Panel/Network or the **winipcfg.exe** utility at each workstation to determine IP address, subnet mask, and default gateway settings
- Use the **Ping** command to test the router and workstation connections
- Use IOS commands to configure routers to the standard lab setup (optional)

Background:

This lab helps you understand how the Cisco lab routers and workstations are configured for the Semester 2 topology (see the previous diagram). You use IOS commands to examine and document the IP network configurations of each router. You also check the IP configuration of each workstation to ensure that there is full connectivity between all nodes in the lab setup. If the routers are not already configured, you can (optionally) use the instructions at the end of the worksheet to configure each router. This requires additional time and probably some assistance from your instructor or a lab assistant because you have not covered this material in the text, labs, or online chapters yet.

Cisco Labs–Semester 2–Router Configuration
LAB 2.2.3.2–ROUTER LAB CONFIGURATION–OVERVIEW

Tools/Preparation:

Prior to starting this lab, you need to have the equipment for the standard five-router lab available (routers, hubs, switch, cables, and so on). The routers should be preconfigured by the instructor or lab assistant with the correct IP interface, settings, and so on, if possible. The workstations should also be preconfigured to have the correct IP address settings prior to starting the lab. The routers, hubs, and workstations should be labeled.

This lab assumes that you have completed Lab 2.2.10.1, and that the lab equipment (routers, hub, workstations, and so on) is assembled and connected in the standard lab topology. Work in teams of three or more. Before beginning this lab, you should refer to the *Cisco Networking Academy Program: First-Year Companion Guide*, Second Edition, and Semester 2 online Chapter 2.

Required Resources:

- Five PC workstations (minimum) with Windows operating system and HyperTerminal installed
- Five Cisco routers (model 1600 series or 2500 series with IOS 11.2 or later)
- Four Ethernet hubs (10Base-T with 4 to 8 ports)
- One Ethernet switch (Cisco Catalyst 1900 or comparable)
- Five serial console cables to connect the workstation to the router console port (with RJ-45 to DB9 converters)
- Three sets of V.35 WAN serial cables (DTE male/ DCE female) to connect from router to router
- CAT5 Ethernet cables wired straight through to connect routers and workstations to hubs and switches
- AUI (DB15) to RJ45 Ethernet transceivers (the quantity depends on the number of routers with AUI ports) to convert router AUI interfaces to 10Base-T RJ-45

Web Site Resources:

- **Routing basics**—www.cisco.com/univercd/cc/td/doc/cisintwk/ito_doc/routing.htm
- **General information on routers**—www.cisco.com/univercd/cc/td/doc/pcat/#2
- **2500 series routers**—www.cisco.com/warp/public/cc/cisco/mkt/access/2500/index.shtml
- **1600 series routers**—www.cisco.com/warp/public/cc/cisco/mkt/access/1600/index.shtml
- **Terms and acronyms**—www.cisco.com/univercd/cc/td/doc/cisintwk/ita/index.htm
- **IP routing protocol IOS command summary**—www.cisco.com/univercd/cc/td/doc/product/ software/ios120/12cgcr/rbkixol.htm

Notes: _____

_____

_____

_____

_____

Cisco Labs–Semester 2–Router Configuration
LAB 2.2.3.2–ROUTER LAB CONFIGURATION–WORKSHEET

Step 1. Verify that all physical connections are correct.
Review the standard Semester 2 lab diagram in the overview section of this lab or the diagram you created in the prior lab and check all physical devices, cables, and connections. Verify that the routers have been configured correctly (physically and internally) by the instructor or lab assistant.

Step 2. Examine and document current router configurations (if the routers have not been configured, skip to Step 5).

A. Log on to the first router, Lab-A.
Verify that you have a good console connection from the workstation to the router, and start the HyperTerminal program (Start/Programs/Accessories/Communications). Enter the password **cisco** if prompted to enter user mode. The prompt should be **Lab-A>**.
B. Enter privileged exec mode.
Type **enable** at the router prompt. Enter the password **class** if prompted. The prompt should now be **Lab-A#**.
C. Gather information about the router.
Physically examine each router and make note of the interfaces (E0, S0, and so on) you see. Enter the **show running-config** command (abbreviated **sh run**) to gather information. The router will respond with the active configuration file currently in RAM.

1. Fill in the following table with IP interface information for each of the five routers.

Cisco Lab Router IP Configuration (answers from router diagram—answers may vary)

Router Name	Lab-A	Lab-B	Lab-C	Lab-D	Lab-E
Model Number					
Interface E0 IP Address					
Interface E0 Subnet Mask					
Interface E1 IP Address					
Interface E1 Subnet Mask					
Interface S0 IP Address					
Interface S0 Subnet Mask					
Interface S0 Clock Rate					
Interface S1 IP Address					
Interface S1 Subnet Mask					
Other Interface(s)					

Cisco Labs–Semester 2–Router Configuration
LAB 2.2.3.2–ROUTER LAB CONFIGURATION–WORKSHEET

2. With the information gathered from the **show running-config** command at router Lab-A, answer the following questions:

   a. What is the routing protocol used? _____

   b. What are the networks that are directly connected to the interfaces?

   _____

   c. What is the clock rate of interface S0 on router Lab-A? _____

   d. What is the password for Telnet lines VTY 0 through 4? _____

Step 3. Examine and document the workstation configurations (if the workstations have not been configured, skip to Step 6).

A. Verify the workstation IP configuration.
Click Start/Settings/Control Panel. Double-click the Network icon. Select the TCP/IP protocol and click the Properties button. For each workstation, click the IP Address tab and record the current settings for IP address and subnet mask in the table below. Click the Gateway tab and record the IP address of the default gateway in the table. (This should be the IP address of the E0 router interface that the hub is connected to for each workstation.) You can also use the **winipcfg.exe** utility at the DOS command prompt to verify settings at each workstation.

3. Fill in the IP configuration with information obtained from each workstation.

Workstation #	Workstation IP Address	Workstation Subnet Mask	Default Gateway IP Address
1			
2			
3			
4			
5			
6			
7			
8			
9			
10			

Cisco Labs–Semester 2–Router Configuration
LAB 2.2.3.2–ROUTER LAB CONFIGURATION–WORKSHEET

Step 4. Test the router lab connectivity.

A. Ping from router to router.
Begin with router Lab-A and use the console workstation connection to it. Start the HyperTerminal program and ping the S1 interface of router Lab-B. This verifies that the WAN link between Lab-A and Lab-B is OK. Ping the serial interfaces of the other routers.

Lab-A> ping 201.100.11.2

4.   Was the ping from router Lab-A to Lab-B successful? _____

B. Ping from workstation to router.
Begin with a workstation connected to the first hub. Click Start/Programs/MS-DOS Prompt and ping the S1 interface of router Lab-B. This will verify that the workstation's IP configuration and the WAN link between Lab-A and Lab-B is OK. Ping the serial interfaces of the other routers.

C:\WINDOWS> ping 201.100.11.2

5.   Was the ping from router Lab-A to Lab-B successful? _____

Step 5. Configure the routers for the standard lab setup (optional).
If the routers need to be configured, you may need to obtain assistance from your instructor or lab assistant.

Step 6. Configure the workstations for the standard lab setup (optional).
If the workstations need to be configured, you may need to obtain assistance from your instructor or lab assistant.

Cisco Labs–Semester 2–Router Configuration
LAB 3.2.1–ROUTER USER INTERFACE–OVERVIEW
(Estimated time: 60 minutes)

Router Name - LAB A
Router Type - 2514
E 0 = 192.5.5.1
E 1 = 205.7.5.1
S 0 = 201.100.11.1
SM = 255.255.255.0

Router Name - LAB C
Router Type - 2503
E 0 = 223.8.151.1
S 0 = 204.204.7.1
S 1 = 199.6.13.2
SM = 255.255.255.0

Router Name - LAB E
Router Type - 2501
E 0 = 210.93.105.2
SM = 255.255.255.0

Router Name - LAB B
Router Type - 2503
E 0 = 219.17.100.1
S 0 = 199.6.13.1
S 1 = 201.100.11.2
SM = 255.255.255.0

Router Name - LAB D
Router Type - 2501
E 0 = 210.93.105.1
S 1 = 204.204.7.2
SM = 255.255.255.0

LEGEND

= ROUTER   User Exec Password = cisco

= HUB   Enable Secret Exec Password = class

= LAN SWITCH   Terminal vty Password = cisco

= CONSOLE CABLE

Objectives:

- Log on to a router in both user and privileged modes
- Use several basic router commands to determine how the router is configured
- Become familiar with the router HELP facility
- Use the command history and editing features
- Log out of the router

Background:

This lab introduces the Cisco Internetwork Operating System (IOS) command-line user interface. You need to log on to the router and use different levels of access to enter commands in user mode and privileged mode. You become familiar with the commands available in each mode (user or privileged) and use the router HELP facility, history, and editing features. The IOS command interface is the most common method of configuring a Cisco router. You will see many commands available, especially in privileged mode. Do not be overwhelmed. As with many things, the 80/20 rule applies. You can do 80 percent of what you need to do on a daily basis with 20 percent of the tools available.

Cisco Labs–Semester 2–Router Configuration
LAB 3.2.1–ROUTER USER INTERFACE–OVERVIEW

Tools/Preparation:
Prior to starting this lab, you need to connect a PC workstation with HyperTerminal to a router using the router's console interface with a roll-over cable. This lab should be done at the router console station. You should refer to the *Cisco Networking Academy Program: First-Year Companion Guide,* Second Edition, and review Semester 1 online Chapter 3 prior to starting this lab. You need to be familiar with these commands:

- ?
- enable
- logout

- show ?
- show running-config
- exit

Required Resources:
- PC with monitor, keyboard, mouse, and power cords
- Windows operating system (Windows 95, 98, NT, or 2000) installed on PC
- HyperTerminal program configured for router console access
- PC connected to the router console port with a roll-over cable

Web Site Resources:
- **Routing basics**—www.cisco.com/univercd/cc/td/doc/cisintwk/ito_doc/routing.htm
- **General information on routers**—www.cisco.com/univercd/cc/td/doc/pcat/#2
- **2500 series routers**—www.cisco.com/warp/public/cc/cisco/mkt/access/2500/index.shtml
- **Terms and acronyms**—www.cisco.com/univercd/cc/td/doc/cisintwk/ita/index.htm
- **IP routing protocol IOS command summary**—www.cisco.com/univercd/cc/td/doc/product/software/ios120/12cgcr/rbkixol.htm

Notes:
_____
_____
_____
_____
_____
_____
_____
_____
_____
_____

Cisco Labs–Semester 2–Router Configuration
LAB 3.2.1–ROUTER USER INTERFACE–WORKSHEET

Step 1. Log on to router.
   Explanation: Connect to the router and log on. If prompted, enter the password **cisco**.

   1. What prompt did the router display? _____ What does it mean?

   _____

Step 2. Enter the help command.
   Task: Enter the help command by typing **?** at the router prompt.
   Explanation: The router will respond with all of the available commands for user mode.

   2. List eight available commands from the router response. Try to pick ones that might be more
      commonly used.

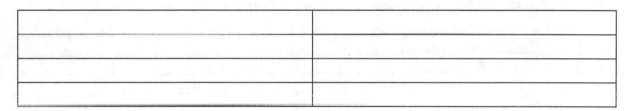

Step 3. Enter enable mode.
   Task:
   a. From user EXEC mode, enter privileged mode by using the **enable** command.
   b. Enter the enable password **class**.
   Explanation: Entering the **enable** command and using the password **class** allows you privileged-
   mode access to the router.

   3. Was **enable** one of the commands available from Step 2? _____

   4. What changed in the router prompt display, and what does it mean? _____

   _____

Step 4. Enter the help command.
   Task: Enter the help command by typing **?** at the router prompt.
   Explanation: The router will respond with all of the available commands for privileged mode.

   5. List ten available commands from the router response. Try to pick ones that might be more
      commonly used.

Cisco Labs–Semester 2–Router Configuration
LAB 3.2.1–ROUTER USER INTERFACE–WORKSHEET

Step 5. List all show commands.
 Task: Enter the **show** command followed by a space and a **?**.
 Explanation: The router will respond with the available subcommands for **show**.

6. Is **running-config** one of the available commands from this user level? _____

Step 6. Look at the running router configuration.
 Task: Enter **show running-config** at the router prompt.
 Explanation: Using the **show running-config** command displays the active configuration file for the router that is stored in RAM.

6a. List six key pieces of information you can get from this command.

Step 7. Continue looking at the configuration.
 Task: When the word **more** appears, press the spacebar.
 Explanation: When you press the spacebar, the router will display the next page of information.

7. What happened when you pressed the spacebar? _____

Step 8. Using the command history.
 Task: Press the up arrow or Ctrl-P.
 Explanation: Ctrl-P or the up arrow lets you review your command history.

8. What happened at the router prompt?

_____

Step 9. Exit the router.
 Task: Enter **exit** at the router prompt.

Cisco Labs–Semester 2 – Router Configuration
LAB 3.2.2–ROUTER USER INTERFACE MODES–OVERVIEW
(Estimated time: 20 minutes)

Objectives
- To identify the six basic and two optional router modes
- To become familiar with the router prompt for each mode
- Use several commands that will enter specific modes

Background:
When using router operating systems, such as Cisco IOS, you must know each of the different user modes a router has and what each one of them is for. Memorizing every command in all of the user modes would be time-consuming and pointless. Try to develop an understanding of what commands and functions are available with each of the modes. There are six main modes available with most routers:

- User EXEC mode
- Privileged EXEC mode (also known as enable mode)
- Global configuration mode
- Router configuration mode
- Interface configuration mode
- Subinterface configuration mode

Cisco Labs–Semester 2–Router Configuration
LAB 3.2.2–ROUTER USER INTERFACE MODES–OVERVIEW

In this lab, you work with the six most common modes, which are listed on the previous page. Two other modes that are used less frequently are RXBoot mode and setup mode. RXBoot is a maintenance mode that can be used for password recovery. Setup mode presents an interactive prompted dialog at the console that helps a new user create a first-time basic configuration. Both RXBoot and setup modes are covered in later labs. You can determine which mode you are in by looking at the prompt. Each of the modes will have a different prompt. Depending on which mode you are in, certain commands may or may not be available. You can always type a question mark (**?**) to see what commands you can use. The most common mistake made when working at the command line with different router modes is to enter a command and get an error when you are in the wrong mode. You need to be familiar with each mode and how to get in and out of each mode.

Tools/Preparation:

Prior to starting this lab, you need to connect a PC with HyperTerminal to a router using the router's console interface with a roll-over cable. Work individually or in teams. Before beginning this lab, you should refer to the *Cisco Networking Academy Program: First-Year Companion Guide*, Second Edition. You should also review online Chapter 3.

Required Resources:

- PC with monitor, keyboard, mouse, and power cords
- Windows operating system (Windows 95, 98, NT, or 2000) installed on PC
- HyperTerminal program configured for router console access
- PC connected to the router console port with a roll-over cable

Web Site Resources:

- **Routing basics**—www.cisco.com/univercd/cc/td/doc/cisintwk/ito_doc/routing.htm
- **General information on routers**—www.cisco.com/univercd/cc/td/doc/pcat/#2
- **2500 series routers**—www.cisco.com/warp/public/cc/cisco/mkt/access/2500/index.shtml
- **Terms and acronyms**—www.cisco.com/univercd/cc/td/doc/cisintwk/ita/index.htm
- **IP routing protocol IOS command summary**—www.cisco.com/univercd/cc/td/doc/product/software/ios120/12cgcr/rbkixol.htm

Notes:

_____

_____

_____

_____

_____

_____

_____

Cisco Labs–Semester 2–Router Configuration
LAB 3.2.2–ROUTER USER INTERFACE MODES–WORKSHEET

Step 1. Identify router modes, prompts, and functions.

For this lab, you and your group should try to discover what each of the modes are and what each of them does. Be sure to note what the prompts on the router look like in each of the modes. For example, when in interface config mode, the prompt is router(config-if)# (where router is the name of the router you work with).

1. Match the different router modes with their appropriate prompts (for example, 1-A, 2-B). Fill in the following table by writing the correct prompt, selecting from the list of choices:

Mode Description	Mode Prompts
1. User EXEC mode	
2. Privileged EXEC mode	
3. Global configuration mode	
4. Router configuration mode	
5. Interface configuration mode	

   A. Router #

   B. Router >

   C. Router (config-if) #

   D. Router (config-router) #

   E. Router (config) #

2. Match the different router modes with their functionality. Fill in the table by writing the letter of the correct choice provided:

Mode Description	Mode Functions
1. User EXEC mode	
2. Privileged EXEC mode	
3. Global configuration mode	
4. Router configuration mode	
5. Interface configuration mode	

   A. Detailed examination of router, debugging, and testing. Remote access.

   B. Setting of IP addresses and subnet masks.

   C. Simple configuration commands.

   D. Limited examination of router. Remote access.

   E. Routing protocols.

3. From the prompt shown, write a command that will allow you to enter the mode listed:

Desired Mode	Current Prompt	Command	Explanation
Privileged EXEC mode	Router>		
Global config. mode	Router#		
Interface config. mode	Router(config)#		
Router config. mode	Router(config)#		

Cisco Labs–Semester 2–Router Configuration
LAB 3.2.2–ROUTER USER INTERFACE MODES –WORKSHEET

Step 2. Diagram a router modes hierarchy.
4. In the space provided, or in your Engineering Journal, draw a hierarchical diagram of the various router modes listed in the background section of this lab. At the top of the hierarchy, you should have the initial router mode that comes up when you boot up the device. The bottom should have more specific modes. If two or more modes have equal priority, choose any order.

Reflection:

In your journal, describe what general function the following modes serve:
1. Config interface: _____
2. Enable mode: _____

Also, answer the following:
1. What did you learn from this lab? _____
2. Where/when did you have difficulties? _____
3. How did you overcome them? _____
4. How can you apply what you learned in this lab toward future labs? _____

Cisco Labs–Semester 2–Router Configuration
LAB 4.2.4–ROUTER SHOW COMMANDS–OVERVIEW
(Estimated time: 90 minutes)

Router Name - LAB A
Router Type - 2514
E 0 = 192.5.5.1
E 1 = 205.7.5.1
S 0 = 201.100.11.1
SM = 255.255.255.0

Router Name - LAB C
Router Type - 2503
E 0 = 223.8.151.1
S 0 = 204.204.7.1
S 1 = 199.6.13.2
SM = 255.255.255.0

Router Name - LAB E
Router Type - 2501
E 0 = 210.93.105.2
SM = 255.255.255.0

Router Name - LAB B
Router Type - 2503
E 0 = 219.17.100.1
S 0 = 199.6.13.1
S 1 = 201.100.11.2
SM = 255.255.255.0

Router Name - LAB D
Router Type - 2501
E 0 = 210.93.105.1
S 1 = 204.204.7.2
SM = 255.255.255.0

LEGEND

= ROUTER   User Exec Password = cisco

= HUB   Enable Secret Exec Password = class

= LAN SWITCH   Terminal vty Password = cisco

= CONSOLE CABLE

Objectives

- Become familiar with the basic router **show** commands
- Retrieve the current running configuration of the router in RAM using **show running-config**
- View the backup configuration file in NVRAM using **show startup-config**
- View the IOS file information using **show flash** and **show version**
- View the current status of the router interfaces using **show interface**
- View the status of any configured layer 3 protocol using **show protocol**

Background:

This lab helps you become familiar with the router **show** commands. The show commands are the most important information-gathering commands available for the router. **show running-config** (or **show run**) is probably the single most valuable command to help determine the current status of a router, because it displays the active configuration file running in RAM. The **show startup-config** (or **show start**) command displays the backup configuration file that is stored in non-volatile RAM (NVRAM). This is the file that will be used to configure the router when it is first started or rebooted with the **reload** command. All the detailed router interface settings are contained in this file.

The **show flash** command is used to view the available flash memory and the amount used. Flash is where the Cisco Internetwork Operating System (IOS) file or image is stored. The **show arp** command displays the router's IP to MAC to interface address mapping. The **show interface** command displays statistics for all interfaces configured on the router. **show protocol** displays global and interface-specific status of configured Layer 3 protocols (IP, IPX, etc.).

Cisco Labs–Semester 2–Router Configuration
LAB 4.2.4–ROUTER SHOW COMMANDS–OVERVIEW

Tools/Preparation:
Prior to starting the lab, you need to connect a PC with HyperTerminal to a router using the router's console interface with a roll-over cable. Work individually or in teams. Before beginning this lab, you should refer to the *Cisco Networking Academy Program: First-Year Companion Guide,* Second Edition. You should also review online Chapter 4. Be familiar with the following **show** commands:

- **show ?**
- **show clock**
- **show hosts**
- **show users**
- **show history**
- **show arp**

- **show flash**
- **show running-config**
- **show startup-config**
- **show interface**
- **show protocol**
- **show version**

Required Resources:
- PC with monitor, keyboard, mouse, and power cords
- Windows operating system (Windows 95, 98, NT, or 2000) installed on PC
- HyperTerminal program configured for router console access
- PC connected to the router console port with a roll-over cable

Web Site Resources:
- **Routing basics**—www.cisco.com/univercd/cc/td/doc/cisintwk/ito_doc/routing.htm
- **General information on routers**—www.cisco.com/univercd/cc/td/doc/pcat/#2
- **2500 series routers**—www.cisco.com/warp/public/cc/cisco/mkt/access/2500/index.shtml
- **1600 series routers**—www.cisco.com/warp/public/cc/cisco/mkt/access/1600/index.shtml
- **Terms and acronyms**—www.cisco.com/univercd/cc/td/doc/cisintwk/ita/index.htm
- **IP routing protocol IOS command summary**—www.cisco.com/univercd/cc/td/doc/product/software/ios120/12cgcr/rbkixol.htm

Notes:
_____
_____
_____
_____
_____
_____
_____
_____
_____
_____
_____
_____
_____

Cisco Labs–Semester 2–Router Configuration
LAB 4.2.4–ROUTER SHOW COMMANDS–WORKSHEET

Step 1. Log on to the router.
Explanation: Connect to the router and log on. If prompted, enter the password **cisco**.

Step 2. Enter the help command.
Task: Enter the help command by typing **?** at the router prompt.
Explanation: The router responds with all commands available in user mode.

1a. What did the router reply with? _____

1b. Are all router commands available at the current prompt? _____

2. Is **show** one of the options available? _____

Step 3. Display help for the show command.
Task: Enter the **show ?** command.
Explanation: The router responds with the **show** subcommands available in user mode.

3. List three user mode **show** subcommands.

show Subcommand	Description

Step 4. Display IOS version and other important information with the show version command.
Task: Enter the **show version** command.
Explanation: The router will return information about the IOS that is running in RAM.

4. With information from the **show version** command, answer these questions:
   a. What is the IOS version? _____
   b. What is the name of the system image (IOS) file? _____
   c. Where was the router IOS image booted from? _____
   d. What type of processor (CPU) and how much RAM does this router have? _____
   _____
   e. How many Ethernet interfaces does this router have? _____ How many serial interfaces? _____
   f. The router backup configuration file is stored in non-volatile random access memory (NVRAM). How much NVRAM does this router have? _____
   g. The router operating system (IOS) is stored in Flash memory. How much Flash memory does this router have? _____
   h. What is the configuration register set to? _____

Cisco Labs–Semester 2–Router Configuration
LAB 4.2.4–ROUTER SHOW COMMANDS–WORKSHEET

Step 5. Display the router's time and date.
   Task: Enter the **show clock** command.
   Explanation: The **show clock** command will show the current time and date.

5.   What information is displayed with **show clock**? _____

Step 6. Display a cached list of host names and addresses.
   Task: Enter the **show hosts** command.
   Explanation: The **show hosts** command displays a cached list of hosts and all of their interface IP addresses.

6.   What information is displayed with **show hosts**? _____

Step 7. Display users who are connected to the router
   Task: Enter the **show users** command.
   Explanation: The **show users** command displays users who are connected to the router.

7.   What information is displayed with **show users**? _____

Step 8. Show the command buffer.
   Task: Enter the **show history** command.
   Explanation: The **show history** command displays a history of commands that have been entered.

8.   What information is displayed with **show history**? _____

Step 9. Enter privileged mode.
   Task: a. From user EXEC mode, enter privileged EXEC mode using the **enable** command.
            b. Enter the enable password **class**.
   Explanation: Enter enable mode from user EXEC mode.

9.
   a.   What command did you use to enter privileged mode? _____
   b.   How do you know if you are in privileged mode? _____

Step 10. Enter the help command.
   Task: Enter the **show ?** command at the router prompt.
   Explanation: The router responds with the **show** subcommands available for privileged mode.

10.
   a.   What did the router reply with? _____
   b.   How is this output different from the one you got in user mode in Step 3? _____
        _____

Step 11. Show the router ARP table.
   Task: Enter the **show arp** command at the router prompt.

Cisco Labs–Semester 2–Router Configuration
LAB 4.2.4–ROUTER SHOW COMMANDS–WORKSHEET

Explanation: The router will respond with its ARP table.

11. What is the ARP table? _____

Step 12. Show information about the Flash memory device.

Task: Enter **show flash** at the router prompt.

Explanation: The router will respond with information about Flash memory and what IOS file(s) are stored there.

12. Document the following information with **show flash**:
   a. How much Flash memory is available and used?_____
   b. What is the file that is stored in Flash memory?_____
   c. What is the size in bytes of the Flash memory? _____

Step 13. Show information about the active configuration file.

Task: Enter **show running-config** (or **show run**) at the router prompt.

Explanation: The router will display information on how it is currently configured.

13. What important information is displayed with **show run**? _____
_____

Step 14. Show information about the backup configuration file.

Task: Enter **show startup-config** (or **show start**) at the router prompt.

Explanation: The router will display information on the backup configuration file stored in NVRAM.

14. What important information is displayed with **show start**, and where is this information kept?
_____

Step 15. Display statistics for all interfaces configured on the router.

Task: Enter **show interface** at the router prompt.

Explanation: The router shows information about the configured interfaces.

15a. Find the following information for interface Ethernet 0 with **show interface**:
   1. What is MTU? _____
   2. What is rely? _____
   3. What is load? _____
   4. What is a runt? _____
   5. What is a giant? _____

15b. Find the following information for interface serial0 with **show interface**:
   1. What is the IP address and subnet mask? _____
   2. What data link layer encapsulation is being used? _____
   3. What does "Serial0 is up, line protocol is up" mean? _____

Step 16. Display the protocols configured on the router.

Task: Enter **show protocol** at the router prompt.

Explanation: This command shows the global and interface-specific status of any configured layer 3 protocols.

16. What important information is displayed? _____

17. Enter **exit** at the router prompt.

Cisco Labs–Semester 2–Router Configuration
LAB 4.3.5–CDP NEIGHBORS–OVERVIEW
(Estimated time: 30 minutes)

Objectives:

- Use CDP commands to get information about neighboring networks and routers
- Display information on how CDP is configured for its advertisement and discovery frame transmission
- Display CDP updates received on the local router

Background:

In this lab, you use the **show cdp** command. Cisco Discovery Protocol (CDP) discovers and shows information about directly connected Cisco devices (routers and switches). CDP is a Cisco proprietary protocol that runs at the data link layer (Layer 2) of the OSI model. This allows devices that might be running different network Layer 3 protocols, such as IP or IPX, to learn about each other. CDP begins automatically upon a device's system startup. However, if you are using Cisco IOS Release 10.3 or a newer version of IOS, you must enable it on each of the device's interfaces by using the **cdp enable** command. Using the command **show cdp interface**, you gather information that CDP uses for its advertisement and discovery frame transmission. Use **show cdp neighbors** and **show cdp neighbors detail** to display the CDP updates received on the local router.

Cisco Labs–Semester 2–Router Configuration
LAB 4.3.5–CDP NEIGHBORS–OVERVIEW

Tools/Preparation:
Prior to starting the lab, you need to connect a PC with HyperTerminal to a router using the router's console interface with a roll-over cable. Work individually or in teams. Before beginning this lab, you should refer to the *Cisco Networking Academy Program: First-Year Companion Guide*, Second Edition. You should also review online Chapter 4. Be familiar with the following **show** commands:

- **show interface**
- **show cdp**
- **show cdp interface**
- **show cdp neighbors**
- **show cdp neighbors detail**

Required Resources:
- PC with Windows operating system and HyperTerminal installed
- Router connected to the PC with a console roll-over cable
- At least three routers interconnected via Ethernet or WAN simulation cables

Web Site Resources:
- **Routing basics**—www.cisco.com/univercd/cc/td/doc/cisintwk/ito_doc/routing.htm
- **General information on routers**—www.cisco.com/univercd/cc/td/doc/pcat/#2
- **2500 series routers**—www.cisco.com/warp/public/cc/cisco/mkt/access/2500/index.shtml
- **1600 series routers**—www.cisco.com/warp/public/cc/cisco/mkt/access/1600/index.shtml
- **Terms and acronyms**—www.cisco.com/univercd/cc/td/doc/cisintwk/ita/index.htm
- **IP routing protocol IOS command summary**—www.cisco.com/univercd/cc/td/doc/product/software/ios120/12cgcr/rbkixol.htm

Notes:
_____
_____
_____
_____
_____
_____
_____
_____
_____
_____
_____
_____
_____
_____

Cisco Labs–Semester 2–Router Configuration
LAB 4.3.5–CDP NEIGHBORS–WORKSHEET

Step 1. Log on to the router.
   Explanation: Connect to the router and log on. If prompted, enter the password **cisco**.

Step 2. Gather information about the router you logged in to by issuing the show interface command.
   Task: Enter the **show interface** command at the router prompt.
   Explanation: The router shows information about the configured interfaces.

1. Document the following information about the router:

   a. What is the name of the router? _____

   b. List IP address and subnet mask of the interfaces.

Interface	IP Address	Subnet Mask

   c. List operational status of each interface.

Interface	Interface Up or Down? (Carrier Detect Signal)	Line Protocol Up or Down? (Keepalives Being Received)

Step 3. Display the values of the CDP timers, interface status, and encapsulation used.
   Task: Enter the **show cdp interface** command at the router prompt.
   Explanation: The router responds with CDP information on all interfaces that have CDP enabled. Global CDP settings can be seen using the **show cdp** command by itself.

2. How often is the router sending CDP packets? _____

3. What is the hold-time value? _____

Step 4. Display the CDP updates received on the local router.
   Task: Enter the **show cdp neighbors** command at the router prompt.
   Explanation: The router responds with information about its neighbors that have CDP enabled.

Cisco Labs–Semester 2–Router Configuration
LAB 4.3.5–CDP NEIGHBORS–WORKSHEET

4. Fill in the following table:

Device and Port ID	Local Interface	Hold Time	Capability	Platform

Step 5. Display details about CDP updates received on the local router.
   Task: Enter **show cdp neighbors detail** from the router prompt.
   Explanation: The router displays the entry address(es), the IOS version, and the same information as the **show cdp neighbors** command.

5. Fill in the following table:

Neighbor device name			
Neighbor device type			
IP address of interface attached to your router			
Port ID of your router that the neighbor is on			
Port ID of neighbor router that your router is on			
IOS version of neighbor router			

Step 6. Telnet to your neighbor router and issue show cdp neighbor.
   Task:
   a. Telnet to the neighboring router by entering **telnet** *hostname of router or IP address*.
   b. Enter the password **cisco**.
   c. Enter **show cdp neighbor** at the router prompt you have telneted to.
Explanation: The router responds with information about its neighbors that have CDP enabled.
Note: Perform this step at router lab-b, lab-c, or lab-d, and telnet to your two neighbors on either side.

Cisco Labs–Semester 2–Router Configuration
LAB 4.3.5–CDP NEIGHBORS–WORKSHEET

6. Fill in the following tables:

First Neighbor

Device and Port ID	Local Interface	Hold Time	Capability	Platform

Second Neighbor

Device and Port ID	Local Interface	Hold Time	Capability	Platform

Cisco Labs–Semester 2–Router Configuration
LAB 4.4.2–REMOTE TELNET ACCESS–OVERVIEW
(Estimated time: 45 minutes)

Router Name - LAB A
Router Type - 2514
E 0 = 192.5.5.1
E 1 = 205.7.5.1
S 0 = 201.100.11.1
SM = 255.255.255.0

Router Name - LAB C
Router Type - 2503
E 0 = 223.8.151.1
S 0 = 204.204.7.1
S 1 = 199.6.13.2
SM = 255.255.255.0

Router Name - LAB E
Router Type - 2501
E 0 = 210.93.105.2
SM = 255.255.255.0

Router Name - LAB B
Router Type - 2503
E 0 = 219.17.100.1
S 0 = 199.6.13.1
S 1 = 201.100.11.2
SM = 255.255.255.0

Router Name - LAB D
Router Type - 2501
E 0 = 210.93.105.1
S 1 = 204.204.7.2
SM = 255.255.255.0

LEGEND

= ROUTER — User Exec Password = cisco

= HUB — Enable Secret Exec Password = class

= LAN SWITCH — Terminal vty Password = cisco

= CONSOLE CABLE

Objectives:

- Use the **telnet** command to remotely access other routers
- Verify that the application layer between source and destination is working properly
- Retrieve information about remote routers using **router show** commands
- Retrieve CDP information from routers not directly connected to you

Background:

In this lab, you work with the **telnet** (remote terminal) utility to access routers remotely. You **telnet** from your local router into another remote router in order to simulate being at the console on the remote router. This procedure uses your router's telnet client software and the remote router's telnet server software. You can also **telnet** from your workstation as a client into any router connected to your network. In addition, you can telnet into Cisco Ethernet switches. You cannot, however, telnet from a router or a workstation into another Windows client or server since the Windows operating system does not support the telnet server daemon. A daemon (pronounced demon) is a UNIX term that refers to a program running on a server that accepts requests for services. You can decide whether to allow others to telnet into your router, or you may require a password for incoming telnet sessions. Telnet connections are referred to as **line VTY 0 4** in the router configuration file. The router can support up to five simultaneous incoming telnet sessions (0 through 4).

Cisco Labs–Semester 2–Router Configuration
LAB 4.4.2–REMOTE TELNET ACCESS–OVERVIEW

Telnet is a good troubleshooting tool because it can be used to access remote routers to gather information when problems occur or when configuration changes are necessary. It also tests from the OSI application layer of the source host down through its Physical layer and then across the network and back up the protocol stack of the destination router. This allows you to verify the application-layer software between source and destination hosts. You use **telnet** to access a remote router and use **show cdp neighbors** to gather information from routers that are not directly connected to you.

Tools/Preparation:

Prior to starting the lab, you need to connect a PC with HyperTerminal to a router using the router's console interface with a roll-over cable. Work individually or in teams. Before beginning this lab, you should refer to the *Cisco Networking Academy Program: First-Year Companion Guide*, Second Edition. You should also review online Chapter 4. Be familiar with the following commands:

- **telnet ?**
- **telnet** *router-name or IP*
- **show CDP neighbors**
- **show interface**

- **show protocols**
- **enable**
- **show running-config**
- **show startup-config**

Required Resources:

- PC with Windows operating system and HyperTerminal installed
- Router connected to the PC with a console roll-over cable
- At least three routers interconnected via Ethernet or WAN simulation cables

Web Site Resources:

- **Routing basics**—www.cisco.com/univercd/cc/td/doc/cisintwk/ito_doc/routing.htm
- **General information on routers**—www.cisco.com/univercd/cc/td/doc/pcat/#2
- **2500 series routers**—www.cisco.com/warp/public/cc/cisco/mkt/access/2500/index.shtml
- **1600 series routers**—www.cisco.com/warp/public/cc/cisco/mkt/access/1600/index.shtml
- **Terms and acronyms**—www.cisco.com/univercd/cc/td/doc/cisintwk/ita/index.htm
- **IP routing protocol IOS command summary**—www.cisco.com/univercd/cc/td/doc/product/software/ios120/12cgcr/rbkixol.htm

Notes:

_____

_____

_____

_____

_____

Cisco Labs–Semester 2–Router Configuration
LAB 4.4.2–REMOTE TELNET ACCESS–WORKSHEET

Step 1. Log on to the router.
    Task: Connect to the router and log on. If prompted, enter the password **cisco**.

    1. What prompt did the router display? _____

Step 2. Enter the help facility.
    Task: Enter **telnet ?** at the router prompt.
    Explanation: The router responds with help with the **telnet** command.

    2. With what did the router reply? _____

    _____

Step 3. Telnet from router to router.
    Task: Enter **telnet *router-name or IP address*** at the router prompt to connect to a remote router.
    Explanation: The router prompts you for user access verification of the router you remotely access. Enter the password **cisco**.

    3. What prompt did the router display? _____

Step 4. Show interfaces.
    Task: Enter **show interface** at the router prompt.
    Explanation: The router responds with information about its interfaces.

    4. List the interfaces, the IP address, and subnet mask.

Interface	IP Address	Subnet Mask

Step 5. Show protocols.
    Task: Enter **show protocols** at the router prompt.
    Explanation: This command shows the global and interface-specific status of any configured Layer 3 protocols.

    5. Fill in the following table with the information generated by the router you remotely access.

Interface	Is there a carrier detect signal?	Are the keepalive messages being received?

Cisco Labs–Semester 2–Router Configuration
LAB 4.4.2–REMOTE TELNET ACCESS–WORKSHEET

Step 6. Enter privileged mode while connected to the remote router with telnet.
   Task:
   a.   Enter **enable** at the command prompt.
   b.   Enter the password **class**.
   Explanation: You use the **enable** command to enter privileged EXEC mode.

   6.   What prompt did the router display? _____ What mode are you in?
        _____

Step 7. Show information about the active configuration file of the remote router.
   Task: Enter **show running-config** at the remote router prompt.
   Explanation: The remote router displays information on how it is currently configured.

   7.   What file are you viewing on the remote router? _____
        Where is this file stored? _____

Step 8. Show information about the backup configuration file of the remote router.
   Task: Enter **show startup-config** at the router prompt.
   Explanation: The remote router displays information on the backup configuration file stored in NVRAM.

   8.   What file are you viewing on the remote router? _____
        Where is this file stored? _____

   9.   What information do you see concerning the **line VTY** connections?
        _____

Step 9. Display the CDP updates received on the local router.
   Task: Enter the **show cdp neighbors** command at the router prompt.
   Explanation: The router responds with information about its neighbors that have CDP enabled.

   10. List all device IDs that are connected to the remote router you have a telnet session with.
        _____
        _____

Cisco Labs–Semester 2–Router Configuration
LAB 4.4.3–ICMP PING–OVERVIEW
(Estimated time: 30 minutes)

Router Name - LAB A
Router Type - 2514
E 0 = 192.5.5.1
E 1 = 205.7.5.1
S 0 = 201.100.11.1
SM = 255.255.255.0

Router Name - LAB C
Router Type - 2503
E 0 = 223.8.151.1
S 0 = 204.204.7.1
S 1 = 199.6.13.2
SM = 255.255.255.0

Router Name - LAB E
Router Type - 2501
E 0 = 210.93.105.2
SM = 255.255.255.0

Router Name - LAB B
Router Type - 2503
E 0 = 219.17.100.1
S 0 = 199.6.13.1
S 1 = 201.100.11.2
SM = 255.255.255.0

Router Name - LAB D
Router Type - 2501
E 0 = 210.93.105.1
S 1 = 204.204.7.2
SM = 255.255.255.0

LEGEND
= ROUTER   User Exec Password = cisco
= HUB   Enable Secret Exec Password = class
= LAN SWITCH   Terminal vty Password = cisco
= CONSOLE CABLE

Objectives:

- Use the **ping** command to send ICMP datagrams to the target host
- Verify that the network layer between source and destination is working properly
- Retrieve information to evaluate the path-to-host reliability
- Determine delays over the path and whether the host can be reached or is functioning

Background:

In this lab, you use ICMP (Internet Control Message Protocol). ICMP gives you the ability to diagnose basic network connectivity. Using **ping** *xxx.xxx.xxx.xxx* sends an ICMP packet to the specified host and then wait for a reply packet from that host. You can ping the host name of a router, but you must have a static host lookup table in the router or DNS server for name resolution to IP addresses.

Ping is an excellent tool for troubleshooting Layers 1 though 3 of the OSI model. If you cannot connect to a host computer (such as a server) but you can ping the server's IP address, your problem is probably not with the physical cabling connections, the NICs, or the routers between you and the server. With this lab, you also have a chance to see the differences between using the **ping** command from a router and from a workstation.

Cisco Labs–Semester 2–Router Configuration
LAB 4.4.3–ICMP PING–OVERVIEW

Tools/Preparation:

Prior to starting the lab, you need to connect a PC with HyperTerminal to a router using the router's console interface with a roll-over cable. You should have access to the standard five-router lab if possible. Work individually or in teams. Before beginning this lab, you should refer to the *Cisco Networking Academy Program: First-Year Companion Guide*, Second Edition, and you should also review online Chapter 4.

Required Resources:

- PC with Windows operating system and HyperTerminal installed
- Router connected to the PC with a console roll-over cable
- At least three routers interconnected via Ethernet or WAN simulation cables

Web Site Resources:

- **Routing basics**—www.cisco.com/univercd/cc/td/doc/cisintwk/ito_doc/routing.htm
- **General information on routers**—www.cisco.com/univercd/cc/td/doc/pcat/#2
- **2500 series routers**—www.cisco.com/warp/public/cc/cisco/mkt/access/2500/index.shtml
- **1600 series routers**—www.cisco.com/warp/public/cc/cisco/mkt/access/1600/index.shtml
- **Terms and acronyms**—www.cisco.com/univercd/cc/td/doc/cisintwk/ita/index.htm
- **IP routing protocol IOS command summary**—www.cisco.com/univercd/cc/td/doc/product/software/ios120/12cgcr/rbkixol.htm

Notes:

_____

_____

_____

_____

_____

_____

_____

_____

_____

_____

Cisco Labs–Semester 2–Router Configuration
LAB 4.4.3–ICMP PING–WORKSHEET

Step 1. Log on to the router.

 Explanation: Connect to the router and log in. Enter the password **cisco** if prompted.

 1.
  a. What prompt did the router display? _____
  b. What does it mean? _____

Step 2. Display a cached list of host names and addresses.

 Task: Enter **show host** at the router prompt.

 Explanation: The router displays information about host to Layer 3 (IP) address mappings, how this information was acquired, and the age of the entry.

 2. List four host names and the first IP address listed for each one.

Host Name	IP Address

Step 3. Test layer 3 addressing ping from router to router.

 Task: Enter **ping** *xxx.xxx.xxx.xxx* where *xxx.xxx.xxx.xxx* is an IP address from one of the other hosts listed above. Repeat with all IP addresses you listed.

 Explanation: The router sends an Internet Control Message Protocol (ICMP) packet to verify the hardware connection and network layer address. Because your PC is acting as the console to the router, you are pinging from your router to another router.

 3. Were you able to ping all the IP addresses? _____

 4. List four important pieces of information that you receive after issuing the **ping** command.

  _____
  _____
  _____
  _____

Cisco Labs–Semester 2–Router Configuration
LAB 4.4.3–ICMP PING–WORKSHEET

Step 4. Examine the output generated by the ping command.

5. Look at the example of the **ping** command generated by a router.

> lab-b#ping 210.93.105.1
>
> Type escape sequence to abort.
> Sending 5, 100-byte ICMP Echoes to 210.93.105.1, timeout is 2 seconds:
> !!!.!
> Success rate is 80 percent (4/5), round-trip min/avg/max = 68/68/168 ms

    a. What does the exclamation point (!) indicate? _____

    b. What does the period (.) indicate? _____

    c. What does the **ping** command test for? _____

Step 5. Access the workstation command prompt.
Task: From a Windows 95/98 or NT workstation, click Start/Programs/MS-DOS Command Prompt. This action opens a command prompt window.
Explanation: Using the command prompt to ping the routers allows you to test that the TCP/IP stack and default gateway on the workstation are configured and working properly.

Step 6. Test the workstation default gateway.
Task: Using the command prompt, enter **ping** and the IP address of the workstation's default gateway. The default gateway is the nearside router interface IP address.
Explanation: By pinging your default gateway, you can test whether you can successfully send packets to and from the router that is directly connected to your LAN.

6. Can you ping your default gateway? _____ (*Hint:* You might need to check the TCP/IP settings using the Windows Control Panel, Network icon.)

Step 7. Test layer 3 addressing from a workstation to a remote router.
Task: At the command prompt, enter **ping** and the IP address of a remote router.
Explanation: This tests Layer 3 connectivity between your workstation and the remote router.

7. Is the output from the workstation's **ping** command the same as the output from the **ping** command from a router? _____

Step 8. Test the connections to other remote routers
Task: At the command prompt, enter **ping** and the IP address of another remote router.
Explanation: This tests Layer 3 connectivity between your workstation and the other remote routers.

8. List the differences between the router's **ping** command and the workstation's **ping** command.

_____

_____

_____

Cisco Labs–Semester 2–Router Configuration
LAB 4.4.4–TRACEROUTE COMMAND–OVERVIEW
(Estimated time: 30 minutes)

Router Name - LAB A
Router Type - 2514
E 0 = 192.5.5.1
E 1 = 205.7.5.1
S 0 = 201.100.11.1
SM = 255.255.255.0

Router Name - LAB C
Router Type - 2503
E 0 = 223.8.151.1
S 0 = 204.204.7.1
S 1 = 199.6.13.2
SM = 255.255.255.0

Router Name - LAB E
Router Type - 2501
E 0 = 210.93.105.2
SM = 255.255.255.0

Router Name - LAB B
Router Type - 2503
E 0 = 219.17.100.1
S 0 = 199.6.13.1
S 1 = 201.100.11.2
SM = 255.255.255.0

Router Name - LAB D
Router Type - 2501
E 0 = 210.93.105.1
S 1 = 204.204.7.2
SM = 255.255.255.0

LEGEND

= ROUTER	User Exec Password = cisco
= HUB	Enable Secret Exec Password = class
= LAN SWITCH	Terminal vty Password = cisco
= CONSOLE CABLE	

Objectives:

- Use the **traceroute** Cisco IOS command from source router to destination router
- Use the **tracert** Windows OS command from source workstation to destination router
- Use the **show ip route** command to display the router's routing table
- Verify that the network layer between source, destination, and each router along the way is working properly. Retrieve information to evaluate the end-to-end path reliability.
- Determine delays at each point over the path and whether the host can be reached

Background:

In this lab, you use the IOS **traceroute** command. The **traceroute** command uses ICMP packets and the error message generated by routers when the packet exceeds its Time-To-Live (TTL). When you initiate the **traceroute** command to a target host, the router sends an ICMP echo-request packet with the TTL set to 1. The first router in the path to the target host receives the ICMP echo-request packet and sets the TTL to 0. The first router then sends an ICMP time-exceeded message back to the source. The source router then sends an ICMP echo-request packet with the TTL set to 2. The first router receives the ICMP echo request and sets the TTL to 1 and sends it to the next router in the path to the target host. The second router receives the ICMP echo request and sets the TTL to 0 and then sends an ICMP time-exceeded message back to the source. The source then sends an ICMP echo request with a TTL set to 3. This cycle continues until an ICMP echo reply is received from the target host or until an ICMP destination-unreachable message is received. This allows you to determine the last router to be reached in the path to the target host. This is a troubleshooting technique called fault isolation.

Cisco Labs–Semester 2–Router Configuration
LAB 4.4.4–TRACEROUTE COMMAND–OVERVIEW

Tools/Preparation:

Prior to starting the lab, you need to connect a PC workstation with HyperTerminal to a router by using the router's console interface with a roll-over cable. This lab should be done at the router console station. You should refer to the *Cisco Networking Academy Program: First-Year Companion Guide*, Second Edition, and review Semester 2 online Chapter 4 prior to starting this lab. Work individually or in teams. Be familiar with the following commands:

- **traceroute ip** *xxx.xxx.xxx.xxx* (where *xxx.xxx.xxx.xxx* is the IP address of the host you want to trace). The **ip** after the command is the default and may be omitted.
- **traceroute** *hostname* (where *hostname* is a name that can be resolved to an IP address). **traceroute** is a Cisco IOS command.
- **tracert** *xxx.xxx.xxx.xxx* (where *xxx.xxx.xxx.xxx* is the IP address of the host you want to trace).
- **tracert** *hostname* (where *hostname* is a name that can be resolved to an IP address). **tracert** is a Windows 95/98 or NT command.
- **show ip route** This shows you the IP routing table. The directions that the router uses determines how it will direct traffic across the network.

Required Resources:

- PC with monitor, keyboard, mouse, and power cords
- Windows operating system (Windows 95, 98, NT, or 2000) installed on PC
- HyperTerminal program
- Access to multiple routers

Web Site Resources:

- **Routing basics**—www.cisco.com/univercd/cc/td/doc/cisintwk/ito_doc/routing.htm
- **General information on routers**—www.cisco.com/univercd/cc/td/doc/pcat/#2
- **2500 series routers**—www.cisco.com/warp/public/cc/cisco/mkt/access/2500/index.shtml
- **1600 series routers**—www.cisco.com/warp/public/cc/cisco/mkt/access/1600/index.shtml
- **Terms and acronyms**—www.cisco.com/univercd/cc/td/doc/cisintwk/ita/index.htm
- **IP routing protocol IOS command summary**—www.cisco.com/univercd/cc/td/doc/product/software/ios120/12cgcr/rbkixol.htm

Notes:

_____

_____

_____

_____

_____

_____

_____

Cisco Labs–Semester 2–Router Configuration
LAB 4.4.4–TRACEROUTE COMMAND–WORKSHEET

Step 1. Log on to the router.
   Explanation: Connect to the router and log on. If prompted, enter the password **cisco**.

1.
   a. What prompt did the router display? _____
   b. What does it mean? _____

Step 2. Enter trace (the abbreviated form of traceroute).
   Task: Enter **trace** at the router prompt.

2. What did the router respond with? _____

Step 3. Enter trace ?.
   Task: Enter **trace ?** at the router prompt.

3. With what did the router respond? _____

Step 4. Get help with the trace ip command.
   Task: Enter **trace ip ?** at the router prompt.

4. With what did the router respond? _____

Step 5. Trace the route from end router to end router.
   Task: Enter **trace ip** *xxx.xxx.xxx.xxx* where *xxx.xxx.xxx.xxx* is the IP address of the target destination. *Note:* You want to do this lab using one of the end routers and **trace ip** to the other end router (ip is the default).
   Explanation: The **trace** command is the ideal tool for finding where data is being sent in your network.

5.
   a. List the hostname and IP address of the routers that the ICMP packet was routed through.

Hostname	IP Address

Step 6. Trace the route to all other routers on your network.
   Task: Repeat Step 5 with all other routers on your network.

Cisco Labs–Semester 2–Router Configuration
LAB 4.4.4–TRACEROUTE COMMAND–WORKSHEET

Step 7. Use tracert from an MS-DOS command prompt.
Task: From the console workstation, click Start/Programs/MS-DOS Command Prompt. An MS-DOS command prompt window opens. Enter **tracert** and the same IP address that you used in Step 5.

Explanation: By using the MS-DOS window, you are using the TCP/IP stack of the workstation to begin the trace to the destination. The first hop will be your default gateway or the near side router interface on the LAN that the workstation is connected to.

6.
   a. List the hostname and IP address of the router that the ICMP packet was routed through.

Hostname	IP Address

   b. Why is there one more entry in the output of the **tracert** command when you trace from the computer command prompt to the target host? _____
   _____

Step 8. Trace a route over the Internet.
Task: From a Windows 95/98 or NT workstation that has Internet access, click Start/Programs/MS-DOS Command Prompt. An MS-DOS command prompt window will open up. Enter **tracert www.cisco.com**.

7.
   a. What is the IP address of **www.cisco.com**? _____

   b. How many hops did it take to get to **www.cisco.com**? If a packet passes through a router, it is considered one hop, and the TTL of the packet is decremented by 1.
   _____

Step 9. View the routing table of the router.
Task: From the router prompt, enter **show ip route**.
Explanation: This shows you the router's routing table.

8. List the IP network number addresses that are directly connected to you.
_____
_____

Cisco Labs–Semester 2–Router Configuration
LAB 4.4.7–SHOW INTERFACE and CLEAR COUNTERS–OVERVIEW
(Estimated time: 30 minutes)

Objectives:

- Use the **show interface** command to display statistics for the router's interfaces
- Use the **clear counters** command to clear statistics for the router's interfaces

Background:

In this lab, you use **show interface** and **clear counters**. The router keeps detailed statistics about data traffic it has sent and received on its interfaces. This is important in troubleshooting a network problem. The **clear counters** command resets the counters that are displayed when you issue the **show interface** command. By clearing the counters, you get a clearer picture of the current status of the network.

Cisco Labs–Semester 2–Router Configuration
LAB 4.4.7–SHOW INTERFACE and CLEAR COUNTERS–OVERVIEW

Tools/Preparation:

Prior to starting the lab, you need to connect a PC workstation with HyperTerminal to a router using the router's console interface with a roll-over cable. This lab should be done at the router console station. You should refer to the *Cisco Networking Academy Program: First-Year Companion Guide*, Second Edition, and Semester 2 online Chapter 4 prior to starting this lab. Work individually or in teams. Be familiar with the following commands:

- **show interface**
- **clear counters**

Required Resources:

- PC with monitor, keyboard, mouse, and power cords
- Windows operating system (Windows 95, 98, NT, or 2000) installed on PC
- HyperTerminal program configured to access the router console port
- PC connected to the router console port with a roll-over cable

Web Site Resources:

- **Routing basics**—www.cisco.com/univercd/cc/td/doc/cisintwk/ito_doc/routing.htm
- **General information on routers**—www.cisco.com/univercd/cc/td/doc/pcat/#2
- **2500 series routers**—www.cisco.com/warp/public/cc/cisco/mkt/access/2500/index.shtml
- **1600 series routers**—www.cisco.com/warp/public/cc/cisco/mkt/access/1600/index.shtml
- **Terms and acronyms**—www.cisco.com/univercd/cc/td/doc/cisintwk/ita/index.htm
- **IP routing protocol IOS command summary**—www.cisco.com/univercd/cc/td/doc/product/software/ios120/12cgcr/rbkixol.htm

Notes:

_____

_____

_____

_____

_____

_____

_____

_____

_____

_____

_____

Cisco Labs–Semester 2–Router Configuration
LAB 4.4.7–SHOW INTERFACE and CLEAR COUNTERS– WORKSHEET

Step 1. Log on to the router.
   Explanation: Connect to the router and log on. If prompted, enter the password **cisco**.

Step 2. Enter the show interface command (abbreviated sh int).
   Task: Enter **show interface** at the command prompt.
   Explanation: The **show interface** command displays packet statistics that reflect router operation since the last time the counters were cleared.

   1. Fill in the following information for all interfaces in use:

Interface	Ethernet 0	Ethernet 1	Serial 0	Serial 1
Hardware address				
Packet input				
Packet output				
Last clearing of counters				

Step 3. Enter the help command.
   Task: Enter the help command by typing **?** at the router prompt.
   Explanation: The router responds with all available commands for user mode.

   2. What is the significance of entering **?** at the command prompt? _____
   _____

Step 4. Enter privileged EXEC mode.
   Task: Enter **enable** at the router prompt. The router asks you for the enable password.
   Enter **class.**
   Explanation: Entering the **enable** command and entering the password **class** allows you privileged mode access to the router.

   3. What prompt is the router showing? _____

Step 5. Get help with the clear command.
   Task: Enter **clear ?** at the router prompt.
   Explanation: The **clear ?** command displays subcommands for **clear**.

   4. Is **counters** one of the subcommands that is listed? _____

   5. What is the description of **counters**? _____

Step 6. Clear all interface counters.
   Task: Enter **clear counters** at the router prompt. The router asks you to confirm with **Y**.
   Explanation: The **clear** command clears all interface statistics on the router.

LAB 4.4.7–SHOW INTERFACE and CLEAR COUNTERS–WORKSHEET

Step 7. Confirm that the counters have been cleared.

Task: Enter **show interfaces** at the router's command prompt.

Explanation: The **show interface** command displays the statistics, which reflect router operation since the last time the counters were cleared.

6.   Have the counters been set to 0? _____

Step 8. Generate network traffic.

Task: Ping all router interfaces in the lab network. Do this several times.

Explanation: By pinging the interfaces of all routers on the labs network, you generate network traffic. You can use the up arrow or Ctrl-P to retrieve previous commands and change the IP address to the next destination.

Step 9. Show interface statistics on the router.

Task: Enter **show interface** at the router prompt.

Explanation: The **show interface** command displays the statistics, which reflect router operation since the last time the counters were cleared.

7.   Fill in the following information in the table for all interfaces:

Interface	Ethernet 0	Ethernet 1	Serial 0	Serial 1
Hardware address				
Packet input				
Packet output				
Last clearing of counters				

Step 10. Show interface statistics terminology.

Task: Enter **show interface** at the router prompt.

Explanation: The router shows information about the configured interfaces. Review the terms used for various interfaces and statistics. These can be helpful in troubleshooting.

8.   Find the following information for interface Ethernet 0 with **show interface**:
   a.   What is MTU? _____
   b.   What is rely? _____
   c.   What is load? _____
   d.   What is a runt? _____
   e.   What is a giant? _____

9.   Find the following information for interface serial 0 with **show interface**:
   a.   What is the IP address and subnet mask? _____
   b.   What data link layer encapsulation is being used? _____
   c.   What does "Serial0 is up, line protocol is up" mean? _____

Cisco Labs–Semester 2–Router Configuration
LAB 4.5.1–TROUBLESHOOTING TOOLS CHALLENGE–OVERVIEW
(Estimated time: 45 minutes)

Objectives:
- Identify what troubleshooting tools (IOS commands) are needed to gather basic information about your network
- Apply what you have learned in past labs to draw a logical diagram of the network

Background:
As you know, having the topology of a network is extremely useful. It allows a network administrator to know exactly what equipment he or she has in what area (for bandwidth needs), how many devices are on the network, and the physical layout of the network. In this lab, you figure out what a topology looks like based on the information you can gather while navigating through the network using IOS commands.

Through the use of **show** commands, you should be able to see which interfaces are up (using **show interface**), what devices the router is connected to (using **show CDP neighbors**), and how the user can get there (using **show protocols**). With the information received from the **show** commands, you should be able to remotely access the neighboring routers (using **telnet**). Through the use of troubleshooting commands (such as **ping** and **trace**), you should be able to see which devices are connected. Your final goal is to construct a logical topology drawing of the network by making use of all of these commands without referring to any diagrams ahead of time.

Cisco Labs–Semester 2–Router Configuration
LAB 4.5.1–TROUBLESHOOTING TOOLS CHALLENGE–OVERVIEW

Tools/Preparation:

Prior to starting this lab, you need to have the equipment for the standard five-router lab available (routers, hubs, switch, cables. etc.). The routers should be preconfigured by the instructor or lab assistant with the correct IP interface settings, etc. The workstations should also be preconfigured to have the correct IP address settings prior to starting the lab. The routers, hubs, and workstations should be labeled. You might also work with a portion of the standard lab setup (three or more of the routers) connected differently than the standard topology if time permits and try to determine the topology.

This lab assumes that you have completed the prior labs 2.2.10.1 and 2.2.10.2 and that the lab equipment (routers, hub, workstations, etc.) is assembled and connected in the standard lab topology. Work in teams of three or more. Before beginning this lab, you should refer to the *Cisco Networking Academy Program: First-Year Companion Guide*, Second Edition, and Semester 2 online Chapters 3 and 4.

Required Resources:

- 5 PC workstations (minimum) with Windows operating system and HyperTerminal installed
- 5 Cisco routers (model 1600 series or 2500 series with IOS 11.2 or later)
- 4 Ethernet hubs (10Base-T with 4 to 8 ports)
- One Ethernet switch (Cisco Catalyst 1900 or comparable)
- 5 serial console cables to connect the workstation to the router console port (with RJ-45 to DB9 converters)
- 3 sets of V.35 WAN serial cables (DTE male/DCE female) to connect from router to router
- CAT5 Ethernet cables wired straight through to connect routers and workstations to hubs and switches
- AUI (DB15) to RJ45 Ethernet transceivers (the quantity depends on the number of routers with AUI ports) to convert router AUI interfaces to 10Base-T RJ-45

Web Site Resources:

- **Routing basics**—www.cisco.com/univercd/cc/td/doc/cisintwk/ito_doc/routing.htm
- **General information on routers**—www.cisco.com/univercd/cc/td/doc/pcat/#2
- **2500 series routers**—www.cisco.com/warp/public/cc/cisco/mkt/access/2500/index.shtml
- **1600 series routers**—www.cisco.com/warp/public/cc/cisco/mkt/access/1600/index.shtml
- **Terms and acronyms**—www.cisco.com/univercd/cc/td/doc/cisintwk/ita/index.htm
- **IP routing protocol IOS command summary**—www.cisco.com/univercd/cc/td/doc/product/software/ios120/12cgcr/rbkixol.htm
- **Beginning IP for new users**—www.cisco.com/warp/public/701/3.html
- **Internetworking design basics**—www.cisco/univercd/cc/td/doc/cisintwk/idg4/nd2002.htm

Cisco Labs–Semester 2–Router Configuration
LAB 4.5.1–TROUBLESHOOTING TOOLS CHALLENGE–
WORKSHEET

Step 1. Gather information about the network.
Use the standard five-router lab setup or a subset of three or more routers. Verify and document the topology of the network that you are working with or have constructed. You will be able to connect to the console of only one of the routers to find out all information about the other routers and other devices connected to you.

    A. Connect as the console to one of the routers in your network. (All information about the physical structure of the network must be obtained from only one console connection.)

        1. What command do you use to enter privileged EXEC mode?

        _____

    B. Gather information about the router you are connected to.

        2. What command do you use to gather information about the router you are on?

        _____

    C. Gather information about the devices that are connected to your router.

        3. What command do you use to gather information about neighboring devices?

        _____

    D. Gather information about devices on your network, but not directly connected to you.

        4. You have gathered information about all interfaces on the router you are working with. You also have the IP address of the devices that are directly connected to the router you are working with. With the information obtained, describe how and what commands you will need to use to gather more detailed information about devices not directly connected to your router.

        _____
        _____
        _____
        _____
        _____
        _____

Step 2. Draw a logical topology of the network.
Using the troubleshooting tools that you have learned from the prior labs in this module, construct a network diagram based on a given topology. In your journal, draw the logical topology of this network. Include all routers, hubs, and switches. Be sure to indicate exactly where there are interfaces. For example, if there is a serial connection from router 1 to router 2, indicate that on the routers. If there is an Ethernet connection to a hub, indicate that. Label the diagram with the proper IP addresses and subnet masks and indicate which end is DCE and which is DTE for each WAN link.

    5. Draw the network diagram with the information you obtained in Step 1.

Cisco Labs–Semester 2–Router Configuration
LAB 5.2.3–ROUTER SETUP COMMAND–OVERVIEW
(Estimated time: 30 minutes)

Router Name - LAB A
Router Type - 2514
E 0 = 192.5.5.1
E 1 = 205.7.5.1
S 0 = 201.100.11.1
SM = 255.255.255.0

Router Name - LAB C
Router Type - 2503
E 0 = 223.8.151.1
S 0 = 204.204.7.1
S 1 = 199.6.13.2
SM = 255.255.255.0

Router Name - LAB E
Router Type - 2501
E 0 = 210.93.105.2
SM = 255.255.255.0

Router Name - LAB B
Router Type - 2503
E 0 = 219.17.100.1
S 0 = 199.6.13.1
S 1 = 201.100.11.2
SM = 255.255.255.0

Router Name - LAB D
Router Type - 2501
E 0 = 210.93.105.1
S 1 = 204.204.7.2
SM = 255.255.255.0

LEGEND

= ROUTER   User Exec Password = cisco

= HUB   Enable Secret Exec Password = class

= LAN SWITCH   Terminal vty Password = cisco

= CONSOLE CABLE

Objectives:

- Become familiar with the router setup mode
- Understand what global parameters can be configured in setup mode
- Understand what interface parameters can be configured in setup mode

Background:

In this lab, you use the command **setup** to enter setup mode. Setup is a Cisco IOS utility (or program) that can help get some of the basic router configuration parameters established. Setup is not intended as the mode for entering complex protocol features in the router. Rather, the purpose of setup mode is to bring up a minimal configuration for any router that cannot find its configuration from some other source.

There are two ways to enter setup mode. If the router cannot find its configuration file, it automatically enters setup mode or the setup dialog. The other way to enter setup mode is to enter the **setup** command at the command line while in privileged mode. The setup dialog prompts you for basic setup options, such as which protocols you will be using and the IP address and subnet mask for each interface the router has. The setup dialog provides default values for most of the configurable options. You can either accept these or enter your own. If setup does not provide a prompted entry for specific interface information, you will have to manually enter those commands at a later time. With this lab, you run the setup utility but will not save the configuration.

Cisco Labs–Semester 2–Router Configuration
LAB 5.2.3–ROUTER SETUP COMMAND–OVERVIEW

Tools/Preparation:

Prior to starting the lab, you need to connect a PC workstation with HyperTerminal to a router using the router's console interface with a roll-over cable. This lab should be done at the router console station. You should refer to the *Cisco Networking Academy Program: First-Year Companion Guide*, Second Edition, and review Semester 2 online curriculum Chapter 5 prior to starting this lab. Work individually or in teams. Be familiar with the following command:

- **setup**

Required Resources:

- PC with monitor, keyboard, mouse, and power cords
- Windows operating system (Windows 95, 98, NT, or 2000) installed on PC
- HyperTerminal program configured for router console access
- PC connected to the router console port with a roll-over cable

Web Site Resources:

- **Routing basics**—www.cisco.com/univercd/cc/td/doc/cisintwk/ito_doc/routing.htm
- **General information on routers**—www.cisco.com/univercd/cc/td/doc/pcat/#2
- **2500 series routers**—www.cisco.com/warp/public/cc/cisco/mkt/access/2500/index.shtml
- **1600 series routers**—www.cisco.com/warp/public/cc/cisco/mkt/access/1600/index.shtml
- **Terms and acronyms**—www.cisco.com/univercd/cc/td/doc/cisintwk/ita/index.htm
- **IP routing protocol IOS command summary**—www.cisco.com/univercd/cc/td/doc/product/software/ios120/12cgcr/rbkixol.htm
- **Beginning IP for new users**—www.cisco.com/warp/public/701/3.html

Notes:

_____

_____

_____

_____

_____

_____

_____

_____

_____

_____

_____

Cisco Labs–Semester 2–Router Configuration
LAB 5.2.3–ROUTER SETUP COMMAND–WORKSHEET

Step 1. Log on to the router.
 Explanation: Connect to the router and log in. If prompted, enter the password **cisco**.

Step 2. Enter privileged mode.
 Task:
   a. Enter **enable** at the command prompt.
   b. Enter the password **class**.
 Explanation: You use the **enable** command to enter privileged EXEC mode

Step 3. Enter the help command.
 Task: Enter the help command by typing **?** at the router prompt.
 Explanation: The router responds with all available commands for privileged mode.

   1. Was **setup** one of the commands available? _____

Step 4. Enter setup mode.
 Task: Enter **setup** at the router prompt.
 Explanation: Entering the **setup** command starts setup mode and executes a question-driven initial configuration routine referred to as the system configuration dialog.

Step 5. Continue with the setup dialog.
 Task: Enter **yes** or press the Enter key to continue with the setup dialog.
 Explanation: The router asks you if you want to continue with the configuration dialog.

   2. What is the importance of the word in the square brackets? _____

Step 6. Show the current interface summary.
 Task: Press the Enter key or type **yes**.
 Explanation: The router asks, "First, would you like to see the current interface summary?" You can press the Enter key to accept the default answers.

   3. Fill in the following table with the information provided.

Interface	IP-Address	OK	Method	Status	Protocol

Cisco Labs–Semester 2–Router Configuration
LAB 5.2.3–ROUTER SETUP COMMAND–WORKSHEET

Step 7. Configure global parameters.
   Task: Configure the router using the default settings for any questions the router asks.
   Explanation: Make sure that you enter **class** as the enable secret password. Make sure you use something different (such as **cisco**) for the enable password.

Step 8. Configure interface parameters.
   Task: Configure the router using the default settings for any questions the router asks.
   Explanation: Setup mode now configures any interfaces present on the router.

Step 9. Configuration command script.
   Task: Answer **no** to the question "Use this configuration?"
   Explanation: The router displays the configuration command script. Then it asks you if you want to save this configuration.

   4.   If you were to answer yes to the question "Use this configuration?", where would this information be saved? _____

Step 10. Enter setup mode.
   Task: Enter setup mode
   Explanation: Repeat this lab, but this time, as you enter setup mode, change the default answers. For the enable secret password, use **class**. Remember to say **no** to the question "Use this configuration?"

Cisco Labs–Semester 2–Router Configuration
LAB 5.3.1–ROUTER SETUP CHALLENGE–OVERVIEW
(Estimated time: 60 minutes)

Router Name - LAB A
Router Type - 2514
E 0 = 192.5.5.1
E 1 = 205.7.5.1
S 0 = 201.100.11.1
SM = 255.255.255.0

Router Name - LAB B
Router Type - 2503
E 0 = 219.17.100.1
S 0 = 199.6.13.1
S 1 = 201.100.11.2
SM = 255.255.255.0

Router Name - LAB C
Router Type - 2503
E 0 = 223.8.151.1
S 0 = 204.204.7.1
S 1 = 199.6.13.2
SM = 255.255.255.0

Router Name - LAB D
Router Type - 2501
E 0 = 210.93.105.1
S 1 = 204.204.7.2
SM = 255.255.255.0

Router Name - LAB E
Router Type - 2501
E 0 = 210.93.105.2
SM = 255.255.255.0

LEGEND

= ROUTER — User Exec Password = cisco

= HUB — Enable Secret Exec Password = class

= LAN SWITCH — Terminal vty Password = cisco

= CONSOLE CABLE

Objectives:

- Apply what you have learned in the *Cisco Networking Academy Program: First-Year Companion Guide*, Second Edition, online Chapter 5, and Lab 5.2.2.1 on the **setup** utility
- Demonstrate your ability to subnet a class B IP address
- Learn to use setup mode to set basic configuration parameters for the router
- Use HyperTerminal to capture the running configuration for the routers

Background:

When you first open a router and the operating system is loaded, you must go through the process of initial setup. In this scenario, you have just received a shipment of new routers, and you need to set up a basic configuration. You have received a class B IP network address of 156.1.0.0, and you need to subnet your Class B address using 5 bits for your subnets. Use the standard five-router diagram above to determine which subnetwork numbers and which IP addresses you will use for the eight networks you need to define. For this lab, set up all five routers. Be sure to configure the router you are using with a console port.

Cisco Labs–Semester 2–Router Configuration
LAB 5.3.1–ROUTER SETUP CHALLENGE–OVERVIEW

Tools/Preparation:

Prior to starting this lab, you need to have the equipment for the standard five-router lab available (routers, hubs, switch, cables, and so on). If the routers are configured, the lab assistant or instructor will have to erase the configuration before you begin. The routers, hubs, and workstations should be labeled.

This lab assumes that you have completed the lab 2.2.10.1 and that the lab equipment (routers, hub, workstations, and so on) is assembled and connected in the standard lab topology. Work in teams of three to five. Before beginning this lab, you should refer to the *Cisco Networking Academy Program: First-Year Companion Guide*, Second Edition, and Semester 2 online Chapter 5.

Required Resources:

- 1 floppy disk
- 5 PC workstations (minimum) with Windows operating system and HyperTerminal installed
- 5 Cisco routers (model 1600 series or 2500 series with IOS 11.2 or later)
- 4 Ethernet hubs (10Base-T with four to eight ports)
- One Ethernet switch (Cisco Catalyst 1900 or comparable)
- 5 serial console cables to connect the workstation to the router console port (with RJ-45 to DB9 converters)
- 3 sets of V.35 WAN serial cables (DTE male/ DCE female) to connect from router to router
- CAT5 Ethernet cables wired straight through to connect routers and workstations to hubs and switches
- AUI (DB15) to RJ45 Ethernet transceivers (the quantity depends on the number of routers with AUI ports) to convert router AUI interfaces to 10Base-T RJ-45

Web Site Resources:

- **Routing basics**—www.cisco.com/univercd/cc/td/doc/cisintwk/ito_doc/routing.htm
- **General information on routers**—www.cisco.com/univercd/cc/td/doc/pcat/#2
- **2500 series routers**—www.cisco.com/warp/public/cc/cisco/mkt/access/2500/index.shtml
- **1600 series routers**—www.cisco.com/warp/public/cc/cisco/mkt/access/1600/index.shtml
- **Terms and acronyms**—www.cisco.com/univercd/cc/td/doc/cisintwk/ita/index.htm
- **IP routing protocol IOS command summary**—www.cisco.com/univercd/cc/td/doc/product/software/ios120/12cgcr/rbkixol.htm

Notes: _____

_____

_____

_____

_____

Cisco Labs–Semester 2–Router Configuration
LAB 5.3.1–ROUTER SETUP CHALLENGE–WORKSHEET

Step 1. Log on to the router in enable mode, and issue the setup command.
If the router has not been configured, it might enter setup automatically. If the router is configured, you need to log on to the router, enter enable mode, and issue the **setup** command.

Step 2. Follow the onscreen prompts, and use the following information.
Use Lab-A to Lab-E as the host names for the routers. The enable secret password should be **class**. Use **IGRP** for your routing protocol with autonomous system number **1**. Be sure to specify the correct IP addresses and number of subnet bits for each interface. When you are asked to "Use this configuration?" answer **yes**.

1. How many subnets can you create with a 5-bit mask and a Class B network address?

    _____

2. How many hosts per subnet ? _____

3. What will the subnet mask be in decimal? _____

Step 3. Document your configuration.
After answering **yes** to "Use this configuration?" you want to capture the output from the **show running-config** command of all five routers to hand in to your instructor. You do this in HyperTerminal by clicking Transfer/Capture Text. In the Capture Text window, you can specify the filename and where you want the capture text to be saved. Save your text to a floppy disk, and name the text file output from each router the same as the router name (lab-a.txt, lab-b.txt, and so on). Then click the start button to start capturing text.

From an enable mode prompt, issue the **show running-config** command. After capturing the running configuration, click Transfer/Capture text/Stop. The output from **show running-config** will be on the floppy disk. Take your floppy disk to a computer that has a printer, and print the captured text or display the text file for your instructor.

Step 4. Repeat for all five routers.

Cisco Labs–Semester 2–Router Configuration
LAB 6.1.2–ROUTER CONFIGURATION with HYPERTERMINAL–OVERVIEW
(Estimated time: 30 minutes)

Router Name - LAB A
Router Type - 2514
E 0 = 192.5.5.1
E 1 = 205.7.5.1
S 0 = 201.100.11.1
SM = 255.255.255.0

Router Name - LAB C
Router Type - 2503
E 0 = 223.8.151.1
S 0 = 204.204.7.1
S 1 = 199.6.13.2
SM = 255.255.255.0

Router Name - LAB E
Router Type - 2501
E 0 = 210.93.105.2
SM = 255.255.255.0

Router Name - LAB B
Router Type - 2503
E 0 = 219.17.100.1
S 0 = 199.6.13.1
S 1 = 201.100.11.2
SM = 255.255.255.0

Router Name - LAB D
Router Type - 2501
E 0 = 210.93.105.1
S 1 = 204.204.7.2
SM = 255.255.255.0

LEGEND

- = ROUTER — User Exec Password = cisco
- = HUB — Enable Secret Exec Password = class
- = LAN SWITCH — Terminal vty Password = cisco
- = CONSOLE CABLE

Objectives:

- Capture the running configuration of a router to an ASCII text file with HyperTerminal
- Edit or modify the captured text file with a text editor such as Notepad
- Upload the text file to configure another router using HyperTerminal

Background:

In this lab, you use the Windows terminal emulation program, HyperTerminal, to capture and upload a router configuration as an ASCII text file. This saved copy can be used as a backup for the current router, or it can be used as a basis for a new router configuration. When adding another router to a network, it is a good idea to base the new configuration on an existing one rather than reinvent the wheel.

You can use any text editor program, such as Notepad or WordPad, to modify the original file. You can use a word processor, such as Word, but you must remember to save the file as a DOS text file. Because each router might have different interfaces, you must analyze the captured router configuration and modify it to suit the new configuration. Additionally, the IP addresses assigned to the interfaces on the new router must be different than those on the original router.

Cisco Labs–Semester 2–Router Configuration

LAB 6.1.2–ROUTER CONFIGURATION with HYPERTERMINAL– OVERVIEW

Tools/Preparation:

Prior to starting the lab, you need to connect a PC workstation with HyperTerminal to a router using the router's console interface with a roll-over cable. This lab should be done at the router console station. You should refer to the *Cisco Networking Academy Program: First-Year Companion Guide*, Second Edition, and review Semester 2 online curriculum Chapter 6 prior to starting this lab. Work individually or in teams. Be familiar with the following commands:

- **show running-config**
- **erase startup-config**
- **reload**
- **configure terminal**
- **copy running-config startup-config**

Required Resources:

- PC with monitor, keyboard, mouse, and power cords
- Windows operating system (Windows 95, 98, NT, or 2000) installed on PC
- HyperTerminal program configured for a console connection
- Notepad or other text editor program
- PC connected to the router console port with a roll-over cable

Notes:

_____

_____

_____

_____

Cisco Labs–Semester 2–Router Configuration
LAB 6.1.2–ROUTER CONFIGURATION with HYPERTERMINAL–WORKSHEET

Step 1. Log on to the router.
    Explanation: Connect to the router and log on. If prompted, enter the password **cisco**.

Step 2. Enter privileged EXEC mode.
    Task:
        a. From user EXEC mode, enter privileged EXEC mode using the **enable** command.
        b. Enter the enable password **class**.
    Explanation: Enter enable mode from user EXEC mode.

Step 3. Enter the show running-config command (abbreviated sh run).
    Task: Enter **show running-config** at the command prompt.
    Explanation: Using the **show running-config** command displays the active configuration file for the router that is stored in RAM.

    1. List all the interfaces on the router (answers will vary). _____

    _____

Step 4. Start capturing the configuration file.
    Task: Start the process of copying the router configuration to a text file.
    Explanation: HyperTerminal captures all text displayed on its screen to a text file.

    In HyperTerminal, select Transfer/Capture Text. When prompted, provide a path and name to capture the configuration to. Use the name of the router for the filename, and use .txt for the extension.

    2. Write down the name and location of this file: _____

Step 5. Enter the show running-config command (abbreviated sh run).
    Task: Enter **show running-config** at the command prompt.
    Explanation: Using the **show running-config** command displays the active configuration file for the router that is stored in RAM.

    Enter the **sh run** command. Press the spacebar when the **– More –** prompt appears.

Step 6. Stop capturing the configuration file.
    Task: Discontinue capturing the router configuration to a text file.
    Explanation: HyperTerminal stops capturing any text displayed on its screen.

    In HyperTerminal, select Transfer/Capture Text. A new menu appears. Click Stop.

Cisco Labs–Semester 2–Router Configuration
LAB 6.1.2–ROUTER CONFIGURATION with HYPERTERMINAL– _WORKSHEET_

Step 7. Clean up the captured configuration file.
Task: Remove any unnecessary information from the captured configuration.
Explanation: The captured text file has information not required for configuring a router, such as the **– More –** prompts. _Note:_ The exclamation mark (!) is the comment command in a router configuration.

Click the Windows Start button, click Run, type **Notepad**, and press the Enter key. In Notepad, select File/Open. Find the file you made note of in Step 4; click Open. Delete the lines that say:

- **sh run**
- **Building configuration...**
- **Current configuration:**

Delete each line that has the **– More –** prompt. _Note:_ There will be characters that appear as black boxes on these lines. Delete any lines that appear after the word **End**. Save the clean version of the configuration by selecting File/Save. Close Notepad (select File/Close) and switch back to HyperTerminal.

Step 8. Erase the startup configuration.
Task: Enter the command **erase startup-config** (abbreviated **erase start**) at the router prompt.
Explanation: The **erase startup-config** command deletes the configuration file from NVRAM. Caution should be used with this command because the router executes it without prompting for confirmation.

Step 9. Confirm that the startup configuration has been deleted.
Task: Enter **show startup-config** (abbreviated **sh start**) at the router prompt.
Explanation: This step confirms that the router's startup configuration will not be available upon restarting of the router.

3. What does the router show after this command is entered? _____
_____

Step 10. Restart the router.
Task: Enter **reload** at the router prompt.
Explanation: The **reload** command will reboot the router.

When asked to proceed with the reload, enter **Y** and press the Enter key. Note that the router displays the message **Notice: NVRAM invalid, possibly due to write erase.** When prompted to enter the initial configuration dialog, type **N** and press Enter. When prompted to terminate autoinstall, type **Y** and press Enter. Press Enter again.

4. What does the prompt look like?
_____

Cisco Workbook–Semester 2–Router Configuration
LAB 6.1.2–ROUTER CONFIGURATION with HYPERTERMINAL– WORKSHEET

Step 11. Reconfigure the router from the text file you saved.
Task: Use the **send file** command in HyperTerminal to copy the new configuration.
Explanation: The cleaned-up version of the router configuration file from Step 7 will be copied into the area of memory known as the clipboard.

In HyperTerminal, enter the command **enable** to change to privileged EXEC mode.

5. Why was a password not required? _____

Enter global config mode by entering the command **configure terminal** (abbreviated **config t**). Select Transfer/Send/Text File. Select the file you saved in Step 4. Each line in the text file will be entered for you, as though you were typing them yourself.

6. What does the router prompt change to? _____

7. What command changes the router prompt? _____

Press Ctrl-Z to exit global configuration mode.

Step 12. Save the new configuration file.
Task: Use the command **copy running-config startup-config** (abbreviated **copy run start**) to save the newly created router configuration.
Explanation: The **copy running-config startup-config** command copies the active router configuration from RAM into NVRAM.

Verify that the running configuration is correct by using the **show running-config** command (abbreviated **show run**). Enter the command **copy start run** at the router prompt.

Step 13. Verify the new configuration.
Task: Use the **reload** command to restart the router.
Explanation: Verify that the new configuration has been saved to NVRAM by restarting the router.

Enter the command **reload**. When prompted to confirm, press **Y** to confirm restarting the router. After the router restarts, press the Enter key.

8. What does the router prompt look like? _____

Cisco Labs–Semester 2–Router Configuration
LAB 6.1.4–ROUTER CONFIGURATION with TFTP–OVERVIEW
(Estimated time: 20 minutes)

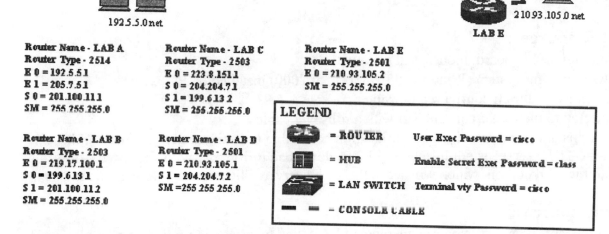

Objectives:

- Copy a router configuration file to a TFTP server
- Configure a router from a TFTP server

Background:

In this lab, you use a Trivial File Transfer Protocol (TFTP) server to save a copy of the router's configuration file. You also configure the router from the TFTP server. Using a TFTP server is an excellent way to keep backup copies of configuration files for routers and other network equipment, such as switches. Additionally, IOS images can be stored on a TFTP server. A TFTP server is simpler to use than a standard FTP server. TFTP does not require a user to have a password, or to navigate between directories. For this reason, it is important to have the TFTP server secure (not available to the general public). TFTP uses UDP rather than TCP like a standard FTP server does. TFTP is a very basic file transfer utility and does not require the guaranteed delivery services of TCP. The TFTP "server" can be a file server, a workstation, or even a Cisco router, and it must have the TFTP utility installed and running. You can download the Cisco TFTP server at no cost from the Web sites listed in the section, "Web Site Resources."

Cisco Labs–Semester 2–Router Configuration
LAB 6.1.4–ROUTER CONFIGURATION with TFTP–OVERVIEW

Tools/Preparation:
Prior to starting the lab, you need to connect a PC workstation with HyperTerminal to a router using the router's console interface with a roll-over cable. This lab should be done at the router console station. Verify that the Cisco TFTP server is installed on a server accessible by the router. You should refer to the *Cisco Networking Academy Program: First-Year Companion Guide*, Second Edition, and review Semester 2 online curriculum Chapter 6 prior to starting this lab. Work individually or in teams. Be familiar with the following commands:

- **copy running-config**
- **erase startup-config**
- **reload**

Required Resources:
- PC with monitor, keyboard, mouse, and power cords
- Windows operating system (Windows 95, 98, NT, or 2000) installed on PC
- HyperTerminal program configured for router console access
- PC connected to the router console port with a roll-over cable
- The TFTP installed and running on a workstation accessible from the router you are working on *Note:* If the TFTP server is not installed, you can download it from the Web site listed below and copy it to the workstation, which will act as the TFTP server. Click the downloaded file to install.

Web Site Resources:
- **Routing basics**—www.cisco.com/univercd/cc/td/doc/cisintwk/ito_doc/routing.htm
- **General information on routers**—www.cisco.com/univercd/cc/td/doc/pcat/#2
- **2500 series routers**—www.cisco.com/warp/public/cc/cisco/mkt/access/2500/index.shtml
- **1600 series routers**—www.cisco.com/warp/public/cc/cisco/mkt/access/1600/index.shtml
- **Terms and acronyms**—www.cisco.com/univercd/cc/td/doc/cisintwk/ita/index.htm
- **IP routing protocol IOS command summary**—www.cisco.com/univercd/cc/td/doc/product/software/ios120/12cgcr/rbkixol.htm
- **Free Cisco TFTP server** (Win 9x version)—ftp.cisco.com/pub/netmgmt/utilities/tftp.zip
- **TFTP command syntax**—www.cisco.com/univercd/cc/td/doc/product/10_100hb/1538m_mh/cli/1538_cli.htm

Notes:
_____
_____
_____
_____
_____

Cisco Labs–Semester 2–Router Configuration
LAB 6.1.4–ROUTER CONFIGURATION with TFTP–WORKSHEET

Step 1. Log on to the router.
Explanation: Connect to the router and log on. If prompted, enter the password **cisco**.

Step 2. Enter privileged EXEC mode.
Task: a. From user EXEC mode, enter privileged EXEC mode using the **enable** command.

b. Enter the enable password **class**.

Explanation: Enter the enable mode from user EXEC mode.

Step 3. Verify connectivity to the TFTP server.
Task: Enter **ping** *xxx.xxx.xxx.xxx* where *xxx.xxx.xxx.xxx* is the IP address of the workstation running the TFTP server.

Explanation: Ensure that you can reach the TFTP server from the router. If you cannot, you first need to check the connections and then check the configurations of the routers in the lab to ensure you can reach the TFTP server. Verify that the workstation has the TFTP server installed and that it is running.

Step 4. Copy the configuration file to the TFTP server.
Task: Enter the command **copy running-config tftp** (abbreviated **copy run tftp**).

Explanation: Start the process of copying the router's running configuration to the TFTP server.

Enter the command **copy running-config tftp** (abbreviated **copy run tftp**). When prompted for the remote host, enter the IP address you verified in Step 3, and press Enter. When prompted for the configuration file to write, the default is the router's name, followed by a dash and the word **confg** (such as **LAB-A-confg**). Accept this name by pressing Enter, or type in a new name and press Enter.

1. What is the name of the configuration file you are writing on the TFTP server? (Answers may vary.) _____

Confirm writing the configuration file to the TFTP server by pressing Enter. You might notice exclamation marks appear on the screen, showing the progress of the TFTP file copy process.

Step 5. Erase the startup configuration.
Task: Enter the command **erase startup-config** (abbreviated **erase start**) at the router prompt.

Explanation: The **erase startup-config** command deletes the contents of NVRAM. Caution should be used with this command because the router executes it without prompting for confirmation.

Step 6. Confirm that the startup configuration has been deleted.
Task: Enter **show startup-config** (abbreviated **show start**) at the router prompt.

Explanation: This step confirms that the router's startup configuration will not be available upon restarting of the router.

2. What does the router show after this command is entered?

_____

Cisco Labs–Semester 2–Router Configuration
LAB 6.1.4–ROUTER CONFIGURATION with TFTP–WORKSHEET

Step 7. Restart the router.
Task: Enter **reload** at the router prompt.
Explanation: The **reload** command reboots the router.

When asked to proceed with the reload, enter **Y** and press the Enter key. *Note:* The router displays the message **Notice: NVRAM invalid, possibly due to write erase.** When prompted to enter the initial configuration dialog, type **N** and press Enter. When prompted to terminate autoinstall, type **Y** and press Enter. Press Enter again.

3.   What does the prompt look like? _____

Step 8. Enter privileged EXEC mode.
Task: From user EXEC mode, enter privileged EXEC mode using the **enable** command.
Explanation: Enter enable mode from user EXEC mode. *Note:* Because the configuration was erased, no password is required.

Step 9. Reconfigure the router Ethernet interface.
Task: Manually reconfigure the IP address and subnet mask of the interface (E0 or E1) used to transfer the backup configuration file to the TFTP server.
Explanation: The router lost its configuration file when NVRAM was erased, and the reloaded configuration of the interface is necessary to re-establish a connection to the TFTP server.

Step 10. Copy the backup configuration file from the TFTP server.
Task: Enter the command **copy tftp running-config** (abbreviated **copy tftp run**).
Explanation: Start the process of copying the router's running configuration to the TFTP server.

Enter the command **copy tftp running-config**. When prompted for the remote host, press Enter to indicate the host configuration file. When prompted for the remote host, enter the IP address you verified in Step 3 and press Enter. When prompted for the configuration file to write, the default is the router's name, followed by a dash and the word **confg** (such as **LAB-A-confg**). Accept this name by pressing Enter, or type in a new name or the name you used in Step 4 and press Enter. Confirm copying the configuration file from the TFTP server by pressing Enter. When the process is complete, the router indicates the amount of RAM used for the configuration file and the total amount of RAM available on the router.

Step 11. Save the new configuration file.
Task: Use the command **copy running-config startup-config** (abbreviated **copy run start**) to save the newly created router configuration.
Explanation: The **copy running-config startup-config** command copies the active router configuration from RAM into NVRAM as a backup.

Verify that the running configuration is correct by using the **show running-config** command (abbreviated **show run**). Enter the command **copy start run** at the router prompt.

Cisco Labs–Semester 2–Router Configuration
LAB 6.2.1–BASIC ROUTER CONFIGURATION–OVERVIEW
(Estimated time: 45 minutes)

Router Name - LAB A
Router Type - 2514
E 0 = 192.5.5.1
E 1 = 205.7.5.1
S 0 = 201.100.11.1
SM = 255.255.255.0

Router Name - LAB B
Router Type - 2503
E 0 = 219.17.100.1
S 0 = 199.6.13.1
S 1 = 201.100.11.2
SM = 255.255.255.0

Router Name - LAB C
Router Type - 2503
E 0 = 223.8.151.1
S 0 = 204.204.7.1
S 1 = 199.6.13.2
SM = 255.255.255.0

Router Name - LAB D
Router Type - 2501
E 0 = 210.93.105.1
S 1 = 204.204.7.2
SM = 255.255.255.0

Router Name - LAB E
Router Type - 2501
E 0 = 210.93.105.2
SM = 255.255.255.0

LEGEND

= ROUTER	User Exec Password = cisco	
= HUB	Enable Secret Exec Password = class	
= LAN SWITCH	Terminal vty Password = cisco	
= CONSOLE CABLE		

Objectives:

- Use router configuration mode to configure the routing protocol
- Configure the router's identification (name)
- Configure a message of the day (motd) banner
- Use interface configuration mode to enter a description for an interface

Background:

In this lab, you use the router's global configuration mode and enter one-line commands that change the entire router. The router's prompt in global configuration mode is ***Router-name*(config)#**. Other configuration modes are used for multiple command lines and detailed configurations as in configuration of interfaces. When working with the interfaces, the router prompt looks like ***Router-name*(config-if)#**. You also configure a message-of-the-day banner using the **banner motd** command in global configuration mode and enter descriptions for the interfaces on the router in interface configuration mode.

Cisco Labs–Semester 2–Router Configuration
LAB 6.2.1–BASIC ROUTER CONFIGURATION–OVERVIEW

Tools/Preparation:

Prior to starting the lab, you need to connect a PC workstation with HyperTerminal to a router using the router's console interface with a roll-over cable. This lab should be done at the router console station. You should refer to the *Cisco Networking AcademyProgram: First-Year Companion Guide*, Second Edition, and review Semester 2 online curriculum Chapter 6 prior to starting this lab. Work individually or in teams. Be familiar with the following commands:

- **enable**
- **show running-config**
- **show startup-config**
- **configure terminal**
- **hostname**

- **banner motd**
- **interface**
- **description**
- **reload**

Required Resources:

- PC with monitor, keyboard, mouse, and power cords
- Windows operating system (Windows 95, 98, NT, or 2000) installed on PC
- HyperTerminal program configured for a console connection
- PC connected to the router console port with a roll-over cable

Web Site Resources:

- **Routing basics**—www.cisco.com/univercd/cc/td/doc/cisintwk/ito_doc/routing.htm
- **General information on routers**—www.cisco.com/univercd/cc/td/doc/pcat/#2
- **2500 series routers**—www.cisco.com/warp/public/cc/cisco/mkt/access/2500/index.shtml
- **1600 series routers**—www.cisco.com/warp/public/cc/cisco/mkt/access/1600/index.shtml
- **Terms and acronyms**—www.cisco.com/univercd/cc/td/doc/cisintwk/ita/index.htm
- **IP routing protocol IOS command summary**—www.cisco.com/univercd/cc/td/doc/product/software/ios120/12cgcr/rbkixol.htm

Notes:

_____
_____
_____
_____
_____
_____
_____
_____

Cisco Labs–Semester 2–Router Configuration
LAB 6.2.1–BASIC ROUTER CONFIGURATION–WORKSHEET

Step 1. Log on to the router.
   Explanation: Connect to the router and log on. If prompted, enter the password **cisco**.

Step 2. Enter privileged mode.
   Task:
   a. Enter **enable** (abbreviated **en**) at the command prompt.
   b. Enter the password **class**.
   Explanation: You use the **enable** command to enter privileged EXEC mode.

   1. What is the router command to view the current running configuration? _____

Step 3. Show the active configuration file.
   Task: Enter **show running-config** (abbreviated **sh run**) at the router prompt.
   Explanation: The router displays information on how it is currently configured from the file that is loaded in RAM (Random Access Memory).

   2. Compare the hostname in the running-config with the router prompt. Are they the same?
   _____

Step 4. Show the backup configuration file.
   Task: Enter **show startup-config** (abbreviated **sh start**) at the router prompt.
   Explanation: The router displays information on the backup configuration file stored in NVRAM (Non-Volatile RAM).

   3. Is the hostname the same as the router prompt? _____

Step 5. Enter global configuration mode.
   Task: Enter **configure terminal** (abbreviated **config t**) at the router prompt.
   Explanation: To configure the router, you must enter global configuration mode. Notice how the router prompt changes after this command.

   4. What does the router prompt look like? _____

Step 6. Enter the help command.
   Task: Enter the help command by typing **?** at the router prompt.
   Explanation: The router responds with all commands available in global configuration mode.

   5. Is **hostname** one of the command options? _____

Step 7. Enter the help command for hostname.
   Task: Enter the help command for **hostname** by entering **hostname ?** at the router prompt.
   Explanation: You can get help with any command by entering the command followed by a space and a **?**.

   6. What did the router respond with? _____

Cisco Labs–Semester 2–Router Configuration
LAB 6.2.1–BASIC ROUTER CONFIGURATION–WORKSHEET

Step 8. Change the hostname of the router.
  Task: Enter **hostname** and *your first name* at the router prompt.
  Explanation: This command changes the router hostname to your first name.

  7.   Did the router's prompt change to the new hostname? _____

Step 9. Show the active configuration file.
  Task:
    a.   Enter **exit** at the router prompt to return to the privileged mode prompt.
    b.   Enter **show running-config** at the router prompt.
  Explanation: To check the running configuration, you first have to exit global configuration mode using **exit**. Then you come to a privileged mode prompt and can issue the **show running-config** command. *Note:* The configuration change (hostname) you just made is in effect until the router is rebooted or reloaded.

  8.   What is the router's hostname? _____

Step 10. Show the backup configuration file.
  Task: Enter **show startup-config** at the router prompt.
  Explanation: The router displays information on the backup configuration file stored in NVRAM.

  9.   Is the hostname the same as the router prompt? _____

Step 11. Enter global configuration mode.
  Task: Enter **configure terminal** (abbreviated **config t**) at the router prompt.
  Explanation: To configure the router, you must enter global configuration mode. Notice how the router prompt changes after this command.

Step 12. Enter a message of the day.
  Task: Enter **banner motd #*This is the Message Of The Day*#** at the router prompt.
  Explanation: This command creates a message-of-the-day banner that displays when someone logs on to the router. *Note:* The message is bracketed by #, which tells the router the beginning and end of the message.

Step 13. Show information about the active configuration file.
  Task:
    a.   Enter **exit** at the router prompt.
    b.   Enter **show running-config** at the router prompt.
  Explanation: To check the running configuration, you first have to exit global configuration mode using **exit**. Then you come to a privileged mode prompt and can issue the **show running-config** command. *Note:* The configuration change you just made is in effect until the router is rebooted or reloaded.

  10. What did the router say the message of the day is? _____

Cisco Labs–Semester 2–Router Configuration
LAB 6.2.1–BASIC ROUTER CONFIGURATION–WORKSHEET

Step 14. Log out of the router.
   Task: Enter **exit** at the router prompt.
   Explanation: To exit the router, you can use either **exit** or **logout** (or **ex** for short).

Step 15. Log on to the router.
   Explanation: Connect to the router and log on. If prompted, enter the password **cisco**.

Step 16. Enter privileged mode.
   Task:
      a.   From user EXEC mode, enter privileged EXEC mode using the **enable** command.
      b.   Enter the enable password of **class**.
   Explanation: Enter enable mode from user EXEC mode.

Step 17. Show the active configuration file.
   Task: Enter **show running-config** at the router prompt.
   Explanation: The router displays information on how it is currently configured.

   11. Is there a description name for interface serial0? _____

Step 18. Enter global configuration mode.
   Task: Enter **configure terminal** at the router prompt.
   Explanation: To configure the router, you must enter global configuration mode. Notice how the router prompt changes after this command.

Step 19. Enter interface configuration mode.
   Task: Enter **interface serial0** at the global configuration prompt.
   Explanation: Entering **interface serial0** at the global configuration prompt allows you to change the configuration for serial0.

   12. What does the router prompt look like in interface configuration mode? _____

Step 20. Enter the help command.
   Task: Enter **?** at the router prompt.
   Explanation: The router responds with a list of available commands to configure interface serial0.

Step 21. Get help for the description command.
   Task: Enter **description ?** at the router prompt.
   Explanation: You can get help with any command at any time using the **?** command.

Step 22. Enter a description for interface serial0.
   Task: Enter **description** *any text you want up to 80 characters* at the router prompt.
   Explanation: This enters a description for interface serial0.

LAB 6.2.1–BASIC ROUTER CONFIGURATION–WORKSHEET

Step 23. Exit configuration mode.
Task:
  a. Enter **exit** in interface configuration mode.
  b. Enter **exit** in global configuration mode.
Explanation: The first **exit** command exits you from interface configuration mode, and the second exits you from global configuration mode. Notice how the router prompt changes after each **exit** command.

Step 24. Show the active configuration file.
Task: Enter **show running-config** at the router prompt.
Explanation: The router displays information on how it is currently configured.

13. What is the description for interface serial0? _____

Step 25. Show the backup configuration file.
Task: Enter **show startup-config** at the router prompt.
Explanation: The router displays information on the backup configuration file stored in NVRAM.

14. Is the interface serial0 description the same as in Step 22? _____

Step 26. Reload the router.
Task: Enter **reload** at the router prompt. When prompted to save changes, answer **no**.
Explanation: All the changes that you made to the router were in effect in the active configuration. When you reload the router, it reloads from the backup configuration file. If you wanted to keep the changes, you would have to use a command to copy the running configuration to the backup configuration file.

15. What is the command to copy the current running configuration to the backup (startup) configuration? _____

LAB 6.2.5–ROUTER INTERFACE CONFIGURATION–OVERVIEW
(Estimated time: 45 minutes)

Router Name - LAB A
Router Type - 2514
E 0 = 192.5.5.1
E 1 = 205.7.5.1
S 0 - 201.100.11.1
SM = 255.255.255.0

Router Name - LAB C
Router Type - 2503
E 0 = 223.8.151.1
S 0 = 204.204.7.1
S 1 - 199.6.13.2
SM = 255.255.255.0

Router Name - LAB E
Router Type - 2501
E 0 = 210.93.105.2
SM = 255.255.255.0

Router Name - LAB B
Router Type - 2503
E 0 = 219.17.100.1
S 0 = 199.6.13.1
S 1 = 201.100.11.2
SM = 255.255.255.0

Router Name - LAB D
Router Type - 2501
E 0 = 210.93.105.1
S 1 = 204.204.7.2
SM = 255.255.255.0

LEGEND

= ROUTER   User Exec Password = cisco

= HUB   Enable Secret Exec Password = class

= LAN SWITCH   Terminal vty Password = cisco

— — = CONSOLE CABLE

Objectives:

- Use interface configuration mode to configure interfaces
- Configure IP address assignments for router interfaces
- Configure subnet mask assignments for router interfaces
- Copy the running configuration to the backup configuration

Background:

In this lab, you use the router's interface configuration mode to configure an IP address and subnet mask for each router interface. You verify that Layer 3 connectivity is okay by using the **ping** command. The **show running-config** command helps make sure the changes you have made are what was intended. You then save the running configuration to the backup configuration.

Cisco Labs–Semester 2–Router Configuration
LAB 6.2.5–ROUTER INTERFACE CONFIGURATION–OVERVIEW

Tools/Preparation:

Prior to starting the lab, you need to connect a PC workstation with HyperTerminal to a router using the router's console interface with a roll-over cable. This lab should be done at the router console station. You should refer to the *Cisco Networking Academy Program: First-Year Companion Guide*, Second Edition, and review Semester 2 online curriculum Chapter 6 prior to starting this lab. Work individually or in teams. Be familiar with the following commands:

- **enable**
- **show running-config**
- **show startup-config**
- **configure terminal**

- **interface**
- **copy**
- **reload**
- **exit**

Required Resources:

- PC with monitor, keyboard, mouse, and power cords
- Windows operating system (Windows 95, 98, NT, or 2000) installed on PC
- HyperTerminal program configured for a console connection
- PC connected to the router console port with a roll-over cable

Web Site Resources:

- **Routing basics**—www.cisco.com/univercd/cc/td/doc/cisintwk/ito_doc/routing.htm
- **General information on routers**—www.cisco.com/univercd/cc/td/doc/pcat/#2
- **2500 series routers**—www.cisco.com/warp/public/cc/cisco/mkt/access/2500/index.shtml
- **1600 series routers**—www.cisco.com/warp/public/cc/cisco/mkt/access/1600/index.shtml
- **Terms and acronyms**—www.cisco.com/univercd/cc/td/doc/cisintwk/ita/index.htm
- **IP routing protocol IOS command summary**—www.cisco.com/univercd/cc/td/doc/product/software/ios120/12cgcr/rbkixol.htm
- **Beginning IP for new users**—www.cisco.com/warp/public/701/3.html

Notes:

_____
_____
_____
_____
_____
_____
_____

Cisco Labs–Semester 2–Router Configuration
LAB 6.2.5–ROUTER INTERFACE CONFIGURATION–WORKSHEET

Step 1. Log on to the router.
   Explanation: Connect to the router and log on. If prompted, enter the password **cisco**.

Step 2. Enter privileged mode.
   Task:
      a. Enter **enable** (abbreviated **en**) at the command prompt.
      b. Enter the password **class**.
   Explanation: You use the **enable** command to enter privileged EXEC mode.

Step 3. Show the active configuration file.
   Task: Enter **show running-config** (abbreviated **sh run**) at the router prompt.
   Explanation: The router displays information on how it is currently configured.

   1. Fill in the following table with the information from the standard five-router lab diagram.

Interface	IP Address	Subnet Mask

Step 4. Ping all interfaces on the router.
   Task: Enter **ping** *xxx.xxx.xxx.xxx* at the router prompt, where *xxx.xxx.xxx.xxx* equals an IP address.
   Explanation: Using ping tests Layer 3 connectivity. *Note:* If the other end of the WAN serial link (to the next router) is not configured correctly, or the other router is not powered on, you might not get a good ping result.

   2. Did all the interfaces ping successfully? _____

Step 5. Enter global configuration mode.
   Task: Enter **configure terminal** (abbreviated **config t**) at the router prompt.
   Explanation: To configure the router, you must start in global configuration mode. Notice how the router prompt changes after this command.

   3. What does the router prompt look like? _____

Step 6. Enter interface configuration mode.
   Task: Enter **interface serial0** (abbreviated **int s0**) at the global configuration prompt.
   Explanation: Entering **interface serial0** at the global configuration prompt allows you to change the configuration for serial0.

   4. What does the router prompt look like? _____

Cisco Labs–Semester 2–Router Configuration
LAB 6.2.5–ROUTER INTERFACE CONFIGURATION–WORKSHEET

Step 7. Configure the IP address for serial0.

Task:

a. Enter **IP address** *xxx.xxx.xxx.xxx yyy.yyy.yyy.yyy* at the router interface mode prompt. *xxx.xxxx.xxx.xxx* is the IP address, and *yyy.yyy.yyy.yyy* is the subnet mask for serial0. Use the IP address and subnet mask from the standard five-router lab setup.

b. Enter **clockrate 56000** to set the DCE clock rate for the WAN link.

Explanation a: This command will set the IP and subnet mask for serial0.

Explanation b: The clock rate must be set on the DCE (female) connection.

Step 8. Exit from interface configuration mode.
Task: Enter **exit** at the router prompt.

Explanation: When you type **exit** in interface configuration mode, it backs you up to a global configuration prompt.

5. What does the router prompt look like? _____

Step 9. Exit from global configuration mode.
Task: Enter **exit** or press Ctrl-Z.

Explanation: When you type **exit** or press Ctrl-Z, the router places you in privileged mode.

6. What does the router prompt look like? _____

Step 10. Show the active configuration file.
Task: Enter **show running-config** at the router prompt.

Explanation: The router displays information on how it is currently configured. Notice that any changes you enter shows up.

7. What did the router say the IP address and subnet mask were for serial0?

_____

Step 11. Test Layer 3 connectivity using ping.
Task: Enter **ping** *xxx.xxx.xxx.xxx* where *xxx.xxx.xxx.xxx* is an IP address of serial0 at the router prompt.

Explanation: This tests serial0 and make sure it is up and running. *Note:* If the other end of the WAN serial link (to the next router) is not configured correctly, or the other router is not powered on, you might not get a good ping result.

Step 12. Copy the running configuration to the backup configuration.
Task: Enter **copy running-config startup-config** at the router prompt.

Explanation: This copies the running configuration to the backup configuration. The next time the router is turned on or reloaded, it will load from the backup configuration.

Cisco Labs–Semester 2–Router Configuration

LAB 6.2.5–ROUTER INTERFACE CONFIGURATION–WORKSHEET

Step 13. Repeat this lab with all interfaces identified in Step 3 (clock rate is set on S0 only).

8. What command tells you how many and what kind of interfaces are on your router?

_____

Step 14. Reload the router's configuration.
   Task: Enter **reload** at the router prompt.
   Explanation: This command reloads the router from the backup configuration.

Step 15. Show information about the active configuration file.

   Task: Enter **show running-config** at the router prompt and compare the results with Step 3.
   Explanation: The router displays information on how it is currently configured.

Step 16. Exit the router.

Cisco Labs–Semester 2–Router Configuration
LAB 6.3.3–ROUTER PASSWORD RECOVERY–OVERVIEW
(Estimated time: 15 minutes)

Router Name - LAB A
Router Type - 2514
E 0 = 192.5.5.1
E 1 = 205.7.5.1
S 0 = 201.100.11.1
SM = 255.255.255.0

Router Name - LAB B
Router Type - 2503
E 0 = 219.17.100.1
S 0 = 199.6.13.1
S 1 = 201.100.11.2
SM = 255.255.255.0

Router Name - LAB C
Router Type - 2503
E 0 = 223.8.151.1
S 0 = 204.204.7.1
S 1 = 199.6.13.2
SM = 255.255.255.0

Router Name - LAB D
Router Type - 2501
E 0 = 210.93.105.1
S 1 = 204.204.7.2
SM = 255.255.255.0

Router Name - LAB E
Router Type - 2501
E 0 = 210.93.105.2
SM = 255.255.255.0

LEGEND

	= ROUTER	User Exec Password = cisco
	= HUB	Enable Secret Exec Password = class
	= LAN SWITCH	Terminal vty Password = cisco
	= CONSOLE CABLE	

Objective:

- Learn the procedure to recover a password when it's forgotten

Background:

Circumstances arise where the password for a router needs to be reset. The password might have been forgotten, or the previous administrator might have left the company that owns the router. The technique described requires physical access to the router so that the console cable may be plugged in. Because this technique is well-known, it is vital that routers are in a secured location, with limited physical access.

The version of HyperTerminal provided with Windows 95, 98, NT, and 2000 was developed for Microsoft by Hilgraeve. This version does not issue a "break" sequence as required for the Cisco router password recovery technique. An upgrade known as HyperTerminal Private Edition (PE) is available free of charge for personal and educational use. Commercial use of the program requires registration with Hilgraeve. The program can be downloaded from the Hilgraeve Web site, listed in the section, "Web Site Resources."

Cisco Labs–Semester 2–Router Configuration
LAB 6.3.3–ROUTER PASSWORD RECOVERY–OVERVIEW

Tools/Preparation:

Prior to starting the lab, you need to connect a PC workstation with HyperTerminal PE to a router using the router's console interface with a roll-over cable. This lab is done at the router console station. You should refer to the *Cisco Networking Academy Program: First-Year Companion Guide*, Second Edition. Work individually or in teams. Be familiar with the following commands:

- **config-register**
- **show version**
- **configure terminal**
- **enable secret**

Required Resources:

- PC with monitor, keyboard, mouse, and power cords ·
- Windows operating system (Windows 95, 98, NT, or 2000) installed on PC
- HyperTerminal PE program configured for router console access
- PC connected to the router console port with a roll-over cable

Web Site Resources:

- **Routing basics**—www.cisco.com/univercd/cc/td/doc/cisintwk/ito_doc/routing.htm
- **General information on routers**—www.cisco.com/univercd/cc/td/doc/pcat/#2
- **2500 series routers**—www.cisco.com/warp/public/cc/cisco/mkt/access/2500/index.shtml
- **1600 series routers**—www.cisco.com/warp/public/cc/cisco/mkt/access/1600/index.shtml
- **Terms and acronyms**—www.cisco.com/univercd/cc/td/doc/cisintwk/ita/index.htm
- **IP routing protocol IOS command summary**—www.cisco.com/univercd/cc/td/doc/product/software/ios120/12cgcr/rbkixol.htm
- **Hilgraeve HyperTerminal PE download**—www.hilgraeve.com
- **IOS password encryption facts**—www.cisco.com/warp/public/701/64.html

Notes:

_____

_____

_____

_____

_____

Cisco Labs–Semester 2–Router Configuration
LAB 6.3.3–ROUTER PASSWORD RECOVERY–WORKSHEET

Step 1. Log on to the router.
  Explanation: Connect to the router and log on. If prompted, enter the password **cisco**.

Step 2. Record the configuration register setting.
  Task: Enter the command **show version** (abbreviated **show ver**).
  Explanation: This displays the current configuration register setting, along with other information.

  1. What is the current configuration register setting? _____

Step 3. Restart the router.
  Task: Turn off the router for a short period of time, and then turn it back on again.
  Explanation: When the router is restarting, the bootup sequence can be interrupted.

Step 4. Interrupt the bootup sequence.
  Task: Within 60 seconds of turning the router back on, press and hold the Ctrl key, and then press the Break key.
  Explanation: A break character is sent to the router, interrupting the bootup sequence.

Step 5. Change the configuration register.
  Task: Enter the commands to change the configuration register.
  Explanation: The configuration register is changed to tell the router to ignore the configuration file in NVRAM on the next startup. The procedure varies, depending on the model of router.

A. 2500 series router:
The prompt will be > with no router name. Type **o/r 0x42** and press Enter (lowercase letter o, slash, lowercase r, space, zero, lowercase x, 4, 2). Type **I** and press Enter to reload the router. Wait until the router has rebooted. Type **N** when prompted to enter the initial configuration. Press Enter to see the **router>** prompt.

B. 1600 series router:
The prompt will be **rommon 1>**. Type **confreg** and type **Y** when asked to change the configuration. Type **N** to all questions except **ignore system config info**. After you respond to the questions, you are prompted to change the configuration again. Type **N**, and then type **reset** to reload the router. Wait until the router reboots. Type **N** when prompted to enter the initial configuration. Press Enter to see the **router>** prompt.

Cisco Labs–Semester 2–Router Configuration
LAB 6.3.3–ROUTER PASSWORD RECOVERY–WORKSHEET

Step 6. Enter privileged EXEC mode.
   Task: From user EXEC mode, enter privileged EXEC mode using the **enable** command.
   Explanation: Enter enable mode from user EXEC mode.

   2. Why was no password required? _____

Step 7. Examine the configuration the router is using.
   Task: Enter the command **show running-config** (abbreviated **sh run**).
   Explanation: Because the configuration registers were set to ignore the configuration file in Step 5, the router has a minimal configuration.

Step 8. Load the router configuration file.
   Task: Type the command **copy startup-config running-config** (abbreviated **copy start run**).
   Explanation: The configuration file is loaded from NVRAM into RAM. This allows you to view and/or modify the router passwords.

   3. How does your router prompt change? _____

Step 9. Look at passwords.
   Task: Enter the command **show running-config** (abbreviated **sh run**).
   Explanation: Passwords that have been encrypted with the **enable secret** command show up as a series of letters, numbers, and symbols (such as 1miYV$i9OOuSBQBde5fzgS3tn8T0). Unencrypted passwords are in plain text.

   4. What passwords do you see? _____

   _____

Step 10. Change passwords.
   Task: Enter the commands to change the appropriate passwords.
   Explanation: Passwords that are set using the **enable secret** command cannot be decrypted, even with third-party software. The only option you have is to change the password to another value.

   Go into global configuration mode by entering the command **configure terminal** (abbreviated **config t**). Enter the command **enable secret mynewpassword**. Press Ctrl-Z to exit global config mode. Type the command **show running-config** (abbreviated **sh run**).

   5. What passwords do you see now? _____

   _____

   6. Has the encrypted password changed from the value in Step 9? _____

Cisco Labs–Semester 2–Router Configuration
LAB 6.3.3–ROUTER PASSWORD RECOVERY–WORKSHEET

Note: For the purposes of this lab, you will not save the router configuration with the new password. You need to change the password back to the value **class**. Enter global config mode by entering the command **config t**. Enter the command **enable secret class** and then press Ctrl-Z to exit global configuration mode. Save the new configuration by entering the command **copy running-config startup-config** (abbreviated **copy run start**).

Step 11. Change the configuration register.
Task: Examine the current status of the configuration register and change it back to its original value.
Explanation: The configuration register is still set to ignore the startup configuration contained in NVRAM. You need to change it back to its original value.

Enter the command **show version** (abbreviated **sh ver**).

7.   What is the value of the configuration register? _____

Enter global config mode by typing the command **config t**. Enter the command **config-register 0x2102**. (*Note:* Use the original value you recorded in Step 2.) Press Ctrl-Z to exit global config mode. Enter the command **sh ver** to see the new value of the configuration register.

8.   What is the new value of the configuration register? _____

Step 12. Verify the new password.
Task:
a.   Enter the command **reload**.
b.   Enter **Y** if prompted to save the new configuration and to proceed with the reload.
Explanation: You need to verify that the new password you created in Step 10 works.

Enter privileged EXEC mode by entering the command **enable** (abbreviated: **en**). Enter the password **class**. If you properly set the enable password, you should see the router prompt change. View the status of the configuration register by entering the command **show version** (abbreviated **sh ver**).

9.   Has the configuration register changed back to the original value you recorded in Step 2?

_____

Cisco Labs–Semester 2–Router Configuration
LAB 6.4.1–ROUTER CONFIGURATION CHALLENGE–OVERVIEW
(Estimated time: 45 minutes)

Router Name - LAB A
Router Type - 2514
E 0 = 192.5.5.1
E 1 = 205.7.5.1
S 0 = 201.100.11.1
SM = 255.255.255.0

Router Name - LAB C
Router Type - 2503
E 0 = 223.8.151.1
S 0 = 204.204.7.1
S 1 = 199.6.13.2
SM = 255.255.255.0

Router Name - LAB E
Router Type - 2501
E 0 = 210.93.105.2
SM = 255.255.255.0

Router Name - LAB B
Router Type - 2503
E 0 = 219.17.100.1
S 0 = 199.6.13.1
S 1 = 201.100.11.2
SM = 255.255.255.0

Router Name - LAB D
Router Type - 2501
E 0 = 210.93.105.1
S 1 = 204.204.7.2
SM = 255.255.255.0

LEGEND

= ROUTER   User Exec Password – cisco

= HUB   Enable Secret Exec Password = class

= LAN SWITCH   Terminal vty Password = cisco

= CONSOLE CABLE

Objectives:

- Demonstrate your ability to configure a router for a remote office
- Configure IP address assignments for router interfaces
- Configure subnet mask assignments for router interfaces
- Use **ping**, **traceroute**, and **tracert** to test connectivity between devices

Background:

You and your group are administrators of a LAN. Due to the rapid expansion of this company, you need to link the headquarters (your group's router) to the rest of the network. You must link the networks via the serial ports, which means that your group is responsible for only your router's connections. Before starting this lab, the lab assistant or instructor should erase the running configuration and the startup configuration for Lab-A only and make sure that the rest of the routers are configured with the standard lab setup. You also need to verify your workstation IP configuration so you can test the connectivity between workstations and routers.

Cisco Labs–Semester 2–Router Configuration
LAB 6.4.1–ROUTER CONFIGURATION CHALLENGE–OVERVIEW

Tools/Preparation:
Prior to starting the lab, you need to connect a PC workstation with HyperTerminal to a router using the router's console interface with a roll-over cable. This lab should be done at the router console station on Lab-A. You should refer to the *Cisco Networking Academy Program: First-Year Companion Guide*, Second Edition, and review Semester 2 online curriculum Chapter 6 prior to starting this lab. Work individually or in teams.

Required Resources:
- Five PC workstations (minimum) with Windows operating system and HyperTerminal installed
- Five Cisco routers (model 1600 series or 2500 series with IOS 11.2 or later)
- Four Ethernet hubs (10Base-T with four to eight ports)
- One Ethernet switch (Cisco Catalyst 1900 or comparable)
- Five serial console cables to connect the workstation to the router console port (with RJ45 to DB9 converters)
- Three sets of V.35 WAN serial cables (DTE male/ DCE female) to connect from router to router
- CAT5 Ethernet cables wired straight through to connect routers and workstations to hubs and switches
- AUI (DB15) to RJ45 Ethernet transceivers (the quantity depends on the number of routers with AUI ports) to convert router AUI interfaces to 10Base-T RJ45

Web Site Resources:
- **Routing basics**—www.cisco.com/univercd/cc/td/doc/cisintwk/ito_doc/routing.htm
- **General information on routers**—www.cisco.com/univercd/cc/td/doc/pcat/#2
- **2500 series routers**—www.cisco.com/warp/public/cc/cisco/mkt/access/2500/index.shtml
- **1600 series routers**—www.cisco.com/warp/public/cc/cisco/mkt/access/1600/index.shtml
- **Terms and acronyms**—www.cisco.com/univercd/cc/td/doc/cisintwk/ita/index.htm
- **IP routing protocol IOS command summary**—www.cisco.com/univercd/cc/td/doc/product/software/ios120/12cgcr/rbkixol.htm

Notes:
_____
_____
_____
_____
_____
_____
_____

Cisco Labs–Semester 2–Router Configuration
LAB 6.4.1–ROUTER CONFIGURATION CHALLENGE–WORKSHEET

Step 1. Connect the Lab-A router to the rest of the network.

Connect to the router. The router should have no configuration prior to starting this lab. Use the standard network diagram to configure the Lab-A router. You can configure the router any way you prefer. Make sure the workstations are configured with an IP address, subnet mask, and default gateway. *Note:* If you are using the **setup** command, you need to add additional commands, because **setup** only does a basic configuration. If you need help, you can type **?** at any time to enter the help facility.

1. Perform the following tests to verify that you have configured Lab-A and the workstation correctly. If any of the tests fail, you must troubleshoot the problem with your router or workstation and document your results in the following table (answers may vary).

Test	Result OK?	Problem
Ping Lab-B		
Ping Lab-C		
Ping Lab-D		
Ping Lab-E		
Traceroute to Lab-E		
Ping a workstation on Lab-B		
Ping a workstation on Lab-C		
Ping a workstation on Lab-D		
Ping from a workstation on Lab-A to a workstation on Lab-E		
Traceroute from a workstation on Lab-A to a workstation on Lab-E		

Cisco Labs–Semester 2–Router Configuration
LAB 6.4.2–CISCO CONFIGMAKER–OVERVIEW
(Estimated time: 30 minutes)

Router Name - LAB A
Router Type - 2514
E 0 = 192.5.5.1
E 1 = 205.7.5.1
S 0 = 201.100.11.1
SM = 255.255.255.0

Router Name - LAB C
Router Type - 2503
E 0 = 223.8.151.1
S 0 = 204.204.7.1
S 1 = 199.6.13.2
SM = 255.255.255.0

Router Name - LAB E
Router Type - 2501
E 0 = 210.93.105.2
SM = 255.255.255.0

Router Name - LAB B
Router Type - 2503
E 0 = 219.17.100.1
S 0 = 199.6.13.1
S 1 = 201.100.11.2
SM = 255.255.255.0

Router Name - LAB D
Router Type - 2501
E 0 = 210.93.105.1
S 1 = 204.204.7.2
SM = 255.255.255.0

LEGEND

= ROUTER   User Exec Password = cisco

= HUB   Enable Secret Exec Password = class

= LAN SWITCH   Terminal vty Password = cisco

= CONSOLE CABLE

Objectives:
- Use Cisco ConfigMaker to configure a router
- Draw a map of a network using Cisco's ConfigMaker
- Print a configuration file created by ConfigMaker

Background:
This lab helps you become familiar with Cisco ConfigMaker. Cisco ConfigMaker is an easy-to-use Windows 95/98/NT application that configures Cisco routers, switches, hubs, and other devices. Using a graphical user interface (GUI), you draw your network, and Cisco ConfigMaker creates the Cisco IOS configuration files for the devices on your network. In addition, you can use Cisco ConfigMaker as an offline tool. You can draw and configure your entire network without having the devices on-hand until you are ready to deliver the configuration files to them. This software has many options, and you are encouraged to "play" with the configuration of the network. This lab takes you through a basic configuration to familiarize you with the software.

Cisco Labs–Semester 2–Router Configuration
LAB 6.4.2–CISCO CONFIGMAKER–OVERVIEW

Tools/Preparation:
Prior to starting this lab, you need to connect a PC with HyperTerminal to a router using the router's console interface with a roll-over cable. You need to download the latest version of Cisco ConfigMaker and install the program on the computer workstation. You need to have at least three routers available. This lab should be done at each router. Work individually or in teams. *Note:* The routers must be running IOS version 11.2 or later in order to deliver the configuration files.

Required Resources:
- PC workstation with Windows operating system and HyperTerminal installed
- Cisco ConfigMaker (latest version)
- IOS version 11.2 or later
- Two Cisco routers—model 1600 series or 2500 series, each with 1 serial and 1 Ethernet interface
- One Cisco router—model 1600 series or 2500 series with 2 serial and 1 Ethernet interface
- Two Ethernet hubs—10Base-T, 4 to 8 ports (use 3 hubs if switch is not available)
- One Ethernet switch (Cisco Catalyst 1900 or similar)
- Three console cables to connect workstation directly to router console port
- Three sets of V.35 WAN serial cables (male/female) to connect from router to router
- Six CAT5 Ethernet cables wired straight through

Web Site Resources:
- **Routing basics**—www.cisco.com/univercd/cc/td/doc/cisintwk/ito_doc/routing.htm
- **General information on routers**—www.cisco.com/univercd/cc/td/doc/pcat/#2
- **2500 series routers**—www.cisco.com/warp/public/cc/cisco/mkt/access/2500/index.shtml
- **1600 series routers**—www.cisco.com/warp/public/cc/cisco/mkt/access/1600/index.shtml
- **Terms and acronyms**—www.cisco.com/univercd/cc/td/doc/cisintwk/ita/index.htm
- **IP routing protocol IOS command summary**—www.cisco.com/univercd/cc/td/doc/product/software/ios120/12cgcr/rbkixol.htm
- **Cisco ConfigMaker information and download**—www.cisco.com/warp/public/cc/cisco/mkt/enm/config/index.shtml

Notes:
_____
_____
_____
_____
_____
_____
_____

Cisco Labs–Semester 2–Router Configuration
LAB 6.4.2–CISCO CONFIGMAKER–WORKSHEET

Step 1. Download and install Cisco ConfigMaker.
Explanation: Check the computer workstation to make sure that the latest version of Cisco ConfigMaker is installed. If it is not installed, or you do not have the latest version, you have to download it from www.cisco.com and install it (the Web site URL is listed in the overview section of this lab). There is no cost for the software.

Step 2. Run Cisco ConfigMaker and start the tutorial.
Task: Double-click the Cisco ConfigMaker icon.
Explanation: This action launches the ConfigMaker program and starts the tutorial automatically (if you choose). You can also run the tutorial at a later time by clicking the tutorial icon on the toolbar.

Step 3. Add routers to your network diagram.
Task: Under Devices, choose the Routers folder and add the routers on your lab setup.
Explanation: After you select the correct model number of the router that you are adding, place the router where you would like it in the network diagram area by dragging it to the network diagram area. You are prompted for configuration information.

1. What other router series can you configure with ConfigMaker?

   _____

Step 4. Configure the router.
Task: Follow the prompts to configure the router.
Explanation: First, you are asked for the name of the router. Enter **Lab-A** and click Next. Then you assign login and enable secret passwords to the router. Enter **cisco** as the password and **class** as the enable, and click Next. Now you need to tell the router what protocol you are going to use. Select **TCP/IP** and click Next and then Finish.

Step 5. Repeat Steps 3 and 4 to add other routers to your network diagram.
Explanation: Add at least two more routers from your lab setup to your network diagram.

Step 6. Add connections to the routers.
Task: In the connections window, click HDLC, Lab-A, and then the connecting device (Lab-B).
Explanation: After you add the HDLC connection from Lab-A to Lab-B, the HDLC wizard opens. Click Next. Now you are asked what serial interface you want to use for this connection. Use Serial0 and click Next. Now you are asked for addressing information for this interface. Enter IP address and subnet mask and click Next. Now ConfigMaker asks you to supply information about the router you are connected to (Lab-B). Select interface Serial1 for Lab-B and enter the IP address, and then click Next. Now you have an opportunity to create a backup connection. For this lab, choose "no backup," click Next, and then Finish. You can click the routers and rearrange them if desired.

2. What other connections can you configure using ConfigMaker?

   _____

   _____

Cisco Labs–Semester 2–Router Configuration
LAB 6.4.2–CISCO CONFIGMAKER–WORKSHEET

Step 7. Repeat Step 6 to add connections from Lab-B to Lab-C.

Step 8. Check/Add to configuration.
Task: Double-click the Lab-A router in your network diagram.
Explanation: This allows you to add or change the configuration for that router. Click the IOS Configuration tab. Compare the IOS configuration for interface Serial0 with the output from the **show running-config** command listed in Lab 4.5.2.1.

3. What command was missing from ConfigMaker's IOS configuration for interface S0?

_____

Step 9. Append configuration commands.
Task: From Lab-A Properties on the IOS Configuration tab, click the Add/Modify IOS commands button.
Explanation: This window lets you enter additional commands for the router. As you probably noticed from Step 8, Lab-A Serial0 is the DCE and should be providing the clock rate. Any commands will be added to the bottom of the configuration list.

4. What commands do you need to add to the router to add clocking for interface S0?

_____

Step 10. Deliver the IOS commands to the router.
Task: Highlight the router into which you want to load the IOS configuration, and click the Deliver button.
Explanation: As long as you have a connection to the router where you are trying to load the IOS configuration, ConfigMaker will attempt to load the IOS config. If there is a problem or an error, ConfigMaker tells you. You can fix the problem and then "deliver" the IOS configuration again.

Step 11. Print your network diagram and router configuration.
Task: Choose File/Print Network or File/Print All.
Explanation: You can print a graphical diagram of the network you have drawn so far or click Print Preview to see what it will look like before printing it. Print All prints the network diagram and a listing of the configuration file for each router.

Step 12. Save the router configuration to a text file.
Task: Right-click the router and choose IOS Configuration. Then choose File/Save As.
Explanation: You might want to save a copy of the configuration file that ConfigMaker generates for later editing with a text editor. You can name the file; it will have a .CFG extension. You can edit it with Notepad. You can also print the config file from here or send it to a router.

Cisco Labs–Semester 2–Router Configuration
LAB 6.4.3–ROUTER CONFIGURATION with a WEB BROWSER– OVERVIEW
(Estimated time: 15 minutes)

Router Name - LAB A
Router Type - 2514
E 0 = 192.5.5.1
E 1 = 205.7.5.1
S 0 = 201.100.11.1
SM = 255.255.255.0

Router Name - LAB C
Router Type - 2503
E 0 = 223.8.151.1
S 0 = 204.204.7.1
S 1 = 199.6.13.2
SM = 255.255.255.0

Router Name - LAB E
Router Type - 2501
E 0 = 210.93.105.2
SM = 255.255.255.0

Router Name - LAB B
Router Type - 2503
E 0 = 219.17.100.1
S 0 = 199.6.13.1
S 1 = 201.100.11.2
SM = 255.255.255.0

Router Name - LAB D
Router Type - 2501
E 0 = 210.93.105.1
S 1 = 204.204.7.2
SM = 255.255.255.0

LEGEND

= ROUTER   User Exec Password = cisco

= HUB   Enable Secret Exec Password = class

= LAN SWITCH   Terminal vty Password = cisco

– – = CONSOLE CABLE

Objectives:
- Configure a router as an HTTP server to accept configuration requests via a Web browser
- Learn what settings on a router can be configured via a Web browser

Background:
With Cisco IOS version 11.0, the **ip http server** command allows the router to act as a limited HTTP (Hypertext Transfer Protocol) Web server. There are no graphics, but rather a series of text color screens that allow the administrator to modify the configuration of and view information about the router. The browser interface to the router supports mouse control and makes it easier to do some tasks without requiring as much knowledge of the CLI (command-line interface). The CLI is available once in browser mode. It is possible to use a browser interface when accessing Cisco switches as well as routers.

A Web browser is more likely to be available on a client computer than a Telnet program. It might be easier in some instances to check on the status of a router and do minor configuration from a Web browser. Because it is relatively easy for someone outside your organization to find out what the IP address of your router is, you might not want to leave this function enabled at all times.

Cisco Labs–Semester 2–Router Configuration
LAB 6.4.3–ROUTER CONFIGURATION with a WEB BROWSER–OVERVIEW

Tools/Preparation:

Prior to starting the lab, you need to connect a PC workstation with HyperTerminal to a router using the router's console interface with a roll-over cable. The workstation needs a current version of a Web browser (Internet Explorer or Netscape Navigator) installed. There must be Ethernet or WAN connectivity between the workstation and the router as well as a console connection. The browser function cannot be used with the console connection, but it is necessary to configure the router to allow a browser connection first using the console connection. You should refer to the _Cisco Networking Academy Program: First-Year Companion Guide_, Second Edition, and review Semester 2 online curriculum, Chapter 6 prior to starting this lab. Work individually or in teams. Be familiar with the following command:

- **ip http server**

Required Resources:

- PC with monitor, keyboard, mouse, and power cords
- Windows operating system (Windows 95, 98, NT, or 2000) installed on PC
- HyperTerminal program configured for a router console connection
- PC connected to the router console port with a roll-over cable
- PC connected to the same hub or switch as the router
- A Web browser (Internet Explorer or Netscape Navigator) installed on the workstation. You must have an Ethernet connection to the router you wish to configure.

Web Site Resources:

- **Routing basics**—www.cisco.com/univercd/cc/td/doc/cisintwk/ito_doc/routing.htm
- **General information on routers**—www.cisco.com/univercd/cc/td/doc/pcat/#2
- **2500 series routers**—www.cisco.com/warp/public/cc/cisco/mkt/access/2500/index.shtml
- **1600 series routers**—www.cisco.com/warp/public/cc/cisco/mkt/access/1600/index.shtml
- **Terms and acronyms**—www.cisco.com/univercd/cc/td/doc/cisintwk/ita/index.htm
- **IP routing protocol IOS command summary**—www.cisco.com/univercd/cc/td/doc/product/software/ios120/12cgcr/rbkixol.htm
- **Command syntax of ip http**—www.cisco.com/univercd/cc/td/doc/product/10_100hb/1538m_mh/cli/1538_cli.htm

Cisco Labs–Semester 2–Router Configuration
LAB 6.4.3–ROUTER CONFIGURATION with a WEB BROWSER–WORKSHEET

Step 1. Log on to the router.
   Explanation: Connect to the router and log on. If prompted, enter the password **cisco**.

Step 2. Enter privileged EXEC mode.
   Task: a.   From user EXEC mode, enter privileged EXEC mode using the **enable** command.
          b.   Enter the enable password **class**.
   Explanation: Enter enable mode from user EXEC mode.

Step 3. Enter global configuration mode.
   Task: Enter the command **configure terminal** (abbreviated **config t**).
   Explanation: Global configuration mode allows you to change settings that affect the router.

Step 4. Enable the HTTP server function.
   Task: Enter the **ip http server** command. Press Ctrl-Z to exit global config mode.
   Explanation: This command allows the router to act as a limited HTTP server on the default HTTP port 80.

Step 5. Access the router via the Web browser.
   Task: Activate the Web browser on your workstation and enter the IP address of the router's Ethernet port into your browser address window.
   Explanation: By entering the IP address of your router's Ethernet interface, you connect to the router as an HTTP client. The HTTP server that you previously activated in the router responds to the browser requests.

   1.   What is the IP address of the Ethernet port? (Answers may vary.) _____

When prompted for a username and password, the username field can be left blank. Enter **class** for the password.

   2.   What options are available? (*Note*: 2500 series routers do not have the **ClickStart** option.)

Cisco Labs–Semester 2–Router Configuration
LAB 6.4.3–ROUTER CONFIGURATION with a WEB BROWSER–
WORKSHEET

Step 6. Examine the available options.
Task: Click each of the options and make notes in your engineering journal.
Explanation: Note the Help Resources listed on the bottom half of the router's home page.

3. Which option on the router's home page has the most suboptions? _____

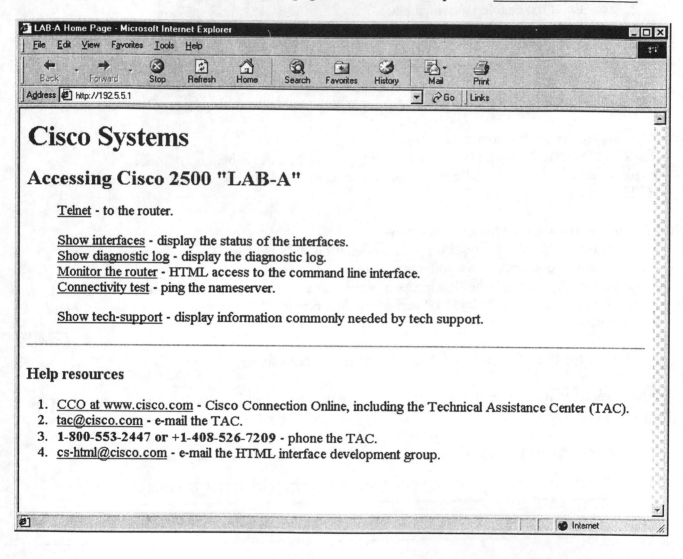

Cisco Labs–Semester 2–Router Configuration
LAB 7.1.3–IOS IMAGE BOOT–OVERVIEW
(Estimated time: 30 minutes)

Router Name - LAB A
Router Type - 2514
E 0 = 192.5.5.1
E 1 = 205.7.5.1
S 0 = 201.100.11.1
SM = 255.255.255.0

Router Name - LAB C
Router Type - 2503
E 0 = 223.8.151.1
S 0 = 204.204.7.1
S 1 = 199.6.13.2
SM = 255.255.255.0

Router Name - LAB E
Router Type - 2501
E 0 = 210.93.105.2
SM = 255.255.255.0

Router Name - LAB B
Router Type - 2503
E 0 = 219.17.100.1
S 0 = 199.6.13.1
S 1 = 201.100.11.2
SM = 255.255.255.0

Router Name - LAB D
Router Type - 2501
E 0 = 210.93.105.1
S 1 = 204.204.7.2
SM = 255.255.255.0

LEGEND
= ROUTER   User Exec Password = cisco
= HUB   Enable Secret Exec Password = class
= LAN SWITCH   Terminal vty Password = cisco
= CONSOLE CABLE

Objectives:
- Display information about the Cisco IOS image (software) that is currently running
- Determine where the IOS is booting from
- Check the amount of RAM, Flash, and NVRAM memory the router has
- Check the IOS image and Flash for space used and available
- Document the parts of the IOS image filename
- Check and document the configuration register settings related to boot method
- Document a fallback boot sequence

Background:
In this lab, you gather information on the version of IOS software that is currently running on the router. You also check the configuration register values to see where the router is currently configured to boot from. Use the **show flash** command to gather information about the Flash memory and see what files and how much memory is free. You also document the commands necessary to change the config register setting and the boot system commands necessary to define a fallback boot source sequence in case the IOS image in Flash is missing or corrupted.

Cisco Labs–Semester 2–Router Configuration
LAB 7.1.3–IOS IMAGE BOOT–OVERVIEW

Tools/Preparation:
Prior to starting the lab, you need to connect a PC workstation with HyperTerminal to a router using the router's console interface with a roll-over cable. This lab should be done at the router console station. You should refer to the *Cisco Networking Academy Program: First-Year Companion Guide*, Second Edition, and review Semester 2 online curriculum Chapter 7 prior to starting this lab. Work individually or in teams. Be familiar with the following commands:

- **enable**
- **show running-config**
- **show startup-config**
- **show flash**

- **show version**
- **boot system**
- **config-register**
- **copy**

Required Resources:
- PC with monitor, keyboard, mouse, and power cords
- Windows operating system (Windows 95, 98, NT, or 2000) installed on PC
- HyperTerminal program configured for router console connection
- PC connected to the router console port with a roll-over cable

Web Site Resources:
- **Routing basics**—www.cisco.com/univercd/cc/td/doc/cisintwk/ito_doc/routing.htm
- **General information on routers**—www.cisco.com/univercd/cc/td/doc/pcat/#2
- **2500 series routers**—www.cisco.com/warp/public/cc/cisco/mkt/access/2500/index.shtml
- **1600 series routers**—www.cisco.com/warp/public/cc/cisco/mkt/access/1600/index.shtml
- **Terms and acronyms**—www.cisco.com/univercd/cc/td/doc/cisintwk/ita/index.htm
- **IP routing protocol IOS command summary**—www.cisco.com/univercd/cc/td/doc/product/software/ios120/12cgcr/rbkixol.htm

Notes:
_____
_____
_____
_____
_____
_____
_____

Cisco Labs–Semester 2–Router Configuration
LAB 7.1.3–IOS IMAGE BOOT–WORKSHEET

Step 1. Log on to the router.
   Explanation: Connect to the router and log on. If prompted, enter the password **cisco**.

Step 2. Enter privileged mode.
   Task:
   a. Enter **enable** at the command prompt.
   b. Enter the password **class**.
   Explanation: You use the **enable** command to enter privileged EXEC mode.

Step 3. Show information about the backup configuration file.
   Task: Enter **show startup-config** at the router prompt.
   Explanation: The router displays information on the backup configuration file stored in NVRAM.

   1. Is there any indication of the configuration register setting? _____

Step 4. Display the IOS version and other important information.
   Task: Enter the **show version** command at the router prompt.
   Explanation: The router returns information about the IOS that is running in RAM..

   2. With the information that the router returns, answer the following questions:

      a   What is the IOS version and rev level? _____
      b. What is the name of the system image (IOS) file? _____
      c. Where was the router IOS image booted from? _____
      d. What type of processor (CPU) and how much RAM does this router have? _____
           _____
      e. What kind of router (platform type) is this? _____
      f.   The router backup configuration file is stored in Non-Volatile Random Access Memory (NVRAM). How much NVRAM does this router have? _____
           _____
      g. The router operating system (IOS) is stored in Flash memory. How much Flash memory does this router have? _____
      h. What is the configuration register set to? _____ What boot type does this setting specify? _____

   3. Assuming the config-register was currently set to 0x2102, write the configuration mode commands to specify that the IOS image should be loaded from:

      a. Flash: _____
      b. ROM monitor: _____
      c. ROM: _____

   4. If the router were in ROM monitor mode, what command would manually boot the Cisco IOS software? _____

Cisco Labs–Semester 2–Router Configuration
LAB 7.1.3–IOS IMAGE BOOT–WORKSHEET

Step 5. Show information about the Flash memory device.
Task: Enter **show flash** at the router prompt.
Explanation: The router responds with information about the Flash memory and what IOS image file(s) are stored there.

5. Document the following information.

   a. How much Flash memory is available and used?_____

   b. What is the file that is stored in Flash memory?_____

   c. What is the size in bytes of the Flash memory? _____

6. What part of the IOS filename **igs-j-1.111-5** identifies the following:

   a. Platform on which the image runs: _____

   b. Special capabilities: _____

   c. Where the image runs and whether it has been zip-compressed: _____

7. To specify a fallback boot sequence, write the configuration command to specify that the IOS image should be loaded from:

   a. Flash: _____

   b. A TFTP server: _____

   c. ROM: _____   Will this be a full IOS image? _____

8. To ensure that these commands are available for the router to use the next time it is restarted, what command would you need to enter next? _____

Cisco Labs–Semester 2–Router Configuration
LAB 7.3.5–IOS IMAGE BACKUP/RESTORE–OVERVIEW
(Estimated time: 30 minutes)

Router Name - LAB A
Router Type - 2514
E 0 = 192.5.5.1
E 1 = 205.7.5.1
S 0 = 201.100.11.1
SM = 255.255.255.0

Router Name - LAB C
Router Type - 2503
E 0 = 223.8.151.1
S 0 = 204.204.7.1
S 1 = 199.6.13.2
SM = 255.255.255.0

Router Name - LAB E
Router Type - 2501
E 0 = 210.93.105.2
SM = 255.255.255.0

Router Name - LAB B
Router Type - 2503
E 0 = 219.17.100.1
S 0 = 199.6.13.1
S 1 = 201.100.11.2
SM = 255.255.255.0

Router Name - LAB D
Router Type - 2501
E 0 = 210.93.105.1
S 1 = 204.204.7.2
SM = 255.255.255.0

LEGEND

= ROUTER — User Exec Password = cisco

= HUB — Enable Secret Exec Password = class

= LAN SWITCH — Terminal vty Password = cisco

= CONSOLE CABLE

Objectives:
- Display information about the Cisco IOS software that is currently running
- Back up the IOS software image from Flash to a TFTP server
- Restore (load) a backup of IOS software image from a TFTP server to Flash

Background:
It is a good idea to keep a backup copy of the IOS image file for each router. You might also want to always back up your current IOS before upgrading to a newer version. In this lab, you use a Trivial File Transfer Protocol (TFTP) server to act as a backup storage location for the IOS image. Production networks usually span wide areas and contain multiple routers. These geographically distributed routers need a source or backup location for software images. Using a TFTP server allows image and configuration uploads and downloads over the network.

In this lab, you check to see how much Flash memory the router has, how much of it is currently used by IOS image, and how much is free. You then copy the current IOS image from the Flash memory of the router to the TFTP server, which can be any workstation running the Cisco TFTP software. This creates a binary backup copy of the router's IOS image on the TFTP server. Assuming the router's Flash image has been damaged, you must restore the IOS image by copying the backup image from the TFTP server back to the router's Flash.

Cisco Labs–Semester 2–Router Configuration
LAB 7.3.5–IOS IMAGE BACKUP/RESTORE–OVERVIEW

Tools/Preparation:

Prior to starting the lab, you need to connect a PC workstation with HyperTerminal to a router using the router's console interface with a roll-over cable. This lab should be done at the router console station. Verify that the Cisco TFTP server is installed on a server accessible by the router. If it is not, you have to download it from the Web site listed in the section, "Web Site Resources." You should refer to the *Cisco Networking Academy Program: First-Year Companion Guide*, Second Edition, and review Semester 2 online curriculum Chapter 7 prior to starting this lab. Work individually or in teams. Be familiar with the following commands:

- **enable**
- **show running-config**
- **show startup-config**
- **show flash**

- **ping**
- **show version**
- **copy**
- **exit**

Required Resources:

- PC with monitor, keyboard, mouse, and power cords
- Windows operating system (Windows 95, 98, NT, or 2000) installed on PC
- HyperTerminal program configured for router console connection
- PC connected to the router console port with a roll-over cable
- PC on a network that the router can send and receive to running a TFTP daemon (server)

Web Site Resources:

- **Routing basics**—www.cisco.com/univercd/cc/td/doc/cisintwk/ito_doc/routing.htm
- **General information on routers**—www.cisco.com/univercd/cc/td/doc/pcat/#2
- **2500 series routers**—www.cisco.com/warp/public/cc/cisco/mkt/access/2500/index.shtml
- **1600 series routers**—www.cisco.com/warp/public/cc/cisco/mkt/access/1600/index.shtml
- **Terms and acronyms**—www.cisco.com/univercd/cc/td/doc/cisintwk/ita/index.htm
- **IP routing protocol IOS command summary**—www.cisco.com/univercd/cc/td/doc/product/ software/ios120/12cgcr/rbkixol.htm
- **WinZip** (to unpack .zip files)—www.winzip.com
- **Free Cisco TFTP server (Windows 9x version)**—ftp.cisco.com/pub/netmgmt/utilities/tftp.zip
- **TFTP command syntax**—www.cisco.com/univercd/cc/td/doc/product/ 10_100hb/1538m_mh/cli/1538_cli.htm

Notes:

_____

_____

_____

_____

Cisco Labs–Semester 2–Router Configuration
LAB 7.3.5–IOS IMAGE BACKUP/RESTORE–WORKSHEET

Step 1. Log on to the router.
  Explanation: Connect to the router and log on. If prompted, enter the password **cisco**.

Step 2. Enter privileged mode.
  Task:
  a. Enter **enable** at the command prompt.
  b. Enter the password **class**.
  Explanation: You use the **enable** command to enter privileged EXEC mode.

Step 3. Show information about the Flash memory device.
  Task: Enter **show flash** at the router prompt.
  Explanation: The router responds with information about the Flash memory and what IOS image file(s) are stored there.

  1. Document the following information from the **show flash** command.

      a. How much Flash memory is used and available? _____
      b. What is the file that is stored in Flash memory? _____
      c. What is the size in bytes of the Flash memory? _____

Step 4. Verify connectivity to the TFTP server.
  Task: Enter **ping *xxx.xxx.xxx.xxx*** where *xxx.xxx.xxx.xxx* is the IP address of the workstation running the TFTP server.
  Explanation: Ensure that you can reach the TFTP server from the router. If you cannot, you first need to check the connections and then check the configurations of the routers in the lab to ensure you can reach the TFTP server. Verify that the workstation has the TFTP server installed and that it is running. You can download the free Cisco TFTP server from the Web site listed in the section, "Web Site Resources."

  2. What was the result of the **ping** command? _____
      _____

Step 5. Verify the TFTP server file location.
  Task: Check the TFTP server root directory location.
  Explanation: The TFTP server root directory is where the IOS image file will be copied. This is where you should look for the file after a successful file copy. Select View/Options and note the location or browse and change the location to another directory.

  3. What is the default location for the TFTP server root directory?
      _____

Cisco Labs–Semester 2–Router Configuration
LAB 7.3.5–IOS IMAGE BACKUP/RESTORE–WORKSHEET

Step 6. Create an IOS software image backup.
  Task:
  a. Enter **copy flash tftp** at the router prompt.
  b. The router asks for the IP address or hostname of the TFTP host. Enter the IP address of the TFTP server.

Explanation: This copies the IOS software to a TFTP host. Before you issue this command, you need to have a TFTP host set up on a network that the router can send data to and receive data from. You also need to know the IP address of that host. You can use a hostname for the TFTP server only if you have a DNS server or proper entry in the host file. *Note:* You can use HyperTerminal or Windows' copy/paste function to capture the copy process as it progresses.

4. What was the IP address of the TFTP server? _____

5. What did you name the file that was written to the TFTP server? _____

6. How did the router respond when copying the file?
    _____

Step 7. Verify the file copied to the TFTP server.
  Task: Check the TFTP server using Windows Explorer, the **DIR** command, or the <u>ls</u> UNIX command for the file you just wrote.

7. What is the size in bytes of the file that was written? _____

Step 8. Restore the IOS software image from backup.
  Task:
  a. Enter **copy tftp flash** at the router prompt.
  b. The router asks for the IP address or hostname of the TFTP host. Enter the IP address of the TFTP server.
  Explanation: This copies the IOS software from a TFTP host to router Flash.

8. If you are copying the same filename as you backed up, the router prompts you to overwrite the existing IOS image. In the lines provided, write some of the prompts and responses you saw on the router screen. *Note:* You can use HyperTerminal or Windows' copy/paste function to capture the copy process as it progresses.

_____
_____
_____
_____
_____
_____
_____
_____
_____

Cisco Labs–Semester 2–Router Configuration
LAB 8.1.2–ROUTER PASSWORD RECOVERY–OVERVIEW
(Estimated time: 15 minutes)

Router Name - LAB A
Router Type - 2514
E 0 = 192.5.5.1
E 1 = 205.7.5.1
S 0 = 201.100.11.1
SM = 255.255.255.0

Router Name - LAB C
Router Type - 2503
E 0 = 223.8.151.1
S 0 = 204.204.7.1
S 1 = 199.6.13.2
SM = 255.255.255.0

Router Name - LAB E
Router Type - 2501
E 0 = 210.93.105.2
SM = 255.255.255.0

Router Name - LAB B
Router Type - 2503
E 0 = 219.17.100.1
S 0 = 199.6.13.1
S 1 = 201.100.11.2
SM = 255.255.255.0

Router Name - LAB D
Router Type - 2501
E 0 = 210.93.105.1
S 1 = 204.204.7.2
SM = 255.255.255.0

LEGEND

= ROUTER	User Exec Password = cisco
= HUB	Enable Secret Exec Password = class
= LAN SWITCH	Terminal vty Password = cisco
= CONSOLE CABLE	

Objective:
- Learn the procedure to recover a password when it is forgotten

Background:
Circumstances arise where the password for a router needs to be reset. The password might have been forgotten, or the previous administrator might have left the company that owns the router. The technique described requires physical access to the router so that the console cable can be plugged in. Because this technique is well-known, it is vital that routers are in a secured location, with limited physical access.

The version of HyperTerminal provided with Windows 95, 98, NT, and 2000 was developed for Microsoft by Hilgraeve. This version does not issue a "break" sequence as required for the Cisco router password recovery technique. An upgrade known as HyperTerminal Private Edition (PE) is available free of charge for personal and educational use. Commercial use of the program requires registration with Hilgraeve. The program can be downloaded from the Hilgraeve Web site, listed in the section, "Web Site Resources."

Cisco Labs–Semester 2–Router Configuration
LAB 8.1.2–ROUTER PASSWORD RECOVERY–OVERVIEW

Tools/Preparation:
Prior to starting the lab, you need to connect a PC workstation with HyperTerminal PE to a router using the router's console interface with a roll-over cable. This lab is done at the router console station. You should refer to the *Cisco Networking Academy Program: First-Year Companion Guide*, Second Edition. Work individually or in teams. Be familiar with the following commands:

- **config-register**
- **show version**
- **configure terminal**
- **enable secret**

Required Resources:
- PC with monitor, keyboard, mouse, and power cords
- Windows operating system (Windows 95, 98, NT, or 2000) installed on PC
- HyperTerminal PE program configured for router console access
- PC connected to the router console port with a roll-over cable

Web Site Resources:
- **Routing basics**—www.cisco.com/univercd/cc/td/doc/cisintwk/ito_doc/routing.htm
- **General information on routers**—www.cisco.com/univercd/cc/td/doc/pcat/#2
- **2500 series routers**—www.cisco.com/warp/public/cc/cisco/mkt/access/2500/index.shtml
- **1600 series routers**—www.cisco.com/warp/public/cc/cisco/mkt/access/1600/index.shtml
- **Terms and acronyms**—www.cisco.com/univercd/cc/td/doc/cisintwk/ita/index.htm
- **IP routing protocol IOS command summary**—www.cisco.com/univercd/cc/td/doc/product/software/ios120/12cgcr/rbkixol.htm
- **Hilgraeve HyperTerminal PE download**—www.hilgraeve.com
- **IOS password encryption facts**—www.cisco.com/warp/public/701/64.html

Notes:
_____
_____
_____
_____
_____

Cisco Labs–Semester 2–Router Configuration
LAB 8.1.2–ROUTER PASSWORD RECOVERY–WORKSHEET

Step 1. Log on to the router.
  Explanation: Connect to the router and log on. If prompted, enter the password **cisco**.

Step 2. Record the configuration register setting.
  Task: Enter the command **show version** (abbreviated **show ver**).
  Explanation: This displays the current configuration register setting, along with other information.

  1. What is the current configuration register setting? _____

Step 3. Restart the router.
  Task: Turn off the router for a short period of time, and then turn it back on again.
  Explanation: When the router is restarting, the bootup sequence can be interrupted.

Step 4. Interrupt the bootup sequence.
  Task: Within 60 seconds of turning the router back on, press and hold the Ctrl key, and then press the Break key.
  Explanation: A break character is sent to the router, interrupting the bootup sequence.

Step 5. Change the configuration register.
  Task: Enter the commands to change the configuration register.
  Explanation: The configuration register is changed to tell the router to ignore the configuration file in NVRAM on the next startup. The procedure varies, depending on the model of router.

  A. 2500 series router:
  The prompt will be > with no router name. Type **o/r 0x42** and press Enter (lowercase letter o, slash, lowercase r, space, zero, lowercase x, 4, 2). Type **I** and press Enter to reload the router. Wait until the router has rebooted. Type **N** when prompted to enter the initial configuration. Press Enter to see the **router>** prompt.

  B. 1600 series router:
  The prompt will be **rommon 1>**. Type **confreg** and type **Y** when asked to change the configuration. Type **N** to all questions except **ignore system config info**. After you finish responding to the questions, you are prompted to change the configuration again. Type **N**, and then type **reset** to reload the router. Wait until the router has rebooted. Type **N** when prompted to enter the initial configuration. Press Enter to see the **router>** prompt.

Cisco Labs–Semester 2–Router Configuration
LAB 8.1.2–ROUTER PASSWORD RECOVERY–WORKSHEET

Step 6. Enter privileged EXEC mode.
Task: From user EXEC mode, enter privileged EXEC mode using the **enable** command.
Explanation: Enter enable mode from user EXEC mode.

2. Why was no password required? _____

Step 7. Examine the configuration the router is using.
Task: Enter the command **show running-config** (abbreviated **sh run**).
Explanation: Because the configuration registers were set to ignore the configuration file in Step 5, the router has a minimal configuration.

Step 8. Load the router configuration file.
Task: Type the command **copy startup-config running-config** (abbreviated **copy start run**).
Explanation: The configuration file is loaded from NVRAM into RAM. This allows you to view and/or modify the router passwords.

3. How does your router prompt change? _____

Step 9. Look at passwords.
Task: Enter the command **show running-config** (abbreviated **sh run**).
Explanation: Passwords that have been encrypted with the **enable secret** command show up as a series of letters, numbers, and symbols (such as 1miYV$i9OOuSBQBde5fzgS3tn8T0). Unencrypted passwords are in plain text.

4. What passwords do you see? _____

_____

Step 10. Change passwords.
Task: Enter the commands to change the appropriate passwords.
Explanation: Passwords that are set using the **enable secret** command cannot be decrypted, even with third-party software. The only option you have is to change the password to another value.

Go into global configuration mode by entering the command **configure terminal** (abbreviated **config t**). Enter the command **enable secret mynewpassword**. Press Ctrl-Z to exit global config mode. Type the command **show running-config** (abbreviated **sh run**).

5. What passwords do you see now? _____

_____

6. Has the encrypted password changed from the value in Step 9? _____

Cisco Labs–Semester 2–Router Configuration
LAB 8.1.2–ROUTER PASSWORD RECOVERY–WORKSHEET

Note: For the purposes of this lab, you do not save the router configuration with the new password. You need to change the password back to the value **class**. Enter global config mode by entering the command **config t**. Enter the command **enable secret class** and then press Ctrl-Z to exit global configuration mode. Save the new configuration by entering the command **copy running-config startup-config** (abbreviated **copy start run**).

Step 11. Change the configuration register.
   Task: Examine the current status of the configuration register and change it back to its original value.
   Explanation: The configuration register is still set to ignore the startup configuration contained in NVRAM. You need to change it back to its original value.

   Enter the command **show version** (abbreviated **sh ver**).

   7.   What is the value of the configuration register? _____

   Enter global config mode by typing the command **config t**. Enter the command **config-register 0x2102**. (**Note:** Use the original value you recorded in Step 2.) Press Ctrl-Z to exit global config mode. Enter the command **sh ver** to see the new value of the configuration register.

   8.   What is the new value of the configuration register? _____

Step 12. Verify the new password.
   Task:
   a.   Enter the command **reload**.
   b.   Enter **Y** if prompted to save the new configuration and to proceed with the reload.
   Explanation: You need to verify that the new password you created in Step 10 works.

   Enter privileged EXEC mode by entering the command **enable** (abbreviated: **en**). Enter the password **class**. If you properly set the enable password, you should see the router prompt change. View the status of the configuration register by entering the command **show version** (abbreviated **sh ver**).

   9.   Has the configuration register changed back to the original value you recorded in Step 2?

   _____

Cisco Labs–Semester 2–Router Configuration
LAB 8.2.1–INDIVIDUAL ROUTER CONFIGURATION–OVERVIEW
(Estimated time: 30 minutes)

Router Name - LAB A
Router Type - 2514
E 0 = 192.5.5.1
E 1 = 205.7.5.1
S 0 = 201.100.11.1
SM = 255.255.255.0

Router Name - LAB B
Router Type - 2503
E 0 = 219.17.100.1
S 0 = 199.6.13.1
S 1 = 201.100.11.2
SM = 255.255.255.0

Router Name - LAB C
Router Type - 2503
E 0 = 223.8.151.1
S 0 = 204.204.7.1
S 1 = 199.6.13.2
SM = 255.255.255.0

Router Name - LAB D
Router Type - 2501
E 0 = 210.93.105.1
S 1 = 204.204.7.2
SM = 255.255.255.0

Router Name - LAB E
Router Type - 2501
E 0 = 210.93.105.2
SM = 255.255.255.0

LEGEND

= ROUTER		User Exec Password = cisco
= HUB		Enable Secret Exec Password = class
= LAN SWITCH		Terminal vty Password = cisco
= CONSOLE CABLE		

Objectives:
- Configure a router for the standard lab setup using only the lab diagram
- Configure the router using only the command-line interface (CLI)
- Configure workstation IP address settings to communicate with the router via Ethernet
- Prepare for Part A of the Final Exam (Timed Router Configuration)

Background:
In this lab, you configure one of the five lab routers from the command line by yourself, without the use of any notes, only the network topology. You can use the router help facility and the router diagram above. Your goal is to configure the router as quickly as possible without errors. You also configure the IP settings for one of the corresponding Ethernet attached workstations.

Tools/Preparation:
Prior to starting this lab, you should have the equipment for the standard five-router lab available. The NVRAM of the router you are configuring should be erased. At the start of this section, the instructor or lab assistant should log on to each router in enable exec mode, issue the **erase startup-config command**, and issue the **reload** command. This forces the routers to come up with a blank configuration. The IP configuration for the associated workstation should also be changed so that it is incorrect. The instructor will review your configuration when you are finished.

Cisco Labs–Semester 2–Router Configuration
LAB 8.2.1–INDIVIDUAL ROUTER CONFIGURATION–WORKSHEET

Step 1. Review the physical connections on the standard lab setup.
Review the standard Semester 2 lab diagram in the overview section of this lab, and check all physical devices, cables, and connections of the physical lab setup to familiarize yourself with them.

Step 2. Console into the router.
Verify that you have a good console connection and that HyperTerminal is configured properly. The router should be booted with no startup configuration file in NVRAM.

Step 3. Identify IP address information.
  1. Fill in the table with IP interface information from the diagram for each of the five routers.

Cisco Lab Router IP Configuration (answers from router diagram–your answers may vary)

Router Name	Lab-A	Lab-B	Lab-C	Lab-D	Lab-E
Model Number					
Interface E0 IP Address					
Interface E0 Subnet Mask					
Interface E1 IP Address					
Interface E1 Subnet Mask					
Interface S0 IP Address					
Interface S0 Subnet Mask					
Interface S0 * Clock Rate					
Interface S1 IP Address					
Interface S1 Subnet Mask					
Other Interface(s)					

* Note: Clock rate must be set on the DCE end (S0) of the WAN link between routers.

Step 4. Configure the router via the console connection.
  2. Select a router and time yourself. Configure the following information for each router: Host name, passwords, IP addresses for interfaces, routing protocol and associated network numbers, IP host lookup table. Repeat with other routers.
  Note: Make sure you copy the running configuration to the startup configuration when you are finished, or you will lose the configuration upon next reboot.

Step 5. Configure the workstation IP settings using the Control Panel's Network icon.
  3. Configure the IP address, subnet mask, and default gateway to be compatible with the router.

Step 6. Test your configuration with ping and telnet
  4. From the PC DOS prompt, use the **ping** and **telnet** commands to test your configuration.

Cisco Labs–Semester 2–Router Configuration
LAB 8.2.1–INDIVIDUAL ROUTER CONFIGURATION–WORKSHEET

The following lists are the outputs from the **show running-config** command for all five routers in the standard lab setup. If you have problems configuring a particular router, refer to these for help. Answers might vary, depending on the router model number and exact configuration of your lab setup.

Router: Lab-A

LAB-A#show run

```
Building configuration...
Current configuration:
version 11.1
service udp-small-servers
service tcp-small-servers
hostname LAB-A
enable secret 5 $1$xT7v$9EC3X5IBHLwq2RehHNvWc0
interface Ethernet0
 ip address 192.5.5.1 255.255.255.0
interface Ethernet1
 ip address 205.7.5.1 255.255.255.0
interface Serial0
 ip address 201.100.11.1 255.255.255.0
 clockrate 56000
interface Serial1
 no ip address
 shutdown
router rip
 network 192.5.5.0
 network 205.7.5.0
 network 201.100.11.0
ip host LAB-B 201.100.11.2 219.17.100.1 199.6.13.1
ip host LAB-C 199.6.13.2 223.8.151.1 204.204.7.1
ip host LAB-D 204.204.7.2 210.93.105.1
ip host LAB-E 210.93.105.2
ip host LAB-A 192.5.5.1 205.7.5.1 201.100.11.1
no ip classless
line con 0
 password cisco
 login
line aux 0
line vty 0 4
 password cisco
 login
!end
```

Cisco Labs–Semester 2–Router Configuration
LAB 8.2.1–INDIVIDUAL ROUTER CONFIGURATION–WORKSHEET

Router: Lab-B

LAB-B#show run

Building configuration...
Current configuration:
version 11.1
service udp-small-servers
service tcp-small-servers
hostname LAB-B
enable secret 5 1xT7v$9EC3X5IBHLwq2RehHNvWc0
interface Ethernet0
 ip address 219.17.100.1 255.255.255.0
 no mop enabled
interface Serial0
 ip address 199.6.13.1 255.255.255.0
 clockrate 56000
interface Serial1
 ip address 201.100.11.2 255.255.255.0
interface BRI0
 no ip address
 shutdown
router rip
 network 219.17.100.0
 network 199.6.13.0
 network 201.100.11.0
ip host LAB-B 201.100.11.2 219.17.100.1 199.6.13.1
ip host LAB-C 199.6.13.2 223.8.151.1 204.204.7.1
ip host LAB-D 204.204.7.2 210.93.105.1
ip host LAB-E 210.93.105.2
ip host LAB-A 192.5.5.1 205.7.5.1 201.100.11.1
no ip classless
snmp-server community public RO
line con 0
 password cisco
 login
line aux 0
line vty 0 4
 password cisco
 login

Cisco Labs–Semester 2–Router Configuration
LAB 8.2.1–INDIVIDUAL ROUTER CONFIGURATION–WORKSHEET

Router: Lab-C

LAB-C#show run

Building configuration...
Current configuration:
version 11.1
service udp-small-servers
service tcp-small-servers
hostname LAB-C
enable secret 5 1xT7v$9EC3X5IBHLwq2RehHNvWc0
interface Ethernet0
 ip address 223.8.151.1 255.255.255.0
interface Serial0
 ip address 204.204.7.1 255.255.255.0
 clockrate 56000
interface Serial1
 ip address 199.6.13.2 255.255.255.0
interface BRI0
 no ip address
 shutdown
router rip
 network 223.8.151.0
 network 199.6.13.0
 network 204.204.7.0
ip host LAB-A 192.5.5.1 205.7.5.1 201.100.11.1
ip host LAB-B 201.100.11.2 219.17.100.1 199.6.13.1
ip host LAB-C 199.6.13.2 223.8.151.1 204.204.7.1
ip host LAB-D 204.204.7.2 210.93.105.1
ip host LAB-E 210.93.105.2
no ip classless
line con 0
 password cisco
login
line aux 0
line vty 0 4
 password cisco
 login
!

Cisco Labs–Semester 2–Router Configuration
LAB 8.2.1–INDIVIDUAL ROUTER CONFIGURATION–WORKSHEET

Router: Lab-D

LAB-D#show run

```
Building configuration...
Current configuration:
version 11.1
service udp-small-servers
service tcp-small-servers
hostname LAB-D
enable secret 5 $1$xT7v$9EC3X5IBHLwq2RehHNvWc0
interface Ethernet0
 ip address 210.93.105.1 255.255.255.0
 no ip mroute-cache
 no ip route-cache
interface Serial0
 no ip address
 no ip mroute-cache
 no ip route-cache
 shutdown
interface Serial1
 ip address 204.204.7.2 255.255.255.0
 no ip mroute-cache
 no ip route-cache
router rip
 network 204.204.7.0
 network 210.93.105.0
ip host LAB-A 102.5.5.1 205.7.5.1 201.100.11.1
ip host LAB-B 201.100.11.2 219.17.100.1 199.6.13.1
ip host LAB-C 199.6.13.2 223.8.151.1 204.204.7.1
ip host LAB-D 204.204.7.2 210.93.105.1
ip host LAB-E 210.93.105.2
no ip classless
line con 0
 password cisco
login
line aux 0
line vty 0 4
 password cisco
login
```

Cisco Labs–Semester 2–Router Configuration
LAB 8.2.1–INDIVIDUAL ROUTER CONFIGURATION–WORKSHEET

Router: Lab-E

LAB-E#show run

Building configuration...
Current configuration:
version 11.1
service udp-small-servers
service tcp-small-servers
hostname LAB-E
enable secret 5 1q/QJ$EA8tfOg1/Rxn/28FSrLgJ/
interface Ethernet0
 ip address 210.93.105.2 255.255.255.0
interface Serial0
 no ip address
 shutdown
interface Serial1
 no ip address
 shutdown
router rip
 network 210.93.105.0
ip host LAB-A 192.5.5.1 205.7.5.1 201.100.11.1
ip host LAB-B 201.100.11.2 219.17.100.1 199.6.13.1
ip host LAB-C 199.6.13.2 223.8.151.1 204.204.7.1
ip host LAB-D 204.204.7.2 210.93.105.1
ip host LAB-E 210.93.105.2
no ip classless
line con 0
 password cisco
login
line aux 0
line vty 0 4
 password cisco
 login
 !

Cisco Labs–Semester 2–Router Configuration
LAB 9.2.4.1–SHOW ARP and CLEAR ARP–OVERVIEW
(Estimated time: 30 minutes)

Router Name - LAB A
Router Type - 2514
E 0 = 192.5.5.1
E 1 = 205.7.5.1
S 0 = 201.100.11.1
SM = 255.255.255.0

Router Name - LAB B
Router Type - 2503
E 0 = 219.17.100.1
S 0 = 199.6.13.1
S 1 = 201.100.11.2
SM = 255.255.255.0

Router Name - LAB C
Router Type - 2503
E 0 = 223.8.151.1
S 0 = 204.204.7.1
S 1 = 199.6.13.2
SM = 255.255.255.0

Router Name - LAB D
Router Type - 2501
E 0 = 210.93.105.1
S 1 = 204.204.7.2
SM =255.255.255.0

Router Name - LAB E
Router Type - 2501
E 0 = 210.93.105.2
SM = 255.255.255.0

LEGEND

= ROUTER   User Exec Password = cisco

= HUB   Enable Secret Exec Password = class

= LAN SWITCH   Terminal vty Password = cisco

= CONSOLE CABLE

Objectives:
- Become familiar with the router's **show arp** command
- Become familiar with the router's **clear arp** command

Background:
In this lab, you view the ARP table stored in the router and clear the router's ARP table. These two commands are important in troubleshooting a network problem. The router keeps detailed information about MAC addresses and associated IP addresses. From time to time, this information can become corrupted and cause packet-delivery problems. When this happens, the router ARP table must be cleared and rebuilt.

Cisco Labs–Semester 2–Router Configuration
LAB 9.2.4.1–SHOW ARP and CLEAR ARP–OVERVIEW

Tools/Preparation:

Prior to starting the lab, you need to connect a PC workstation with HyperTerminal to a router using the router's console interface with a roll-over cable. This lab should be done at the router console station. You should refer to the *Cisco Networking Academy Program: First-Year Companion Guide*, Second Edition, and review Semester 2 online curriculum Chapter 9 prior to starting this lab. Work individually or in teams. Be familiar with the following commands:

- **enable**
- **show arp**

- **clear arp**
- **ping**

Required Resources:

- PC with monitor, keyboard, mouse, and power cords
- Windows operating system (Windows 95, 98, NT, or 2000) installed on PC
- HyperTerminal program configured for router console access
- PC connected to the router console port with a roll-over cable

Web Site Resources:

- **Routing basics**—www.cisco.com/univercd/cc/td/doc/cisintwk/ito_doc/routing.htm
- **General information on routers**—www.cisco.com/univercd/cc/td/doc/pcat/#2
- **2500 series routers**—www.cisco.com/warp/public/cc/cisco/mkt/access/2500/index.shtml
- **1600 series routers**—www.cisco.com/warp/public/cc/cisco/mkt/access/1600/index.shtml
- **Terms and acronyms**—www.cisco.com/univercd/cc/td/doc/cisintwk/ita/index.htm
- **IP routing protocol IOS command summary**—www.cisco.com/univercd/cc/td/doc/product/software/ios120/12cgcr/rbkixol.htm

Notes:

_____
_____
_____
_____
_____
_____
_____
_____
_____

Cisco Labs–Semester 2–Router Configuration
LAB 9.2.4.1–SHOW ARP and CLEAR ARP–WORKSHEET

Step 1. Log on to the router.
   Explanation: Connect to the router and log on. If prompted, enter the password **cisco**.

Step 2. Show the router's ARP table.
   Task: Enter **show arp** at the router prompt.
   Explanation: The router responds with the ARP table that shows IP address to MAC address to interface number.

   1.   What three important pieces of information are displayed? _____

   _____

Step 3. Enter privileged mode.
   Task:
   a.   Enter **enable** at the command prompt.
   b.   Enter the password **class**.
   Explanation: You use the **enable** command to enter privileged EXEC mode.

Step 4. Enter the help command.
   Task: Enter the help command by typing **?** at the router prompt.
   Explanation: The router responds with all commands available in privileged mode.

   2.
       a.   What is the significance of entering **?** at the router prompt? _____
       b.   Does the **clear** command appear as an option? _____

Step 5. Clear the ARP table.
   Task: Enter the **clear arp** command at the router prompt.
   Explanation: The router clears the ARP table.

Step 6. Show the ARP table.
   Task: Enter the **show arp** command at the router prompt.
   Explanation: The router responds with the ARP table.

   3.   Are there any entries in the ARP table? _____

   4.   Looking at the IP address of the ARP entries, what are the entries for? _____

Cisco Labs–Semester 2–Router Configuration
LAB 9.2.4.1–SHOW ARP and CLEAR ARP–WORKSHEET

Step 7. Generate network traffic.
  Task: Ping all interfaces on the network.
  Explanation: This generates network traffic between routers.

Step 8. Show the ARP table.
  Task: Enter the **show arp** command at the router prompt.
  Explanation: The router will respond with the ARP table.

5. Are there any new entries in the ARP table? _____

Step 9. Generate network traffic.
  Task: Open an MS-DOS command prompt (select Start/Programs/MS-DOS Command Prompt). Ping all the workstations on the lab network. *Note:* Make sure that all workstations have proper IP addressing for the network they are connected to and a default gateway.
  Explanation: This generates network traffic from workstation to workstation.

Step 10. Show the ARP table.
  Task: Enter the **show arp** command at the router prompt.
  Explanation: The router responds with the ARP table.

6. Are there any new entries in the ARP table? _____

7. Explain why there were no new entries in Step 8 but there were in Step 10.

Step 11. Exit the router.

Cisco Labs–Semester 2–Router Configuration
LAB 9.2.4.2–ARP CHALLENGE–OVERVIEW
(Estimated time: 30 minutes)

Router Name - LAB A
Router Type - 2514
E 0 = 192.5.5.1
E 1 = 205.7.5.1
S 0 = 201.100.11.1
SM = 255.255.255.0

Router Name - LAB C
Router Type - 2503
E 0 = 223.8.151.1
S 0 = 204.204.7.1
S 1 = 199.6.13.2
SM = 255.255.255.0

Router Name - LAB E
Router Type - 2501
E 0 = 210.93.105.2
SM = 255.255.255.0

Router Name - LAB B
Router Type - 2503
E 0 = 219.17.100.1
S 0 = 199.6.13.1
S 1 = 201.100.11.2
SM = 255.255.255.0

Router Name - LAB D
Router Type - 2501
E 0 = 210.93.105.1
S 1 = 204.204.7.2
SM = 255.255.255.0

LEGEND

= ROUTER   User Exec Password = cisco

= HUB   Enable Secret Exec Password = class

= LAN SWITCH   Terminal vty Password = cisco

= CONSOLE CABLE

Objective:
- Practice working with ARP tables

Background:
You and your group have been assigned to help a system administrator of a network for XYZ Company. The system administrator of this network would like to know the MAC addresses of each of the Ethernet interfaces on the routers

Tools/Preparation:
Prior to starting this lab, you need to have the equipment for the standard five-router lab available (routers, hubs, switch, cables, etc.). The routers should be preconfigured by the instructor or lab assistant with the correct IP interface settings, etc. The workstations should also be preconfigured to have the correct IP address settings prior to starting the lab. The routers, hubs, and workstations should be labeled.

This lab assumes that you have completed lab 2.2.10.1 and that the lab equipment (routers, hub, workstations, etc.) is assembled and connected in the standard lab topology. Work in teams of three or more. Before beginning this lab, you should refer to the *Cisco Networking Academy Program: First-Year Companion Guide*, Second Edition, and Semester 2 online Chapter 9.

Cisco Labs–Semester 2–Router Configuration
LAB 9.2.4.2–ARP CHALLENGE–OVERVIEW

Required Resources:

- Five PC workstations (minimum) with Windows operating system and HyperTerminal installed
- Five Cisco routers (model 1600 series or 2500 series with IOS 11.2 or later)
- Four Ethernet hubs (10Base-T with 4 to 8 ports)
- One Ethernet switch (Cisco Catalyst 1900 or comparable)
- Five serial console cables to connect the workstation to the router console port (with RJ-45 to DB9 converters)
- Three sets of V.35 WAN serial cables (DTE male/ DCE female) to connect from router to router
- CAT5 Ethernet cables wired straight through to connect routers and workstations to hubs and switches
- AUI (DB15) to RJ-45 Ethernet transceivers (the quantity depends on the number of routers with AUI ports) to convert router AUI interfaces to 10Base-T RJ-45

Web Site Resources:

- **Routing basics**—www.cisco.com/univercd/cc/td/doc/cisintwk/ito_doc/routing.htm
- **General information on routers**—www.cisco.com/univercd/cc/td/doc/pcat/#2
- **2500 series routers**—www.cisco.com/warp/public/cc/cisco/mkt/access/2500/index.shtml
- **1600 series routers**—www.cisco.com/warp/public/cc/cisco/mkt/access/1600/index.shtml
- **Terms and acronyms**—www.cisco.com/univercd/cc/td/doc/cisintwk/ita/index.htm
- **IP routing protocol IOS command summary**—www.cisco.com/univercd/cc/td/doc/product/ software/ios120/12cgcr/rbkixol.htm

Notes:

_____

_____

_____

_____

_____

_____

_____

_____

_____

_____

_____

_____

_____

Cisco Labs–Semester 2–Router Configuration
LAB 9.2.4.2–ARP CHALLENGE–WORKSHEET

Step 1. Find the MAC address for all Ethernet interfaces.

Verify that the routers and workstations are set up according to the standard five-router lab diagram. When you are done with this, view the ARP tables and find out the MAC address of all surrounding routers. Be sure to record the ARP tables of the other group's routers. This will allow you to construct a diagram of all the routers and their IPs with MAC addresses. You might want to write down a quick step-by-step example of how you found the MAC address to one of the routers.

1. List the following MAC addresses for the routers:

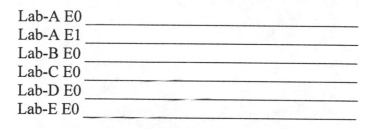

  Lab-A E0 _____
  Lab-A E1 _____
  Lab-B E0 _____
  Lab-C E0 _____
  Lab-D E0 _____
  Lab-E E0 _____

Step 2. Generate network traffic.

From the workstations, ping another workstation on a different router. Then, from the router, issue the **show arp** command from a privileged prompt.

2. List the MAC addresses for the workstations that are connected to the router.

  _____

Cisco Labs–Semester 2–Router Configuration
LAB X.X.X.X–NETWORK TROUBLESHOOTING CHALLENGE–
OVERVIEW
(Estimated time: 45 minutes)

Objectives:

- Use IOS informational and troubleshooting commands to identify network problems
- Investigate and verify physical network connections
- Demonstrate your ability to work as a team to troubleshoot network problems

Background:

With this lab, you use your knowledge of the router lab setup and various information such as **show version**, **show running-config**, **show interface**, and **show ip route**, as well as troubleshooting commands such as **ping**, **telnet**, and **traceroute**. You need to group into two teams (Team A and Team B) with three to five members on each team. Team A will select a problem from the Problem List to introduce into the network. Team B will then have to troubleshoot the network, find the problem, and correct it.

Your goal is to ping from a workstation on LAN A, which router Lab-A connects to, to a workstation on LAN E, which router Lab-E connects to. After you document the problem and your team's solution on the worksheet, Team B will introduce a problem for Team A to troubleshoot and correct. The resources you have available are the standard lab diagram shown here and the help commands at the command-line interface (CLI). You can use the console connections at all five routers.

Cisco Labs–Semester 2–Router Configuration
LAB X.X.X.X–NETWORK TROUBLESHOOTING CHALLENGE–OVERVIEW

Tools/Preparation:

Prior to starting this lab, you need to have the equipment for the standard five-router lab available (routers, hubs, switch, cables, and so on). The routers should be preconfigured by the instructor or lab assistant with the correct IP interface settings, and so on. The workstations should also be preconfigured to have the correct IP address settings prior to starting the lab. The routers, hubs, and workstations should be labeled. The team that introduces the problem into the lab setup should discuss it with the lab assistant or instructor, who can provide coaching and assistance to the team trying to find the problem.

This lab assumes that you have completed Lab 2.2.10.1 and that the lab equipment (routers, hub, workstations, and so on) are assembled and connected in the standard lab topology. Work in teams of three to five.

Required Resources:

- Five PC workstations (minimum) with Windows operating system and HyperTerminal installed
- Five Cisco routers (model 1600 series or 2500 series with IOS 11.2 or later)
- Four Ethernet hubs (10Base-T with 4 to 8 ports)
- One Ethernet switch (Cisco Catalyst 1900 or comparable)
- Five serial console cables to connect the workstation to the router console port (with RJ-45 to DB9 converters)
- Three sets of V.35 WAN serial cables (DTE male/DCE female) to connect from router to router
- CAT5 Ethernet cables wired straight through to connect routers and workstations to hubs and switches
- AUI (DB15) to RJ-45 Ethernet transceivers (the quantity depends on the number of routers with AUI ports) to convert router AUI interfaces to 10Base-T RJ-45

Web Site Resources:

- **Routing basics**—www.cisco.com/univercd/cc/td/doc/cisintwk/ito_doc/routing.htm
- **General information on routers**—www.cisco.com/univercd/cc/td/doc/pcat/#2
- **2500 series routers**—www.cisco.com/warp/public/cc/cisco/mkt/access/2500/index.shtml
- **1600 series routers**—www.cisco.com/warp/public/cc/cisco/mkt/access/1600/index.shtml
- **Terms and acronyms**—www.cisco.com/univercd/cc/td/doc/cisintwk/ita/index.htm
- **IP routing protocol IOS command summary**—www.cisco.com/univercd/cc/td/doc/product/software/ios120/12cgcr/rbkixol.htm

Notes: _____

_____

_____

_____

_____

Cisco Labs–Semester 2–Router Configuration
LAB X.X.X.X–NETWORK TROUBLESHOOTING CHALLENGE– WORKSHEET

Step 1. The first team introduces a problem.
Chose two from the following ten possible problems to introduce into the network, and write down which problems you introduced and where they were introduced. Discuss these with the instructor or lab assistant so they can provide assistance if necessary.

1. Change the TCP/IP configuration on a workstation (IP address, default gateway, subnet mask).

2. Change the IP address or subnet mask of an interface on one of the routers.

3. Take down an interface on a router.

4. Remove the clocking signal on one of the DCE interfaces.

5. Add an incorrect static route to misdirect traffic.

6. Remove the RIP or IGRP routing protocol from a router.

7. Change the IP host table to remove a host or change an IP address.

8. Disconnect an Ethernet cable from a hub or router.

9. Turn off one of the routers.

10. Turn off one of the hubs.

Step 2. The second team troubleshoots and fixes the problem.

1. Try to telnet from a workstation on the router Lab-A network to router Lab-E using the router's name. Always remember when troubleshooting to start with router-to-router connections and troubleshoot systematically from router Lab-A to router Lab-E. Then begin testing from workstations connected to the router Lab-A LAN to other routers. Then test from workstation to workstation. Document your results.

   _____

   _____

2. Document how and what you had to change to fix the two problems introduced.
   A. _____
   B. _____

Cisco Labs–Semester 2–Router Configuration
LAB X.X.X.X–NETWORK TROUBLESHOOTING CHALLENGE–
WORKSHEET

3. Fill in the checklist to make sure you have connectivity to all nodes in the network.
    - Ping all routers' interfaces.
    - Ping all workstations.
    - Ping from one workstation to all other workstations.
    - Traceroute from router Lab-A to router Lab-E.
    - Traceroute from one workstation to all other workstations.
    - Telnet to all other routers.

Step 3. Repeat the lab with the second team introducing two of the networking problems and the first team troubleshooting the network.

Cisco Labs–Semester 2–Router Configuration
LAB 10.1.4–IP ADDRESSING AND SUBNETS CHALLENGE– OVERVIEW
(Estimated time: 30 minutes)

Router Name - LAB A
Router Type - 2514
E 0 = 192.5.5.1
E 1 = 205.7.5.1
S 0 = 201.100.11.1
SM = 255.255.255.0

Router Name - LAB B
Router Type - 2503
E 0 = 219.17.100.1
S 0 = 199.6.13.1
S 1 = 201.100.11.2
SM = 255.255.255.0

Router Name - LAB C
Router Type - 2503
E 0 = 223.8.151.1
S 0 = 204.204.7.1
S 1 = 199.6.13.2
SM = 255.255.255.0

Router Name - LAB D
Router Type - 2501
E 0 = 210.93.105.1
S 1 = 204.204.7.2
SM = 255.255.255.0

Router Name - LAB E
Router Type - 2501
E 0 = 210.93.105.2
SM = 255.255.255.0

LEGEND
= ROUTER   User Exec Password = cisco
= HUB   Enable Secret Exec Password = class
= LAN SWITCH   Terminal vty Password = cisco
= CONSOLE CABLE

Objectives:
- Design and implement a five-router network topology
- Develop an IP addressing scheme based on the topology
- Use a single Class C network address with subnets for LANs and WANs
- Assign IP addresses to router interfaces and hosts
- Diagram the network using ConfigMaker

Background:
In this lab, you work with other group members to design a five-router network topology and an IP addressing scheme. You must come up with a proper IP addressing scheme using a single Class C network address (204.204.7.0) and multiple subnets. You then use ConfigMaker to diagram the network you designed. You have creative freedom in designing your network.

Cisco Labs–Semester 2–Router Configuration
LAB 10.1.4–IP ADDRESSING AND SUBNETS CHALLENGE– OVERVIEW

Tools/Preparation:

Prior to starting this lab, you should have the equipment for the standard five-router lab available (routers, hubs, switch, cables, and so on). Because this is a challenge lab, the routers may or may not be preconfigured with the correct IP interface settings, and so on. If they are, you need to change the IP addresses to be different from those of the standard lab setup. The workstations might also be preconfigured to have the correct IP address settings prior to starting the lab. The IP addressing configuration of the workstations will need to be changed. If the actual lab equipment is not available to configure, design the network using the worksheets provided in this lab. Work in teams of five or more.

Required Resources:

- Five PC workstations (minimum) with Windows operating system and HyperTerminal installed
- Five Cisco routers (model 1600 series or 2500 series with IOS 11.2 or later)
- Four Ethernet hubs (10Base-T with 4 to 8 ports)
- One Ethernet switch (Cisco Catalyst 1900 or comparable)
- Five serial console cables to connect the workstation to the router console port (with RJ-45 to DB9 converters)
- Four sets of V.35 WAN serial cables (DTE male/DCE female) to connect from router to router
- CAT5 Ethernet cables wired straight through to connect routers and workstations to hubs and switches
- AUI (DB15) to RJ-45 Ethernet transceivers (the quantity depends on the number of routers with AUI ports) to convert router AUI interfaces to 10Base-T RJ-45

Web Site Resources:

- **Routing basics**—www.cisco.com/univercd/cc/td/doc/cisintwk/ito_doc/routing.htm
- **General information on routers**—www.cisco.com/univercd/cc/td/doc/pcat/#2
- **2500 series routers**—www.cisco.com/warp/public/cc/cisco/mkt/access/2500/index.shtml
- **1600 series routers**—www.cisco.com/warp/public/cc/cisco/mkt/access/1600/index.shtml
- **Terms and acronyms**—www.cisco.com/univercd/cc/td/doc/cisintwk/ita/index.htm
- **IP routing protocol IOS command summary**—www.cisco.com/univercd/cc/td/doc/product/ software/ios120/12cgcr/rbkixol.htm
- **Cisco ConfigMaker information and download**—www.cisco.com/warp/public/cc/cisco/ mkt/enm/config/index.shtml

Notes:

_____

_____

_____

_____

Cisco Labs–Semester 2–Router Configuration
LAB 10.1.4–IP ADDRESSING AND SUBNETS CHALLENGE–WORKSHEET

Step 1. Design the physical topology of the network.
You should have at least five routers in different geographical locations. You should have at least one Ethernet LAN off of each router. Sketch out the topology as you go. Answer the following questions to assist in planning:

1. How many routers will you have? _____

2. Where will the routers be located? _____

3. How many switches will you have? _____

Step 2. Develop an IP addressing scheme.
Review your topology sketch from Step 1. Using a single Class C address of 204.204.7.0, create a subnetwork design for your topology. Document your scheme by indicating where you will put each of the subnets. Answer the following questions to assist in planning:

4. How many LANs are there? _____

5. How many WANs are there? _____

6. How many unique subnets will you need? _____

7. How many hosts per subnet (LAN and WAN) will you have? _____

8. How many IP addresses (hosts and router interfaces) will be required? _____

9. What is your Class C network address? _____

10. How many bits will you borrow from the host portion of the network address? _____

11. What will your subnet mask be? _____

12. How many total useable subnets will this allow for? _____

13. How many hosts per subnet will this allow for? _____

Cisco Labs–Semester 2–Router Configuration
LAB 10.1.4–IP ADDRESSING AND SUBNETS CHALLENGE–WORKSHEET

Step 3. Assign IP addresses to each device interface.
Using the following table, assign an IP address to each device interface or range of devices (hosts) that will require an IP address. Switches do not require an IP address, but you can assign one if you want. Hubs will not have an IP address. (Answers may vary.)

Device Name/Model	Interface	IP Address	Subnet Mask	Default Gateway

14. Which interfaces will require clock rate to be set? _____

Step 4. Diagram the network using ConfigMaker.
Use Cisco ConfigMaker to create a network diagram and add all configuration information, such as IP addresses and subnet masks. ConfigMaker allows you to enter all interface IP addresses and helps you create a finished diagram. You should be familiar with ConfigMaker if you completed lab 6.5.2.2. Use the Web site listed in the section, "Web Site Resources," to download ConfigMaker if you do not have it.

Reflection:

_____
_____
_____
_____
_____
_____

Answers may vary widely. Students should ping and then telnet across the network to check if connections and configurations are properly implemented.

Cisco Labs–Semester 2–Router Configuration
LAB 10.4.1–SEMESTER 2 TOPOLOGY CHALLENGE–OVERVIEW
(Estimated time: 30 minutes)

Router Name - LAB A
Router Type - 2514
E 0 = 192.5.5.1
E 1 = 205.7.5.1
S 0 = 201.100.11.1
SM = 255.255.255.0

Router Name - LAB C
Router Type - 2503
E 0 = 223.8.151.1
S 0 = 204.204.7.1
S 1 = 199.6.13.2
SM = 255.255.255.0

Router Name - LAB E
Router Type - 2501
E 0 = 210.93.105.2
SM = 255.255.255.0

Router Name - LAB B
Router Type - 2503
E 0 = 219.17.100.1
S 0 = 199.6.13.1
S 1 = 201.100.11.2
SM = 255.255.255.0

Router Name - LAB D
Router Type - 2501
E 0 = 210.93.105.1
S 1 = 204.204.7.2
SM = 255.255.255.0

LEGEND
= ROUTER   User Exec Password = cisco
= HUB   Enable Secret Exec Password = class
= LAN SWITCH   Terminal vty Password = cisco
= CONSOLE CABLE

Objectives:
- Design an IP addressing scheme based on a given network topology
- Use multiple Class C network addresses for LANs and WANs
- Assign IP addresses to router interfaces
- Diagram the network using ConfigMaker

Background:
You and your group members have just received your Cisco certification. Your first job is to work with other group members in designing a topology and IP addressing scheme. It will be a five-router topology similar to the standard five-router lab diagram shown above, but with a few changes. Refer to the modified five-router lab diagram shown in the worksheet. You must come up with a proper IP addressing scheme using multiple Class C addresses that are different from those of the standard lab setup. You will then use ConfigMaker to do your own diagram of the network. You can do this lab using the worksheets or work with the actual lab equipment if it is available.

Cisco Labs–Semester 2–Router Configuration
LAB 10.4.1–SEMESTER 2 TOPOLOGY CHALLENGE–OVERVIEW

Tools/Preparation:

Prior to starting this lab, you should have the equipment for the standard five-router lab available (routers, hubs, switch, cables, and so on). Because this is a challenge lab, the routers may or may not be configured with IP interface settings, and so on. If they are, you need to change the IP addresses to be different from those of the standard lab setup. The IP address configuration of the workstations will also need to be changed. If the actual lab equipment is not available to configure, design the network using the worksheets provided in this lab. Work in teams of five or more.

Required Resources:

- Five PC workstations (minimum) with Windows operating system and HyperTerminal installed
- Five Cisco routers (model 1600 series or 2500 series with IOS 11.2 or later)
- Four Ethernet hubs (10Base-T with 4 to 8 ports)
- One Ethernet switch (Cisco Catalyst 1900 or comparable)
- Five serial console cables to connect the workstation to the router console port (with RJ-45 to DB9 converters)
- Four sets of V.35 WAN serial cables (DTE male/DCE female) to connect from router to router
- CAT5 Ethernet cables wired straight through to connect routers and workstations to hubs and switches
- AUI (DB15) to RJ-45 Ethernet transceivers (the quantity depends on the number of routers with AUI ports) to convert router AUI interfaces to 10Base-T R-J45
- Cisco ConfigMaker software version 2.3 or later (see the next section for the Web site)

Web Site Resources:

- **Routing basics**—www.cisco.com/univercd/cc/td/doc/cisintwk/ito_doc/routing.htm
- **General information on routers**—www.cisco.com/univercd/cc/td/doc/pcat/#2
- **2500 series routers**—www.cisco.com/warp/public/cc/cisco/mkt/access/2500/index.shtml
- **1600 series routers**—www.cisco.com/warp/public/cc/cisco/mkt/access/1600/index.shtml
- **Terms and acronyms**—www.cisco.com/univercd/cc/td/doc/cisintwk/ita/index.htm
- **IP routing protocol IOS command summary**—www.cisco.com/univercd/cc/td/doc/product/software/ios120/12cgcr/rbkixol.htm
- **Cisco ConfigMaker information and download**—www.cisco.com/warp/public/cc/cisco/mkt/enm/config/index.shtml

Notes:

_____

_____

_____

Cisco Labs–Semester 2–Router Configuration
LAB 10.4.1–SEMESTER 2 TOPOLOGY CHALLENGE–WORKSHEET

Step 1. Review the physical connections on the standard lab setup.
Review the standard Semester 2 lab diagram in the overview section of this lab, and check all physical devices, cables, and connections if the physical lab setup is available.

Step 2. Develop an IP addressing scheme.
With the standard five-router lab configuration shown in the overview section, there are eight networks. Five of these are Ethernet local-area networks (LANs), and three of them are serial wide-area networks (WANs). Review the modified setup of the lab diagrammed below. Using multiple Class C addresses similar to the existing standard lab, select addresses and document the IP addressing scheme by indicating where you will put each of the Class C addresses. Answer the following questions to assist your team in planning the network IP address scheme.

1. How many LANs are there? _____

2. How many WANs are there? _____

3. How many unique Class C network addresses will you need? _____

4. How many devices are there? _____

5. How many device interfaces will require IP addresses? _____

Cisco Labs–Semester 2–Router Configuration
LAB 10.4.1–SEMESTER 2 TOPOLOGY CHALLENGE–WORKSHEET

Step 3. Assign IP addresses to each device interface.
Use the following table to identify each router interface that will require an IP address. Switches do not require an IP address, but you can assign one if you want. Hubs will not have an IP address.

Device Name/ Model	Interface	IP Address	Subnet Mask	Default Gateway

6. Which interfaces will require clock rate to be set? _____

Step 4. Diagram the network using ConfigMaker.
Use Cisco ConfigMaker to recreate the network diagram in the worksheet and add all configuration information, such as IP addresses and subnet masks. ConfigMaker allows you to enter all interface IP addresses and helps you create a finished diagram. Choose your own device names.

Reflection:
What did you learn from designing a topology with such a large group of people?
_____

_____

In what router mode did you spend most of your time? _____
Could you have done it any other way? If so, how? _____

_____

When doing this lab, how could a TFTP server have been useful? _____

_____

Cisco Labs–Semester 2–Router Configuration
LAB 12.1.5–STATIC ROUTES–OVERVIEW
(Estimated time: 30 minutes)

Router Name - LAB A
Router Type - 2514
E 0 = 192.5.5.1
E 1 = 205.7.5.1
S 0 = 201.100.11.1
SM = 255.255.255.0

Router Name - LAB B
Router Type - 2503
E 0 = 219.17.100.1
S 0 = 199.6.13.1
S 1 = 201.100.11.2
SM = 255.255.255.0

Router Name - LAB C
Router Type - 2503
E 0 = 223.8.151.1
S 0 = 204.204.7.1
S 1 = 199.6.13.2
SM = 255.255.255.0

Router Name - LAB D
Router Type - 2501
E 0 = 210.93.105.1
S 1 = 204.204.7.2
SM = 255.255.255.0

Router Name - LAB E
Router Type - 2501
E 0 = 210.93.105.2
SM = 255.255.255.0

LEGEND

= ROUTER	User Exec Password = cisco
= HUB	Enable Secret Exec Password = class
= LAN SWITCH	Terminal vty Password = cisco
= CONSOLE CABLE	

Objectives:
- Configure a static route between direct neighboring routers using the **ip route** command
- Copy the running configuration to the startup configuration

Background:
In this lab, you configure a static route between neighboring routers. Static routes are routes that cause packets moving between a source and a destination to take a specified path. They are typically defined manually by a network administrator. Routing updates are not sent on a link if it is only defined by a static route, thereby conserving bandwidth. Another application for a static route is security because dynamic routing tends to reveal everything known about a network. Static routes are sometimes used for remote sites and for testing of a particular link or series of routers in your internetwork.

Cisco Labs–Semester 2–Router Configuration
LAB 12.1.5–STATIC ROUTES–OVERVIEW

Tools/Preparation:

Prior to starting the lab, you need to connect a PC workstation with HyperTerminal to a router using the router's console interface with a roll-over cable. This lab should be done at the router console station. You should refer to the *Cisco Networking Academy Program: First-Year Companion Guide*, Second Edition, and review Semester 2 online curriculum Chapter 12 prior to starting this lab. Work individually or in teams. Be familiar with the following commands:

- enable
- show arp
- show startup-config
- configure terminal

- IP route
- show running-config
- copy
- ping

Required Resources:

- PC with monitor, keyboard, mouse, and power cords
- Windows operating system (Windows 95, 98, NT, or 2000) installed on PC
- HyperTerminal program configured for router console connection
- PC connected to the router console port with a roll-over cable

Web Site Resources:

- **Routing basics**—www.cisco.com/univercd/cc/td/doc/cisintwk/ito_doc/routing.htm
- **General information on routers**—www.cisco.com/univercd/cc/td/doc/pcat/#2
- **2500 series routers**—www.cisco.com/warp/public/cc/cisco/mkt/access/2500/index.shtml
- **1600 series routers**—www.cisco.com/warp/public/cc/cisco/mkt/access/1600/index.shtml
- **Terms and acronyms**—www.cisco.com/univercd/cc/td/doc/cisintwk/ita/index.htm
- **IP routing protocol IOS command summary**—www.cisco.com/univercd/cc/td/doc/product/software/ios120/12cgcr/rbkixol.htm

Notes:

_____
_____
_____
_____
_____
_____

Cisco Labs–Semester 2–Router Configuration
LAB 12.1.5–STATIC ROUTES–WORKSHEET

Step 1. Log on to the router.
Explanation: Connect to the router and log on. If prompted, enter the password **cisco**.

Step 2. Test Layer 3 (network) connectivity.
Task: Enter **ping *xxx.xxx.xxx.xxx***.
Explanation: *xxx.xxx.xxx.xxx* is the IP address of one of your neighboring routers that is directly connected to you.

1. Did the router's interface respond with a successful ping? _____

_____

Step 3. Enter privileged mode.
Task:
   a. Enter **enable** at the command prompt.
   b. Enter the password **class**.
Explanation: You use the **enable** command to enter privileged EXEC mode.

Step 4. Show the backup configuration file.
Task: Enter **show startup-config** (abbreviated **show start**) at the router prompt.
Explanation: The router displays information on the backup configuration file stored in NVRAM.

2. Are there any routing protocols or static routes defined? _____

Step 5. Enter global configuration mode.
Task: Enter **configure terminal** (abbreviated **config t**) at the router prompt.
Explanation: To configure the router, you must enter global configuration mode. Notice how the router prompt changes after this command.

3. What does the router prompt look like? _____

Step 6. Enter the help facility.
Task: Enter the **IP route ?** command at the router prompt.
Explanation: The router responds with the description available for **IP route**.

4. What was the router's response? _____

Step 7. Enter the help facility.
Task: Enter **IP route *xxx.xxx.xxx.xxx* ?** at the router prompt.
Explanation: *xxx.xxx.xxx.xxx* is the network address you want a static route for.

5. What was the router's response? _____

Cisco Labs–Semester 2–Router Configuration
LAB 12.1.5–STATIC ROUTES–WORKSHEET

Step 8. Enter the help facility.
   Task: Enter **ip route** *xxx.xxx.xxx.xxx yyy.yyy.yyy.yyy* at the router prompt.
   Explanation: *xxx.xxx.xxx.xxx* is the network address of the destination network, and *yyy.yyy.yyy.yyy* is the subnet mask of the destination network.

   6. What was the router's response? _____

Step 9. Enter a static route.
   Task: Enter **IP route** *xxx.xxx.xxx.xxx yyy.yyy.yyy.yyy zzz.zzz.zzz.zzz* at the router prompt..
   Explanation: *xxx.xxx.xxx.xxx* is the network address of the destination network, and *yyy.yyy.yyy.yyy* is the subnet mask of the destination network. *zzz.zzz.zzz.zzz* is the IP address of the direct neighbor interface.

Step 10. Exit the router's global configuration mode.
   Task: Enter **exit** at the router prompt.
   Explanation: The router exits global configuration mode.

   7. What does the router prompt look like? _____

Step 11. Show the running configuration.
   Task: Enter **show running-config** at the router prompt.
   Explanation: The router shows the active configuration file.

   8. Was there an IP route with the static route you configured in the active configuration file?

   _____

Step 12. Copy the active configuration to the backup configuration.
   Task: Enter **copy running-config startup-config** at the router prompt.
   Explanation: This command permanently writes the configuration change to memory.

Step 13. Test the static route with the ping command.
   Task: Enter **ping** *xxx.xxx.xxx.xxx* at the router prompt.
   Explanation: *xxx.xxx.xxx.xxx* is the neighboring router you set up a static route to.

   9. Was the neighboring router interface reachable?

Step 14. Exit the router.

Cisco Labs–Semester 2–Router Configuration
LAB 12.3.5–RIP ROUTING–OVERVIEW
(Estimated time: 45 minutes)

Router Name - LAB A
Router Type - 2514
E 0 = 192.5.5.1
E 1 = 205.7.5.1
S 0 = 201.100.11.1
SM = 255.255.255.0

Router Name - LAB C
Router Type - 2503
E 0 = 223.8.151.1
S 0 = 204.204.7.1
S 1 = 199.6.13.2
SM = 255.255.255.0

Router Name - LAB E
Router Type - 2501
E 0 = 210.93.105.2
SM = 255.255.255.0

Router Name - LAB B
Router Type - 2503
E 0 = 219.17.100.1
S 0 = 199.6.13.1
S 1 = 201.100.11.2
SM = 255.255.255.0

Router Name - LAB D
Router Type - 2501
E 0 = 210.93.105.1
S 1 = 204.204.7.2
SM = 255.255.255.0

LEGEND

= ROUTER   User Exec Password = cisco

= HUB   Enable Secret Exec Password = class

= LAN SWITCH   Terminal vty Password = cisco

= CONSOLE CABLE

Objective:
- Configure RIP as your routing protocol

Background:
In this lab, you configure RIP as the routing protocol. RIP is a distance-vector routing protocol. Hop count is used as the metric for path selection. It has a maximum allowable hop count of 15. RIP broadcasts routing updates consisting of its routing table to its neighbors every 30 seconds by default. RIP is a standard protocol that is appropriate for relatively small homogeneous networks.

Cisco Labs–Semester 2–Router Configuration
LAB 12.3.5–RIP ROUTING–OVERVIEW

Tools/Preparation:

Prior to starting the lab, the instructor or lab assistant has to log on to each router and delete all router RIP and static route entries from all the routers. You need to connect a PC workstation with HyperTerminal to a router using the router's console interface with a roll-over cable. This lab should be done at the router console station. You should refer to the *Cisco Networking Academy Program: First-Year Companion Guide*, Second Edition, and review Semester 12 online curriculum Chapter 12 prior to starting this lab. Work individually or in teams. Be familiar with the following commands:

- **enable**
- **show IP route**
- **show startup-config**
- **configure terminal**
- **network**

- **show running-config**
- **copy**
- **show IP protocols**
- **router RIP**

Required Resources:

- PC with monitor, keyboard, mouse, and power cords
- Windows operating system (Windows 95, 98, NT, or 2000) installed on PC
- HyperTerminal program configured for a router console connection
- PC connected to the router console port with a roll-over cable

Web Site Resources:

- **Routing basics**—www.cisco.com/univercd/cc/td/doc/cisintwk/ito_doc/routing.htm
- **General information on routers**—www.cisco.com/univercd/cc/td/doc/pcat/#2
- **2500 series routers**—www.cisco.com/warp/public/cc/cisco/mkt/access/2500/index.shtml
- **1600 series routers**—www.cisco.com/warp/public/cc/cisco/mkt/access/1600/index.shtml
- **Terms and acronyms**—www.cisco.com/univercd/cc/td/doc/cisintwk/ita/index.htm
- **IP routing protocol IOS command summary**—www.cisco.com/univercd/cc/td/doc/product/software/ios120/12cgcr/rbkixol.htm

Notes:

_____
_____
_____
_____
_____
_____
_____

Cisco Labs–Semester 2–Router Configuration
LAB 12.3.5–RIP ROUTING–WORKSHEET

Step 1. Log on to the router.
   Explanation: Connect to the router and log on. If prompted, enter the password **cisco**.

Step 2. Test Layer 3 connectivity.
   Task: Enter **ping** *xxx.xxx.xxx.xxx*.
   Explanation: Ping all interfaces on your router and direct neighboring routers.

   1. Did all interfaces respond with a successful ping? _____

Step 3. View the routing table.
   Task: Enter **show IP route** at the router prompt.
   Explanation: The router responds with its routing table.

   2. Is there any routing protocol defined? _____

Step 4. Enter privileged mode.
   Task:
      a. Enter **enable** at the command prompt.
      b. Enter the password **class**.
   Explanation: You use the **enable** command to enter privileged EXEC mode.

Step 5. Show information about the active configuration file.
   Task: Enter **show running-config** at the router prompt.
   Explanation: The router displays information on the active configuration file.

   3. Are there any static routes defined? _____

Step 6. Enter global configuration mode.
   Task: Enter **configure terminal** at the router prompt.
   Explanation: To configure the router, you must enter global configuration mode. Notice how the router prompt changes after this command.

   4. What does the router prompt look like? _____

Step 7. Enable RIP as your routing protocol.
   Task: Enter the **router RIP** command at the router prompt.
   Explanation: This enables RIP on the router.

   5. What changed in the router prompt? _____

Step 8. Enable RIP routing on a particular IP network.
   Task: Enter **network** *xxx.xxx.xxx.xxx* at the router prompt.
   Explanation: *xxx.xxx.xxx.xxx* is the network address you want to enable RIP on.

Step 9. Enable RIP routing on a particular IP network
   Task: Repeat Step 8 for all the networks directly connected to the router.

Cisco Labs–Semester 2–Router Configuration
LAB 12.3.5–RIP ROUTING–WORKSHEET

Step 10. Exit router configuration mode.
 Task: Enter **exit** at the router prompt.
 Explanation: The router exits router configuration mode, and you will be in global configuration mode.

Step 11. Exit the router's global configuration mode.
 Task: Enter **exit** at the router prompt.
 Explanation: The router exits global configuration mode.

Step 12. Show the running configuration.
 Task: Enter **show running-config** at the router prompt.
 Explanation: The router shows the active configuration file.

 6. Is the router RIP protocol turned on and advertising the networks you defined? _____

Step 13. Copy the active configuration to the backup configuration.
 Task: Enter **copy running-config startup-config** at the router prompt.
 Explanation: This command permanently writes the configuration change to memory.

 7. What does this command do? _____
 _____

Step 14. View the IP protocols.
 Task: Enter **show IP protocols** at the router prompt.
 Explanation: The router displays values about routing timers and network information associated with the entire router.

 8. When is the next update due? _____

Step 15. View the routing table.
 Task: Enter **show IP route** at the router prompt.
 Explanation: The router displays its routing table.

 9. How many routes were discovered by RIP? _____

Step 16. Display the status and global parameters.
 Task: Enter **show IP interface** at the router prompt.
 Explanation: The router displays the status and global parameters associated with an interface.

 10. What information did you receive from this command? _____
 _____

Cisco Labs–Semester 2–Router Configuration
LAB 12.3.5–RIP ROUTING–WORKSHEET

Step 17. Display RIP routing updates as they are sent and received.
    Task: Enter **debug IP RIP** at the command prompt.
    Explanation: This command allows you to display RIP routing updates as they are sent and received.

    11. What important information did you receive from this command? _____

Step 18. Turn off debug for RIP.
    Task: Enter **no debug IP RIP** at the router prompt.
    Explanation: This command turns off the debugging for RIP.

Step 19. Exit the router.

Cisco Labs–Semester 2–Router Configuration
LAB 12.5.1–RIP CONVERGENCE–OVERVIEW
(Estimated time: 60 minutes)

Objectives:

- Gain experience with and knowledge of routing protocols
- Work with and compare static routes and dynamic routes
- Understand the process of convergence

Background:

As a system administrator, there will be times when configuring static routes can be very useful. Static routes are useful for stub networks because there is only one way to get to that network. Security is another reason to use static routes. If you have a network or networks that you don't want the rest of the network to "see," you would not want RIP or other routing protocols sending periodic updates to other routers. With simple networks (few routers), it is sometimes more efficient to use static routes since this conserves bandwidth on WAN links. In this lab, you use static routes for troubleshooting purposes and to see their relationship to dynamic routes and routing protocols.

Cisco Labs–Semester 2–Router Configuration
LAB 12.5.1–RIP CONVERGENCE–OVERVIEW

Tools/Preparation:

Prior to starting this lab, you need to have the equipment for the standard five-router lab available (routers, hubs, switch, cables, and so on). The routers should be preconfigured by the instructor or lab assistant with the correct IP interface settings, and so on. RIP should be enabled on all routers. The workstations should also be preconfigured to have the correct IP address settings prior to starting the lab. The routers, hubs, and workstations should be labeled.

This lab assumes that you have completed lab 2.2.10.1 and that the lab equipment (routers, hub, workstations, and so on) is assembled and connected in the standard lab topology. Work in teams of three or more. Before beginning this lab, you should refer to the *Cisco Networking Academy Program: First-Year Companion Guide*, Second Edition, and Semester 2 online Chapter 12.

Required Resources:

- Five PC workstations (minimum) with Windows operating system and HyperTerminal installed
- Five Cisco routers (model 1600 series or 2500 series with IOS 11.2 or later)
- Four Ethernet hubs (10Base-T with 4 to 8 ports)
- One Ethernet switch (Cisco Catalyst 1900 or comparable)
- Five serial console cables to connect the workstation to the router console port (with RJ-45 to DB9 converters)
- Three sets of V.35 WAN serial cables (DTE male/DCE female) to connect from router to router
- CAT5 Ethernet cables wired straight through to connect routers and workstations to hubs and switches
- AUI (DB15) to RJ-45 Ethernet transceivers (the quantity depends on the number of routers with AUI ports) to convert router AUI interfaces to 10Base-T RJ-45

Web Site Resources:

- **Routing basics**—www.cisco.com/univercd/cc/td/doc/cisintwk/ito_doc/routing.htm
- **General information on routers**—www.cisco.com/univercd/cc/td/doc/pcat/#2
- **2500 series routers**—www.cisco.com/warp/public/cc/cisco/mkt/access/2500/index.shtml
- **1600 series routers**—www.cisco.com/warp/public/cc/cisco/mkt/access/1600/index.shtml
- **Terms and acronyms**—www.cisco.com/univercd/cc/td/doc/cisintwk/ita/index.htm
- **IP routing protocol IOS command summary**—www.cisco.com/univercd/cc/td/doc/product/software/ios120/12cgcr/rbkixol.htm

Notes: _____

_____

_____

_____

_____

_____

_____

Cisco Labs–Semester 2–Router Configuration
LAB 12.5.1–RIP CONVERGENCE–WORKSHEET

Step 1. Show the IP route.
Verify that RIP is enabled and that no static routes are on any of the routers. If there are static routes, remove them with the **no IP route** *xxx.xxx.xxx.xxx* command in global config mode.

Step 2. Enable debugging on Lab-D.
When you use the command **debug ip rip**, you are able to see all routing updates the router is receiving and sending. Turn on debugging for Lab-D.

Step 3. Shut down the serial 1 interface on Lab-B.
Shut down the serial 1 interface on Lab-B with the **shutdown** command. Watch the debugging information on Lab-D, and issue the **show ip route** command there.

1. Has the output from the command **show ip route** changed from when you issued the command in Step 1? _____

2. What networks are inaccessible?
_____

Step 4. Converged network.
After about five minutes, issue the **show ip route** command on Lab-D.

3. Are the networks that were inaccessible in Question 2 listed in the output from the **show ip route** command? _____

Step 5. Enter static routes.
Bring Lab-B's serial 1 interface back up. Then enter static routes for all five routers, leaving RIP enabled. Issue the **show ip route** command. Your output from the **show ip route** command should look like the following (*Note:* There are no R-RIP entries in the routing table):

```
Lab-D#show ip route
Codes: C - connected, S - static, I - IGRP, R - RIP, M - mobile, B - BGP
       D - EIGRP, EX - EIGRP external, O - OSPF, IA - OSPF inter area
       N1 - OSPF NSSA external type 1, N2 - OSPF NSSA external type 2
       E1 - OSPF external type 1, E2 - OSPF external type 2, E - EGP
       i - IS-IS, L1 - IS-IS level-1, L2 - IS-IS level-2, * - candidate default
       U - per-user static route, o - ODR

Gateway of last resort is not set
C    204.204.7.0/24 is directly connected, Serial1
S    223.8.151.0/24 [1/0] via 204.204.7.1
S    201.100.11.0/24 [1/0] via 204.204.7.1
S    219.17.100.0/24 [1/0] via 204.204.7.1
S    192.5.5.0/24 [1/0] via 204.204.7.1
S    199.6.13.0/24 [1/0] via 204.204.7.1
S    205.7.5.0/24 [1/0] via 204.204.7.1
C    210.93.105.0/24 is directly connected, Ethernet0
```

LAB 12.5.1–RIP CONVERGENCE–WORKSHEET

Step 6. Shut down the serial 1 interface on Lab-B.
After you shut down the serial 1 interface on Lab-B, watch the debugging information on Lab-D.

4. Do you see any information that would let you know that Lab-B's serial 1 interface is down?
   _____

5. Why or why not? _____
   _____
   _____

Step 7. Turn off debugging on Lab-D.
Turn off debugging on Lab-D using the **undebug all** command.

6. Now that you have a good understanding of what static routes are, what are the benefits of dynamic routes?
   _____
   _____
   _____
   _____
   _____

Cisco CCNA Labs–Semester 2–Router Configuration
LAB 12.5.2–ROUTING LOOPS CHALLENGE–OVERVIEW
(Estimated time: 30 minutes)

Objectives:
- Configure a WAN connection between Lab-A and Lab-E
- Demonstrate your ability to configure serial interfaces

Background:
In this lab, you set up a WAN connection between Lab-A and Lab-E to create alternate paths in the standard router lab setup. Using a set of WAN serial cables, connect Lab-A Serial 1 to Lab-E Serial 0. Remember to set the clock rate on the DCE side of the cable (Lab-E's Serial 0 interface).

Tools/Preparation:
Prior to starting this lab, you need to have the equipment for the standard five-router lab available (routers, hubs, switch, cables, and so on). The routers should be preconfigured by the instructor or lab assistant with the correct IP interface settings, and so on. The workstations should also be preconfigured to have the correct IP address settings prior to starting the lab. The routers, hubs, and workstations should be labeled.

This lab assumes that you have completed lab 2.2.10.1 and that the lab equipment (routers, hub, workstations, and so on) is assembled and connected in the standard lab topology. Work in teams of three or more. Before beginning this lab, you should refer to the *Cisco Networking Academy Program: First-Year Companion Guide*, Second Edition, and Semester 2 online Chapter 12.

Cisco Labs–Semester 2–Router Configuration
LAB 12.5.2–ROUTING LOOPS CHALLENGE–OVERVIEW

Required Resources:
- Five PC workstations (minimum) with Windows operating system and HyperTerminal installed
- Five Cisco routers (model 1600 series or 2500 series with IOS 11.2 or later)
- Four Ethernet hubs (10Base-T with 4 to 8 ports)
- One Ethernet switch (Cisco Catalyst 1900 or comparable)
- Five serial console cables to connect the workstation to the router console port (with RJ-45 to DB9 converters)
- Four sets of V.35 WAN serial cables (DTE male/ DCE female) to connect from router to router
- CAT5 Ethernet cables wired straight through to connect routers and workstations to hubs and switches
- AUI (DB15) to RJ-45 Ethernet transceivers (the quantity depends on the number of routers with AUI ports) to convert router AUI interfaces to 10Base-T RJ-45

Web Site Resources:
- **Routing basics**—www.cisco.com/univercd/cc/td/doc/cisintwk/ito_doc/routing.htm
- **General information on routers**—www.cisco.com/univercd/cc/td/doc/pcat/#2
- **2500 series routers**—www.cisco.com/warp/public/cc/cisco/mkt/access/2500/index.shtml
- **1600 series routers**—www.cisco.com/warp/public/cc/cisco/mkt/access/1600/index.shtml
- **Terms and acronyms**—www.cisco.com/univercd/cc/td/doc/cisintwk/ita/index.htm
- **IP routing protocol IOS command summary**—www.cisco.com/univercd/cc/td/doc/product/software/ios120/12cgcr/rbkixol.htm

Notes: _____

_____

_____

_____

_____

_____

_____

Cisco Labs–Semester 2–Router Configuration
LAB 12.5.2–ROUTING LOOPS CHALLENGE–WORKSHEET

Step 1. Verify that all physical connections are correct.
Review the standard Semester 2 lab diagram in the overview section of this lab. You will add a fourth set of V.35 WAN serial cables (DTE male/DCE female) to connect from router Lab-A interface S1 to router Lab-E interface S0.

Step 2. Configure Lab-A Serial 1 interface.
Log on to the router and enter interface configuration mode. Configure interface Serial 1 with the following information (this is a new Class C IP address):

- IP address 220.68.33.2
- Subnet mask 255.255.255.0
- Bandwidth of 56

Step 3. Configure IP host and RIP networks.
After you finish the configuration for the interface, you need to add the 220.68.33.0 network with the **network** command to all five routers. Also add the new IP address to the host table entry for routers Lab-A and Lab-E for name resolution to all routers.

Step 4. Configure Lab-E Serial 0 interface.
Repeat Steps 2 and 3 for Lab-E interface Serial 0 with the following information:

- IP address 220.68.33.1
- Subnet mask 255.255.255.0
- Clock rate 56000
- Bandwidth of 56

Step 5. Test your setup.
After you configure Lab-A's and Lab-E's interfaces, check off the items in this list:

- Ping from all routers to 220.68.33.1
- Ping from all routers to 220.68.33.2
- Ping from all Workstations to 220.68.33.1
- Ping from all Workstations to 220.68.33.2
- Telnet from Lab-C to 220.68.33.1
- Telnet from Lab-C to 220.68.33.2
- Telnet from Workstation to 220.68.33.1
- Telnet from Workstation to 220.68.33.2

Step 6. Troubleshooting.
If you were not able to finish Step 5, use your troubleshooting skills learned in previous labs to correct the problem. After you successfully finish Step 5, save the running configuration to the startup configuration for all routers. You will use this new configuration for Lab 12.9.2.1.

Cisco Labs–Semester 2–Router Configuration
LAB 12.5.3–ROUTING LOOPS PREVENTION CHALLENGE–OVERVIEW
(Estimated time: 45 minutes)

Router Name - LAB A
Router Type - 2514
E 0 = 192.5.5.1
E 1 = 205.7.5.1
S 0 = 201.100.11.1
SM = 255.255.255.0

Router Name - LAB B
Router Type - 2503
E 0 = 219.17.100.1
S 0 = 199.6.13.1
S 1 = 201.100.11.2
SM = 255.255.255.0

Router Name - LAB C
Router Type - 2503
E 0 = 223.8.151.1
S 0 = 204.204.7.1
S 1 = 199.6.13.2
SM = 255.255.255.0

Router Name - LAB D
Router Type - 2501
E 0 = 210.93.105.1
S 1 = 204.204.7.2
SM = 255.255.255.0

Router Name - LAB E
Router Type - 2501
E 0 = 210.93.105.2
SM = 255.255.255.0

LEGEND

= ROUTER   User Exec Password = cisco

= HUB   Enable Secret Exec Password = class

= LAN SWITCH   Terminal vty Password = cisco

= CONSOLE CABLE

Objectives:

- Understand methods of controlling routing loops, including holddown timers, defining a maximum hop count, counting to infinity, poison reverse, and split-horizon
- Adjust the RIP maximum hop count to control routing loops

Background:

In the previous challenge lab, you saw how long it took to converge when a link went down. In this lab, your task is to find out how to prevent and control routing loops. The use of holddown timers, defining a maximum hop count, counting to infinity, poison reverse, and split-horizon are all methods of controlling routing loops. You use the RIP hop count metric to control routing loops in this lab. You should have finished lab 12.8.2.1 and have the fourth set of WAN cables connected from Lab-A Serial 1 to Lab-E Serial 0.

Tools/Preparation:

Prior to starting this lab, you need to have the equipment for the standard five-router lab available. The routers and workstations should be preconfigured by the instructor or lab assistant with the correct IP settings prior to starting the lab. Before beginning this lab, you should refer to the *Cisco Networking Academy Program: First-Year Companion Guide*, Second Edition, and Semester 2 online Chapter 12.

Cisco Labs–Semester 2–Router Configuration
LAB 12.5.3–ROUTING LOOPS PREVENTION CHALLENGE–
OVERVIEW

Required Resources:

- Five PC workstations (minimum) with Windows operating system and HyperTerminal installed
- Five Cisco routers (model 1600 series or 2500 series with IOS 11.2 or later)
- Four Ethernet hubs (10Base-T with 4 to 8 ports)
- One Ethernet switch (Cisco Catalyst 1900 or comparable)
- Five serial console cables to connect the workstation to the router console port (with RJ-45 to DB9 converters)
- Four sets of V.35 WAN serial cables (DTE male/DCE female) to connect from router to router
- CAT5 Ethernet cables wired straight through to connect routers and workstations to hubs and switches
- AUI (DB15) to RJ-45 Ethernet transceivers (the quantity depends on the number of routers with AUI ports) to convert router AUI interfaces to 10Base-T RJ-45

Web Site Resources:

- **Routing basics**—www.cisco.com/univercd/cc/td/doc/cisintwk/ito_doc/routing.htm
- **General information on routers**—www.cisco.com/univercd/cc/td/doc/pcat/#2
- **2500 series routers**—www.cisco.com/warp/public/cc/cisco/mkt/access/2500/index.shtml
- **1600 series routers**—www.cisco.com/warp/public/cc/cisco/mkt/access/1600/index.shtml
- **Terms and acronyms**—www.cisco.com/univercd/cc/td/doc/cisintwk/ita/index.htm
- **IP routing protocol IOS command summary**—www.cisco.com/univercd/cc/td/doc/product/ software/ios120/12cgcr/rbkixol.htm

Notes: _____

_____

_____

_____

_____

_____

_____

Cisco Labs–Semester 2–Router Configuration
LAB 12.5.3–ROUTING LOOPS PREVENTION CHALLENGE–WORKSHEET

Step 1. Turn on debugging.
Working with router Lab-C, turn on debugging with the **debug ip rip** command.

Step 2. Shut down Lab-A's Ethernet 0 interface.
Shut down Lab-A's Ethernet 0 interface. From Lab-C, watch the routing information, and use the **show ip route** command to see how many routing updates it takes to flush out Lab-A's Ethernet 0 network.

    1.   How many updates did it take to converge? _____

Step 3. Enable Lab-A's Ethernet 0 interface.
On Lab-A, bring Ethernet 0 back up, and allow enough time for the network to converge.

Step 4. Configure default metric timers basic and split-horizon on Lab-C.
There are other timers that can be modified to help avoid routing loops. This lab focuses on hop count. Change the RIP maximum hop count on router Lab-C to 10 (the default is 16) and adjust the routing timers and split horizon using the following commands:

```
Lab-C#conf t
Lab-C(config)#router rip
Lab-C(config-router)#default-metric 10
Lab-C(config-router)#timers basic 30 60 150 30
Lab-C(config-router)#exit
Lab-C(config)#int s0
Lab-C(config-if)#ip split-horizon
Lab-C(config-if)#int s1
Lab-C(config-if)#ip split-horizon
Lab-C(config-if)#^Z
Lab-C#
```

Step 5. Shut down Lab-A's Ethernet 0 interface.
Shut down Lab-A's Ethernet 0 interface. From Lab-C, watch the routing information, and use the **show ip route** command to see how many routing updates it takes to flush out Lab-A's Ethernet 0 network.

    2.   How many updates did it take to converge? _____

    3.   Compare Questions 1 and 2 and explain why the network converged faster after you changed the default metric timers and split horizon.

Cisco Labs–Semester 2–Router Configuration
LAB 13.1.6–TROUBLESHOOTING 5-ROUTER NETWORK–OVERVIEW
(Estimated time: 30 minutes)

Objectives:

- Troubleshoot problems in the five-router lab network
- Document the problems found and the corrective action taken
- Prepare for Part B of the Final Exam (Router Lab Troubleshooting)

Background:

For this lab, your instructor or lab assistant creates/introduces multiple problems in the network. You have a limited amount of time in which to find and solve the problems so that you can get your entire network up and running. The tools that you can use for the hardware are in your tool kit. The tools that you can use for the software (IOS) include **ping**, **trace ip route**, **telnet**, and **show arp**. You can use your Engineering Journal and any Web-based resources (including the curriculum) that are available. As you discover the problems, document them along with what you did to correct them.

Tools/Preparation:

Prior to starting this lab, you should have the equipment for the standard five-router lab available. All routers and workstations should be properly configured. You are asked to leave the room, and your instructor or lab assistant induces between three and five problems into the lab setup.

Cisco Labs–Semester 2–Router Configuration
LAB 13.1.6–TROUBLESHOOTING 5-ROUTER NETWORK– WORKSHEET

Step 1. Review the physical connections on the standard lab setup.
Review the standard Semester 2 lab diagram in the overview section of this lab, and check all physical devices, cables, and connections if the physical lab setup is available.

Step 2. Troubleshooting introduced network problems.
Basic problem descriptions:
   a. We cannot ping a host on Lab-E's network from a host on Lab-A's network.
   b. We cannot telnet from one router to another router's hostname.
The instructor introduces multiple problems (three to five) into the network that can cause these high-level symptoms. Your team has a fixed time period (20 to 30 minutes) to correct the problems. You can use your journals and toolkits to troubleshoot the problems.

Step 3. Document the problems discovered.
Write down the problems as you encounter them, and then indicate what you did to correct them. When you are able to ping from a Lab-A workstation to a Lab-E workstation and telnet from one router to another router's hostname, have the instructor or lab assistant verify that you have corrected all problems.

Problem #	Problem Discovered	Solution	Instructor Verification
1			
2			
3			
4			
5			

About the CD

Cisco Networking Academy Program: Lab Companion, Volume I, Second Edition, is supplemented with a CD-ROM. Materials on the CD-ROM are presented in an interactive multimedia format. The CD-ROM contains e-lab activities, which are aligned to the content in the textbooks. These e-lab activities effectively support self-directed learning by allowing you to engage in your skill building. As a result, the e-lab activities provide the following:

- An easy-to-use graphical user interface
- Accuracy and conciseness feedback
- Frequency interaction with content
- Support for guided and exploratory navigation
- Guidance and external control over navigation
- Direction and support
- Flexibility to learners at different levels of expertise

NOTES